A Family
of Value

A Family of Value

by
John Rosemond

Andrews and McMeel
A Universal Press Syndicate Company
Kansas City

Library of Congress Cataloging-in-Publication Data

Rosemond, John K., 1947—
A family of value / John Rosemond.
p.   cm.
Includes bibliographical references (p.   ).
ISBN 0-8362-0505-7 (pbk)
1. Child rearing — United States.
2. Parenting — United States. I. Title.
HQ778.63.R67   1995
649'.1—dc20   95-23829
CIP

First Printing, October 1995
Fourth Printing, October 1997

To John McHenry Rosemond

Contents

Thanks!

Donna Martin, Tom Thornton, Matt Lombardi, Ann Hall, Patty Donnelly, and all the other supportive folks at Andrews and McMeel; Gary Nielson at the *Charlotte Observer,* for invaluable support and assistance; Kate Greer, Lisa Fann, and Randy Johnson at *Hemispheres,* for putting up with me; Barb Palar at *Better Homes and Gardens,* for understanding; Jamie Hoover and the fabulous "Spongetones," for allowing me to work out my rock 'n' roll fantasies; Janet Moss and Mary Ellen Dillon, for making sure that life "on the road" is always a pleasure; Nancy, for going above and beyond; and most of all, Willie, with whom all things are possible.

A Family
of Value

I, Heretic

If you cannot answer a man's argument, do not panic.
You can always call him names.

—*Oscar Wilde*

Since I began writing my syndicated newspaper column in 1976, it has become increasingly clear to me that the psychological community often functions more like a political party or a religion than a science. For example, although it often pretends to matters of fact, psychology consists of nothing more than a set of highly speculative (and constantly changing) theories concerning human behavior. Believing in these theories requires faith, and psychology certainly has its share of true believers. These theories constitute psychology's ideology or canon, and as is the case concerning an organized political party or religion, they are the subject of constant intraprofessional debate. There is, however, an unwritten rule that no party to these debates may ever say that another party is dead *wrong*. One may express skepticism, or reserve judgment, or politely disagree, but one may not scoff. Consequently, conflict among members of the profession almost always takes place with extreme respect for form, and always within the context of a certain agreed-upon "party line." Psychologists may sneer at the ideas and methods of mainstream psychiatry, but they may not sneer at mainstream psychology. Not without penalty, that is.

This is much the way political and religious debate is conducted. Catholics, for example, may differ greatly with Jews concerning spiritual matters, but a Catholic expresses public opinion inconsistent with church canon at the risk of sanction of one sort or another. Likewise, Democrats may disagree on how to implement welfare, but a Democratic politician who desires continuing party support does not dare offer that welfare itself is an evil. In each case, deviation from the implicit limits imposed upon any debate is considered heresy, and even in America, where freedom of speech is supposedly guaranteed by the Constitution, professional heresy is always subject to censure, whether formal or informal.

I know this because I am a heretic within my profession. My views on child rearing and family life are "psychologically incorrect." They rock the boat, upset applecarts, and provoke often vitriolic response. The simple explanation is that I have been willing to publicly state my disdain for the child-rearing ideology propounded since the 1950s by mainstream psychology. Furthermore, I go so far as to propose that previous generations of American parents reared children generally well. There was a little room for improvement, to be sure, but there was never any call to toss the baby out with the bathwater. As the reader will see, I am basically restating what our ancestors took for granted concerning family life, and the parent-child relationship in particular. I am relegitimizing their attitudes, their beliefs, their values, and their practices. As long as there are psychologists who believe they have better ideas concerning child rearing than were held by our forebears, there will be psychologists who think I am a menace, and who display, in their denouncements, their intolerance for ideas inconsistent with their own parochial philosophy. In that context, I accept that I am a heretic. I not only accept it, I am proud of it, and I will continue to be a heretic until psychology gets its head out of the clouds and its feet on the ground. In anticipation of that, I'm not holding my breath.

The Heretic's Tale

This book extends the chronicle of a personal and professional revolution that began in 1972, three years after the birth of our first child, Eric, and continues today. During graduate school, I had been successfully indoctrinated into the "nouveau" ideology concerning child rearing then being advanced by mainstream psychology. Central to this ideology was a nebulous psychic ether that psychologists were calling "self-esteem," which adults were obligated to activate in children by "making them feel good about themselves." This, said psychologists and other "helping" professionals, was accomplished via massive, ongoing doses of praise and attention. Like most of my professional peers, I regarded myself as an apostle sent out from academia to spread the gospel of this secular religion. I was convinced that psychology was capable of saving humanity from destruction by its own hand. If enough people would listen to psychology's high priests and priestesses and practice its prescriptions for living, we could create a nearly perfect world! Or so I thought.

Unlike many novice psychologists, however, I was a parent in the early 1970s. Eric Brian Rosemond was born in 1969, during my tenure as a graduate student. Determined not to repeat the grievous errors we had been led to understand our parents had made with us, my wife, Willie, and I were rearing Eric "by the book." It slowly dawned on us, however, that the promises of nouveau child rearing were clashing with the reality of Eric's behavior. He was, as my grandmother would have said, a "holy terror." He threw wild, violent tantrums when thwarted in any way, refused to cooperate with most of our instructions (the exceptions being those along the lines of "C'mon, Eric, let's go get some ice cream"), was loudly demanding, and was stuck in warp drive most of the time. Otherwise, he was a wonderful, charming child. Especially when he was asleep.

Willie and I reached the end of our rope when Eric was three. Everything was going wrong, and our well-intentioned efforts at correcting the situation were having no positive effect. Around then, Willie became pregnant again. That caused us to wake up to the fact that we had an obligation to our second child to set things right in our family, and less than eight months (from the time of confirmation) in which to do so. In subsequent discussion, we came to the conclusion that Willie and John Rosemond were not the problem. We were as capable, we decided, as any other two people of doing a good job of rearing children. The problem was the road map we were trying to follow. It kept leading us into one dead end after another. This road map consisted of books like Selma Fraiberg's *The Magic Years* (1959), psychologist Thomas Gordon's *Parent Effectiveness Training* (1970), and family counselor Dorothy Briggs's *Your Child's Self-Esteem* (1970). These authors railed against traditional child rearing. They proposed that the traditional autocratic family be replaced by the "democratic" family, one in which parents and children cohabitated on a level playing field. Gordon had written that democratic child rearing was the only context in which children's emotional development could be properly nurtured because "they like so much to be trusted and to be treated as an equal." Briggs had warned that the workings of democracy in government would have little meaning to a child "unless he feels the daily benefits of it at home." She went on to say:

> Discipline is democratic when parents share power, when adults and children work together to establish rules that protect the rights of all. In democratic homes, children have an equal part in working out limits.

Like most young parents of our generation, Willie and I had been impressed by this rhetoric. We had tried to create democracy, but we finally realized that we had failed. We had instead created a state of tyranny. In this case, the tyrant was three years old. Eric terrorized us from the time he awoke in the morning until we had successfully negotiated a bedtime with him. Any time he didn't like a decision we made or were trying to persuade him to cooperate with, he would throw himself to the floor and begin screaming and thrashing about like the inmate of a medieval insane asylum.

Our method of coping with his fits was to do what I now refer to as the "Tantrum Dance." It went something like this: We would make, or propose, a decision. Eric would begin to scream and thrash. We would immediately begin to "dance" about until we found a place to stand that Eric approved of. He would, thenceforth, stop screaming and all was well until the next time, which was always imminent. The problem, of course, was that the more we danced, the more he screamed; and the more he screamed, the more we danced.

Willie and I lived in fear of Eric. We were certain that his frequent, wild tantrums were evidence of bad parenting. After all, Gordon and his co-revisionists had as much as said that democratic child-rearing methods guaranteed a happy child. It was easy to see that Eric was often not very happy. He seemed, in fact, more relaxed with other people than with us. Willie and I blamed ourselves, or one another, for this ever-worsening debacle. But Willie's second pregnancy changed all that.

Coming at last to our senses, we realized that for all the things our parents had supposedly done wrong, we hadn't turned out badly at all. If our parents' child rearing had worked for us, we reasoned, maybe it would work with Eric. So, we shifted gears and began relating to and dealing with him in much the same manner our parents had dealt with us. We began insisting that he do as he was told, and punished him when he didn't. We began putting him in his room when he threw tantrums, and if he came out before a tantrum had run its course, we spanked him and put him back. We stopped trying to make him happy and began devoting ourselves to making him civilized. (I've since made the observation that the most happy children *are* well-behaved. And when I ask their parents, as I often do, "How did you go about making this wild thing so pleasantly civilized?" they always credit old-fashioned child-rearing methods.)

Slowly, but surely, Eric began coming around. But Willie and I had "missed the boat" and as a consequence were paddling upstream. Making matters worse, we initially fooled ourselves into thinking that there were certain parts of nouveau "parenting" that were, indeed, worthwhile. It took us a while to understand that because it was founded on a false premise—specifically, that it was possible to democratize the parent-child relationship—nothing of enduring value could be squeezed out of it. To make a long story short, the rehabilitation of our child rearing, and therefore our family, took a good six years. During that time, we transformed ourselves from being child-centered to being marriage-centered, we embraced distinctly old-fashioned attitudes toward and methods of discipline, and we stopped taking ourselves so seriously.

In the meantime, I had become thoroughly disenchanted with the advice psychologists and other "helping" professionals were dispensing to America's parents and resolved to become a proverbial "voice in the wilderness" in advocacy of traditional child rearing. Willie and I had tried it both ways, and it was obvious that the better way was the old way. At the urging of several colleagues who felt similarly, I approached Bill Williams, the editor-in-chief of my hometown newspaper, the *Gastonia Gazette*, and asked him for fifteen column inches a week within which to dispense child-rearing advice. I am forever indebted to Bill, who has since retired, for recognizing that despite my academic training, I still had vestiges of common sense. I began writing the column in July of 1976, while employed as director of early-intervention services at Gastonia's mental health center.

Two years later, the *Charlotte Observer* took notice of the column, and in March of 1978 the column began running in their Sunday "Living" section. In 1979, my editor at the *Observer* submitted the column to Knight-Ridder for syndication, and they began distributing it to their subscribers.

In 1981, *Parent Power!* was published by East Woods Press, a small house in Charlotte. As with all of my subsequent books, I sought to provide a counterpoint to the ideas then being advanced by mainstream psychology. The "democratic family" was a myth conjured out of thin air, I said. The choice open to parents was a simple one: either create a "benevolent dictatorship" or fling wide the door to family anarchy. From all over the country, parents began writing and calling to thank me for putting into words what they had felt all along was the right way to rear kids, but didn't feel they had permission to do. Psychologists and other mental health professionals, however, were not so enthused. My colleagues around the country, for the most part, were outraged that I had the chutzpah to take such blatant potshots at accepted psychological doctrine. I suddenly found myself at the center of a cyclone that's been raging ever since, and the more widely read and widely spoken I've become,* the more violently it has raged.

I threaten America's mental health industry because I attempt through my work to convince parents that whether they realize it or not, they are competent to solve 95 percent of child-rearing prob-

---

*At this writing, my newspaper column appears in more than one hundred newspapers, including the Pacific edition of *Stars and Stripes.* I write monthly articles for both *Better Homes and Gardens* and *Hemispheres,* United Air Lines' in-flight magazine. I now have seven books to my credit, including this one and an updated edition of *Parent Power!* Beginning in 1990, the year I left private practice to devote myself to writing and public speaking, I've been making more than two hundred presentations a year to parent and professional groups around the country.

lems on their own, without professional help. Mental health professionals, on the other hand, have spent enormous energy trying to convince the American public they are indispensable to nearly every aspect of child rearing. I'm willing to concede that some mental health professionals can, in some cases, be helpful, but then so can a co-worker, your barber, your grandmother, a neighbor, or your best friend. Unlike the case with doctors, dentists, and automobile mechanics, however, there is no evidence that mental health professionals have improved the overall quality of life in America. In short, if by some miracle they all disappeared from the face of the planet, life would go on, and suffering would not increase significantly. Trust me on this. Remember, I am a psychologist. If I disappeared from the face of the earth, life would go on, although the mean "humor quotient" of the world would drop ever so slightly.

Like I said, I'm a heretic, and upsetting people is what heresy is all about. It's not about being *wrong*. It's about violating implicit rules concerning what can and can't be said within a given discipline or organization. I violate the rules, therefore, I'm a heretic. There's a lot of people that would like for me to shut up and go away. But I'm not gonna. Heresy is a dirty job, but someone's got to do it.

The State of the Family

My sixth book, *To Spank or Not to Spank* (1994), represented my first foray into political territory. Nearly a third of it dealt with the rise in America of a powerful antispanking movement, consisting of various "helping" professionals and children's rights advocates. In the course of researching that issue, I became increasingly aware that the American family has become a political battleground. Ultraliberal elements are clearly attempting to control what takes place within the family, especially how children are reared, and they are receiving support and assistance from high places, including the current inhabitants of the White House. Conservatives, meanwhile, are equally determined to defend the sanctity of the traditional family. They understand that the autonomous, self-governing family unit, as English historian Paul Johnson has said, is the last defense against an "overweening state."

For nearly thirty years, the traditional family (two heterosexual, married parents and one or more children) and the values it represents have been under assault by deconstructionist forces within our culture. A few examples:

❑ No-fault divorce laws have transformed marriage from a sacrament into a legal contract subject to negotiation, renegotiation, and nullification, thus weakening the commitment of the people involved and cheapening marriage's cultural value. In the words of UCLA professor James Q. Wilson, author of *The Moral Sense* (1994), "It is now easier to renounce a marriage than a mortgage." Indeed, as any banker will tell you, people are more likely to divorce than to default on a home loan.

❑ Radical feminists have characterized males as pathological by nature, determined to subjugate females by any means necessary and prone to physical/sexual violence toward them. As hysterical demonizing to this effect achieved politically correct status, women's liberation, which had begun as a legitimate struggle for workplace equity, quickly became a war for freedom from men, thus lending further faux legitimacy to America's "divorce culture."

❑ School curriculums abound with instruction in such pseudosubjects as "human sexuality," "AIDS awareness," "conflict resolution," "diversity appreciation," "family life education," and other equally frivolous offerings, none of which are more than disingenuous means of promoting ultraliberal social propaganda.

❑ For three decades, mental health professionals have been characterizing the traditional nuclear family as a breeding ground of personal and interpersonal pathologies. The current term is "dysfunctional," which noted family counselor and author John Bradshaw *(Bradshaw on the Family: A Revolutionary Way of Self-Discovery)*, has said describes nearly all American families. Mental health professionals further told baby boomers they had been psychologically damaged by traditional child-rearing practices and entreated them not to rear their children likewise. Most of the blame for the supposed dysfunctionality of American families was assigned to men. The popularization of this sort of disingenuous propaganda had the effect of undermining marriage formation and marriage stability.

❑ A number of mainline churches caved in to political correctness by conferring legitimacy upon homosexual unions. The term used, "committed relationship," implies that this sort of capricious arrangement is equal in value and status to a heterosexual marriage. A rose by any other name is, indeed, a rose, but calling a dandelion a rose does not make it a rose.

❑ The passage of "homosexual rights" laws have made it possible for homosexuals to adopt children, have children via artificial insemination, and retain custody of biological children by previous heterosexual unions. "Gay and lesbian parenting" is the subject of several books published since 1990, the authors of which are not only unanimous in denying that being reared by homosexual parents poses a risk to normal heterosexual development, but also are unabashed in claiming that a child reared by homosexual parents is probably going to grow up more tolerant, more sensitive, and more creative, as well as devoid of any traits that might lend themselves to sexism, racism, or aggression. In short, we are to believe that homosexual families are *better* for children than traditional families!

❑ Most public school sex education programs have promoted the cynical notion that teenagers are going to engage in premarital sex, no matter what; therefore, said these programs' designers and advocates, it was "unrealistic" to encourage abstinence until marriage. Condom distribution and instruction in other forms of supposedly "safe" sex has become the norm. It is apparently okay to tell kids to "just say no" when it comes to drugs, but not when it comes to sex.

❑ An implicit antimarriage bias has seeped into many public school curricula. Protecting the "self-esteem" of children requires that they not be told that a family headed by two permanently married heterosexuals has numerous economic, emotional, and social advantages over single-parent families, stepfamilies, blended families, or "families" formed by adults in "committed relationships." In the New York City schools, an elementary reader entitled *Heather Has Two Mommies,* about a little girl being reared by two lesbians in a "committed relationship" was disallowed in the curriculum only because a disgruntled and more-than-slightly irate electorate brought about a change in school board composition.

❑ Many of the motion picture and music industry movers and shakers of Hollywood and New York make their livings peddling images and messages which are not only inconsistent with, but also blatantly deny the validity of traditional family values. Time Warner, for example, not only markets so-called "gangsta rap," the lyrics of which typically (a) glorify rape and other forms of violence toward women, (b) justify racist hate toward Caucasians, and (c) encourage law breaking, even the murder of police, but also defends the "free speech" rights of the scum who spout this sort of trash. On the typical "family sitcom" (e.g., *Rosanne*), children talk to their parents with sarcastic disrespect as the laugh track rolls. In 1991, Vice President Dan Quayle was roasted by the major media for denouncing the glorification and unrealistic representation of unwed motherhood portrayed on the television series *Murphy Brown*. Three years later, many of his detractors, even President Clinton, were admitting Quayle was right.

❑ Among the Hollywood elite, parenthood without the responsibility of marriage has become the vogue. Several well-known actresses have demonstrated their "solidarity" with unwed welfare mothers and their contempt for traditional family values by having children out of wedlock. In most cases, they not only refused to identify the fathers, but also made it perfectly clear they had no intention whatsoever of getting married. This highlights a growing trend further legitimized in *Single Parents by Choice* (1992) by Naomi Miller and glorified by Single Mothers by Choice, a national organization founded and directed by a female social worker. The fact is that the overwhelming majority of women who read the former and/or join the latter are capable of making this choice without experiencing economic hardship. In other words, they represent a small minority of single female parents, most of whom are struggling to keep their children adequately fed and clothed. The point, of course, behind the aforementioned book and organization is that fathers are irrelevant.

❑ Definitions of child abuse have slowly expanded to encompass disciplinary methods used routinely by parents of previous generations, including spanking. At the same time, government social workers charged with investigating child abuse reports have adopted a zealous attitude toward their responsibilities, apparently believing their own disapproval of a parent's discipline justifies forcing entry into the family in question and disrupting the lives therein.

❑ Meanwhile, psychologists and other "helping" professionals have been helping to drive the dramatic increase of single-parent families by failing to support marriage. In many cases, marriage counseling, rather than being an attempt to salvage a potentially viable relationship, focuses instead on helping the two parties understand one another such that they can obtain an amicable divorce. The leader of a marriage-counseling workshop I attended in the early '80s began by saying, "Let's face it, in most cases our job is not to save the marriage, but to assist in a friendly divorce, *one that doesn't harm the children*" (emphasis mine). In addition, the "party line" in the mental health professions has been that children are no less psychologically well off with one parent than with two. The most important things, said mental health professionals, were (1) that children not feel "responsible" for their parents' divorce, (2) that the parents continue to communicate well concerning the children, and (3) that the children see the father on a regular basis.

Undermining the strength and legitimacy of the traditional family has become a cultural sport that by the 1990s has taken on the character of a riot. As a result, America's long-standing culture of marriage has been slowly but surely replaced with a culture of divorce, unwed parenthood, and "committed relationships." Beginning in 1975, the marriage rate for previously unmarried women ages fifteen to forty-four began to fall. By 1988, it had reached an all-time low of ninety-one per thousand. From 1970 to 1990, the percentage of married adults dropped from 72 to 62 percent and is still falling. As the rate of marriage has fallen, the rate of divorce has risen, along with the percentage of children born to unwed mothers. From 1960 to 1990, the percentage of families headed by a single parent more than tripled, from 9 to 28 percent. One of the more insidious precipitates of the divorce revolution has been the fatherless home. Nine of ten single-parent homes are fatherless today, and more than one-third (36 percent) of children are living apart from their biological fathers. It is projected that only 6 percent of black children and 30 percent of white children born in 1980 will live with both biological parents through age eighteen. The comparable figures for children born in 1950 were 52 and 81 percent, respectively.

The consequences to children of this nouveau social experiment have been nothing short of disastrous. In recent years, it has become increasingly and painfully evident that children fare significantly better in every conceivable way—developmentally, emotionally, economically, socially, and academically—when they are reared by two permanently married heterosexuals. Since the 1950s, when, according to nearly an entire generation of mental health professionals, almost all families were dysfunctional, child-rearing methods were harmful, and schools were not meeting the needs of many students, *nearly every indicator of positive mental health in children has been in precipitous decline* (the sole exception being drug and alcohol use, which has leveled off since 1980). For example:

❑ Violent crimes (murders, forcible rapes, aggravated assaults) committed by juveniles have increased sixfold, and this statistic is based solely on arrest records. It's fairly safe to say, therefore, that this statistic is conservative. In any case, children are the fastest growing segment of America's criminal population.

❑ Violence on the part of children against their parents and teachers—something almost unheard of forty years ago—has become a serious problem.

❑ Although alcohol and/or drug use among teens is, by all accounts, less of a problem today than was the case in the '70s and '80s, it continues to be a factor in more than half of all teenage deaths. Alarmingly, while high school seniors report consuming fewer drugs and less alcohol than ever, the rate of use among eighth graders is rising slightly. In 1990, an estimated 1.6 million teens needed treatment for alcohol and other drug abuse.

❑ The rate of births to unmarried teens has increased almost 200 percent. In 1990, more than two-thirds of all births to teens were to unmarried girls, compared to less than one-third in 1970, and even less in the '50s.

❑ Since 1960, the rate of teen suicide has more than tripled. Suicide is now the second leading cause of death among teenagers.

❑ Eating disorders have soared among adolescent girls.

❑ Teenage depression has become almost epidemic.

❑ SAT test scores have declined nearly eighty points, even though the test has been renormed to artificially inflate the numbers. At the same time, per capita student expenditures (in constant 1993 dollars) have increased threefold, the ratio of pupils to teachers has dropped in all fifty states, and the educational level of the average teacher has markedly increased.

❏ Classroom disciplinary problems are much worse, and much more serious. In the '50s, the top disciplinary problems according to public school teachers were talking out of turn, chewing gum, and cutting in line. In 1990, teachers named drug and alcohol use, assault (against both peers and teachers), and robbery among their most serious disciplinary concerns.

There's no two ways about it: The American family is in a state of deepening crisis (and so is the American school), and as a consequence, America's children are in more trouble and at more risk than ever before.

The conclusions, all of which belie professional propaganda to the contrary, are inescapable: The predominant family of the 1950s was a healthier place for children than is the confusion of families they grow up in today. As a child, the typical baby boomer was far more secure than his child is likely to be. Not only were the "Ozzies and Harriets" of the '50s doing a better job than today's parents (Ozzie and Harriet's kids!), but America's schools were doing a much better job educating America's children with—get this—less money, more crowded classrooms, and less well-educated teachers! Mental health professionals would like us to believe that anyone who thinks the "good old days" were actually better days is looking at the 1950s through rose-colored glasses. But the numbers tell the story: The cynics are wrong. Dead wrong.

It's time we baby boomers owned up to the fact that we've made, as a generation, some very big mistakes. The biggest mistake of all was letting the wrong people give us our marching orders. Much of the blame for the cultural debacle in which we are currently enmired, I'm afraid, falls on the shoulders of people in my profession and related professions. They're not the only culprits, of course. Included in the "rogues' gallery" are politicians of all stripes, feminists, lawyers, jurists, educational policy makers, church leaders, the media, and even well-intentioned children's rights advocates. We allowed these people to orchestrate chaos, and it's now time we removed them, as politely as possible, from their podiums.

It then becomes imperative that we fix what we let fall into disrepair. We started the dominoes falling, and it is now necessary that we not only stop the chain reaction, but set the dominoes—marriage, the traditional family, and traditional, old-fashioned child rearing—upright again. The responsibility is ours for both a moral reason—we rejected our upbringing and allowed ourselves to be led astray—and for a practical one as well—we are the last generation to remember what it was like before the dominoes began tumbling; therefore, we can understand the goals in concrete terms. Many of our children will be able understand them in the abstract only—if they ever understand them at all.

Marriage, the traditional family, and traditional, old-fashioned child rearing are what this book is all about. They constitute what I call "A Family of Value." I coined the term to refer to a family that is of optimal value to our culture, of optimal and enduring value to its members, and that succeeds at endowing children with the values that comprise good citizenship. Once upon a time not so long ago, the typical American family fit that description, which is not to say that the typical family was faultless, *because it is impossible for human beings to do anything that is without fault.* As Judeo-Christian scripture tells us, every human being is fraught with fault; therefore, everything human beings do is faulted. Our marriages are faulted, our families are faulted, our child rearing is faulted. For the most part, however, this is not dysfunction; it's simply reality. And furthermore, the notion that enough therapy with the right therapist will "resolve" the fault in a family is absurd. There has never been, and there will never be, a perfect family. Every human starts life with one strike against him. In the course of being raised in an imperfect family, by imperfect parents, he acquires another strike. Those first two strikes can't be avoided. A child has no choice where they are concerned. The challenge that lies before each and every one of us, once we reach adulthood, is to not acquire a third strike, the strike of choice.

Despite its faults, the family of the '50s was about as good as it's ever going to get. This book is a celebration of that fact, and it is my small contribution to helping us get back on that right track.

PART ONE
Through the Looking Glass

CHAPTER ONE

Have We Hit Bottom Yet?

Prior to World War II, young parents who met with difficulty in the course of rearing their children didn't take themselves or their kids to therapists of one sort or another. Instead, they sought out older, wiser members of their extended families—people who lived within walking distance. They consulted their favorite aunts, their own parents, grandparents, older cousins, or perhaps even close family friends who were considered "family" in the figurative sense. These were people whom they trusted and respected and who, furthermore, were recognized within the community as bona fide "experts" on the rearing of children. They were considered experts not because they had gone to college and done great study on the subject, not because they were doctors of this or that, but because they had proven, beyond a shadow of doubt, their "hands-on" competence as parents. They had reared children who had become, as adults, upstanding members of the community; upstanding not in the sense of having attained great wealth and status (although that would not have been a disqualification), but in that they were thought of as responsible, hard-working, and productive; in short, good citizens. Throughout this book, I will refer to these genuine experts as "Grandma."

Grandma gave advice to young parents that was based *on a life she had led.* As such, it was firmly rooted in the soil of *common* (as in commonly held and commonly regarded as indisputable) sense. It was down-to-earth, practical, and easy to understand. You didn't need a college degree or a dictionary to figure out what Grandma was talking about. Perhaps more important than anything else, her advice was reassuring. In one way or another, Grandma told her young petitioners that although they might be feeling overwhelmed by whatever problem or problems they were encountering, there was, in fact, *nothing a child could do that was bigger than his or her parents' ability to successfully deal with it*. Absolutely nothing. And so these young parents left Grandma's possessed of not only a clear sense of direction, but also a renewed sense of confidence in themselves.

Grandma's advice reflected a body of traditional understandings that had been implicit to the rearing of American children since before the signing of the Declaration of Independence. These understandings constituted America's child-rearing model, or paradigm. According to that paradigm, a parent's primary responsibility was seeing to it that his or her children were endowed with those traits of character that constituted good citizenship: specifically, *respect* for persons in positions of legitimate authority; a willingness to accept *responsibility* for one's own social behavior as well as for assignment from authority figures; and *resourcefulness,* a hang-in-there, tough-it-out, try-and-try-again attitude toward the many challenges of life. Respect, responsibility, resourcefulness: I refer to these timeless values as the "Three Rs" of child rearing.

The teaching of these values began at home. Respect was developed first toward one's parents, whose responsibility it was to command (not *demand*) it by being authoritative models and directors of proper moral behavior. Having been successfully "rooted," respect extended outward to include other authority figures—teachers, police, lawmakers, employers—then further still to include every honest, law-abiding person regardless of background or station in life. Finally, this respect would come full circle back to the child, now perhaps in his or her late adolescence, as a relatively mature sense of *self-respect*. It is, after all, a scriptural truth that in order to achieve respect for self, one must first give respect away, not selectively, but universally. To "love thyself" you must first "love thy neighbor" and "love thy God." In the final analysis, then, self-respect is something *earned,* not something that can be either learned or given.

Responsibility was learned through the doing of chores in and around the home. These acts were to be selfless; in other words, they were not compensated with money. The child was to do them because, and only because, he was a member of the family. As such, he shared in the family's work as well as its bounty. Through the doing of chores, the child learned the value of contribution, a prime tenet of good citizenship. The child's contributions to the family uplifted not only his own value within the family, but also the value of the family to him. This sharing, this mutuality of value, bonded the child to the *values* that defined the family, thus forming *A Family of Value.*

Resourcefulness—the ability to do a lot with relatively little— was neither earned nor learned, but rather brought forth. It is, after all, every child's nature to be resourceful. It is *not* human nature to be respectful or responsible, but resourcefulness is a different matter. To bring forth the resourcefulness of a child, parents of not so long ago provided the child with everything he *needed* along with a small—very small, in most cases—amount of what he *wanted.* In short, they said "no" more often than they said "yes." Thus "creatively deprived," the child had to learn to solve problems on his own. He had to do his own homework, occupy himself, solve his own social conflicts, and so on. He had to *invent* solutions to problems in these areas because adults, for the most part, would not solve those problems for him. Adults wanted the child to learn to "stand on his own two feet"; therefore, they were quite conservative when it came to letting him stand on theirs.

These were the standards of good child rearing. Parents were not measured by the grades their children earned in school. Everyone knew that a child possessed of the "Three Rs" would do his or her best in school, and that was sufficient. Neither were parents measured in terms of how exhausted they made themselves in the course of driving their children from one after-school activity to another. In fact, parents were not supposed to do much of that sort of thing at all. For the most part, children were to come home from school, change their clothes, and find something to do. Their parents were not to find the something for them. Nor were parents measured in terms of how *involved* they became in such things as their children's homework. Children were to do their own homework, as they were to find their own after-school occupation, as they were to fight their own battles, as they were to stew in their own juices, as they were to lie in the beds they made, and so on. Parents of generations past were measured against the standard of the

"Three Rs." If, as a parent during those times, you had succeeded in the eyes of your peers at endowing your children with adequate amounts of each "R"—and whether you had succeeded or not was self-evident—your child-rearing skills would be held in high esteem. Your friends and neighbors, therefore, would have said you "were doing a good job." Whether your child grew up to become a doctor or a janitor was secondary to the fact that your good child rearing had all but guaranteed that whatever path he chose to walk, he would be an asset to the community.

Losing It

Every culture has its own unique child-rearing paradigm. In fact, a culture's child-rearing paradigm is the centerpiece of the culture—its axis, if you will. Since in the final analysis a culture is defined by its child-rearing practices, a stable child-rearing paradigm—one that is handed down intact from generation to generation—is essential to ongoing cultural stability. If deconstructionist forces succeed at subverting a culture's child-rearing paradigm by creating doubt concerning its validity, the culture will be disrupted in many significant ways. This process is akin to shaking the culture by its axis, the destabilizing tremors of which will be felt throughout all of its institutions, but especially in those two institutions which are primarily responsible for the socialization of children: the family and the school. That, unfortunately, is exactly what has happened in these United States since the 1950s.

In the aftermath of World War II, extended family clusters, which had once been the demographic norm, began breaking up into nuclear family units that dispersed across the American landscape. Suddenly, young parents found themselves living not across the street from Grandma, but hundreds, if not thousands, of miles away. As extended family supports became less and less readily available, young parents began turning to various professionals—psychologists, family counselors, clinical social workers, and other members of the so-called "helping" professions—for child-rearing support.

The problem—it was a problem from the outset, and it continues to be a problem today—is that professionals have not, by and large, dispensed advice based on lives they have led. Rather, their advice has been based on *books they have read*. Their perspective has been shaped less by real-life experience and more by an academic one. As a consequence, their "take" on child rearing has been intellectual rather than commonsensical; more "in the clouds" than down to earth. "Helping" professionals have created a child-rearing jargon that is full of abstractions and speculative theories. It is difficult to understand, imprecise, confusing, and for all of these reasons, it has not been reassuring. It is an undeniable fact that since professional advice achieved dominance in the "parenting marketplace," American parents—and especially those who, like yourself, dear reader, consume this advice—have become the most insecure, anxious, indecisive, guilt-ridden bunch of parents ever to inhabit any culture on earth at any time in history.

As "helping" professionals played with the awesome power parents were granting them concerning how America's children were reared—*again, the process most critical to our culture's continued stability*—they made it seem as if the rearing of children was extremely complicated. Perusing the "Child Care" section of any large bookstore, you will find books on how to rear the child with attention deficit disorder, the child with learning disabilities, the adopted child, the gifted child (always a best-seller), the strong-willed child, the difficult child, the only child, the middle child, the stepchild, the child born to older parents, and so on. Today's parent has been led to believe that in order to rear a child properly, you must first find out what *kind* of child you have. If you cannot figure it out on your own, you can pay a "helping" professional upward of one hundred dollars an hour to make the determination. Once you have discovered what *category* of child you are rearing, you go to the bookstore and buy every book available on the category in question, and—voilà!—you now have your very own customized child-rearing kit which you then share with your child's teachers so that they will have sufficient appreciation of his "special needs."

Professionals have taken the "whole" of childhood and sliced it into ever-thinner sections, then held each section up to the light of psychological scrutiny and analysis. In the process of all of this dissecting, theorizing, and intellectualizing, professionals seem to have lost sight of the fact—and have caused American parents to lose sight of it as well—that *a child, regardless of prefix, is first and foremost a child.*

But American parents no longer think in terms of "child." They think in terms of categories of "child." Representative of this mindset, a woman in Dubuque, Iowa, approached me after a speaking engagement, asking, did I have a book that dealt with the ADD (attention deficit disorder) child? I told her that nothing I'd written was specific to ADD, but any of my books would deal with the issue in general terms.

"No," she said, "that won't do. I need something specific."

"Why?" I asked, curious regarding her urgency.

"Because my eight-year-old son *is* ADD," she answered (emphasis hers).

Oh, my. This woman thinks her son *is*, in his entirety, in every fiber of his being, in every aspect of who he is and can ever hope to become, ADD. He is nothing more and nothing less than ADD. He is no longer simply a child. He has become a category, a subset, of child. He *is* a prefix. He *is* ADD.

This woman, like so many American parents of her generation, has gone to a professional who has rendered this diagnosis concerning her son. I am not questioning the diagnosis. I might have suggested it myself. But I would have told the woman this: "Do not be misled by this diagnosis, this condition we're going to call attention deficit disorder. It constitutes perhaps 10 percent of your son's overall makeup. The other 90 percent of him is just like every other eight-year-old child in the world. If you forget that, you do so at his, and your, peril."

That is obviously not what this mother was told. Whatever the diagnosing professional said, she came away with the impression that her son *is* ADD. Consequently, this diagnosis does not help her see her son more clearly or understand him better. It is a distorting lens through which she views him and all that he does. As a result of holding this lens up in front of her, she sees her son *less* clearly. She does not understand that he is first and foremost a child, more *like* other children than different. Much more. And because she now thinks she's rearing a child who is more *different* than alike, her child rearing is way off the mark. It's "aimed" at the 10 percent rather than the 90. This is nothing but sad.

My encounter with this woman was far from unique. In the course of my extensive travels as a public speaker, I encounter parents nearly every day who think they are rearing prefixes rather than children. They think they're rearing adopteds or gifteds or steps or onlys or whatevers. They don't understand that the prefix, whatever it is, never constitutes much more than 10 percent, if that.

I get the impression, furthermore, that many of today's parents don't even want to rear unprefixed children. That's too ordinary. They feel almost left out if their children aren't identified as "special" in some prefixable way. It especially pumps them up if their children are discovered to be "gifted," as if that means they must be the world's best parents or something. Then again there are those (and these two categories are not mutually exclusive) who seem to relish being victims of their children's "specialness." Within a minute of being introduced to someone, the parent-victim almost always finds a way of revealing that his or her child *is* ADD or learning disabled or strong-willed or something that's supposed to evoke much sympathy for what the parent in question has to endure, day in, day out.

"Bill," says their mutual friend, "I'd like you to meet Martha."

"Hi, Martha," says Bill, "I've heard a lot about you."

"Well then," says Martha, "I guess you know that all three of my children are ADD, and so is my husband, and we're beginning to suspect that our dog is, too."

Making matters worse, there are separate books on how to accomplish every task involved in the rearing of children, from weaning to toilet training, to enrolling them in school, to going on vacation with them, to putting them in the hospital, to getting them to do their homework (e.g., *Ending the Homework Hassle*, by yours truly), to teaching them about the birds and the bees, to all of the little mundane things previous generations of parents regarded as "all in a day's work." Parents of bygone eras simply taught their children how to do such things as use the toilet. They didn't think about it much. They just knew it had to be done, so they did it. They also knew that human children are smart. A child who was old enough to "get it" didn't need to be shown something more than once or twice in order to do so. The combination of parental resolve and human intelligence rendered such matters almost trivial. Today's parents agonize over such things. They think and think and think and think, and in the process they hesitate and vacillate and procrastinate, and they miss boat after boat, and find themselves paddling upstream chasing a veritable armada of "issues."

Capping all this off, there are separate books on how to rear children in single-parent families and stepfamilies and adoptive families and blended families and double-blended, single-sided, half-gainer-with-a-double-back-flip stepfamilies, and my gawd! there are even books on how to rear children in "gay" families. Aaaaagggrrrhhhhhh!

This embarrassment of babble has mystified the rearing of children. It has transformed something that previous generations of parents thought was just "something you did" into something incredibly complex, arcane, stupefying, and difficult. Oh, yes, difficult. "The hardest thing I've ever done," says today's exhausted parent who, if she wasn't a hopelessly obsessive-compulsive neurotic before she had kids, is certainly one now.

As part and parcel of this mystification, *helping professionals successfully marketed a nouveau child-rearing paradigm to America's parents.* By the late '60s, psychologists, etc. had persuaded America's parents that the ultimate goal of "parenting"—as child rearing was now being called—was something called "self-esteem." And thus was child rearing uprooted from the soil of common sense and sent into orbit in the nebulo-sphere.

You didn't need a psychologist to tell you if your child was sufficiently endowed with the "Three Rs" of Respect, Responsibility, and Resourcefulness. Anyone who knew your child even slightly could pass accurate judgment on that matter. But what, pray tell, is "self-esteem," and how is one to know whether one's child has enough of it? Those questions only mental health professionals could answer. Or so America's parents were led to believe.

Parents asked these professionals, "Oh, great learned ones, what is this thing you are calling self-esteem?"

And the "experts" said, "It's all about making children feel *good* about themselves." (By the way, I know what they were saying because, to remind you, I happen to be a psychologist, and I, too, was saying this stuff before I awoke to the healing power of common sense.)

"And what," parents asked, "are we lowly parents to do in order to bring that about?"

And mental health professionals answered that self-esteem accrued as a result of parents who:

(1) paid a lot of attention to their children. The more attention a parent pays, the psychologists said, the better the parent. The latest spin on this notion has it that parents should become "highly involved" with their children.

(2) praised their children a lot, while ignoring their inappropriate behavior. Parents were to "catch their children being good" and give them lots and lots of "warm fuzzies." The child who is given a surplus of "warm fuzzies," wrote one psychologist, turns around and gives them to other people. And oh, what a wonderful world this would be, tra la la! It was also, of course, essential that parents not make mention of inappropriate behavior, lest it be given "attention" that would make it likely to happen again. Besides, telling a child he did something wrong would make the child "feel bad about himself," thus sending his "self-esteem" into a tailspin from which it might never recover.

(3) protected their children from frustration and failure. This particular aspect of the mythology of self-esteem found its most welcome home in America's public schools. Educators—who seem to be even more impressionable than parents—jumped on this bandwagon with both feet and began immediately trying to figure out ways to take the frustration and failure out of school and learning and make both the place and the process "fun." This was accomplished, of course, by dumbing down the entire spectrum of the curriculum (except for kindergarten which, curiously enough, became *more* difficult), grading students according to ability rather than performance if not tossing grades out completely, and promoting students from one grade to the next whether they had mastered the material or not.

To give but one example of the ludicrousness that passed for logic where these matters were concerned: In one study purporting to prove that being retained (held back) damaged children's "self-esteem," children who had been retained were solicited as to their feelings about it. Guess what they said! They said things like "It was embarrassing" and "I don't like to talk about it" and "I didn't like it." Conclusion: Their "self-esteem" had been damaged; therefore, concluded the authors of the study, children should not be retained. Similar perversions of "logic" and "science" were used to justify eliminating grades and to implement such educational fads as "cooperative learning," wherein children are not graded according to individual achievement; rather, they work on problems in groups and the group, as a whole, receives the "grade." Huh? So how, one might ask, do teachers know who are the better students? The theory, at least, is that they won't. That's the point, you see. No one is better than anyone else; therefore, no one's "self-esteem" suffers because of unfavorable comparisons. And one might also ask, does not this "cooperative" arrangement result in the brightest, most motivated child in any given group doing most, if not all, of the work? The answer to that is obvious: One child ends up pulling the load for four others. But no one's "self-esteem" suffers, and that's the most important thing (ha!). In this and numerous other ways, public (the operative word) schools were transformed from places of learning to places of coddling, and their primary mission, once to educate, became that of doing therapy. It can accurately be said that in today's public school, seeing to it that children acquire "good self-esteem" is the primary objective, not seeing to it that children learn basic skills. More on all this later.

Fairy Tales

Persuading America's parents to embrace the "self-esteem paradigm" required that the child-rearing paradigm of tradition—the "Three Rs paradigm"—be discredited. The new parenting "experts" began this campaign of disinformation by charging that traditional approaches to child rearing were psychologically damaging. In 1959, child-development specialist Selma Fraiberg's *The Magic Years*, which became a million-seller, used Sigmond Freud as chief "witness for the prosecution." Prior to this, Freud's rather idiosyncratic (a.k.a. bizarre) theories concerning such things as "Oedipus complexes" and "penis envy" and "id" and "repression" had achieved great acceptance among intellectuals; Fraiberg, however, introduced them into the mainstream. In so doing, she implied—without ever saying so directly—that parental authority was more destructive than constructive. Therefore, before exercising it, parents had to *think,* lest they damage the child's most fragile psyche. They had to think of the ramifications and the permutations and the Freudian symbolicisms and then, after much cogitation, cogitate some more.

As other prominent child-rearing "experts" jumped on this very intellectual bandwagon (yelling, "I'm smart, too!"), a climate of anxiety began to permeate the rearing of children. Parents began to question their approaches to matters previous generations had considered mundane. Every aspect of the parent-child relationship took on great psychological significance. Most of this anxiety centered around Freud's idea that children "repressed" traumatic memories associated with certain early experiences—toilet training in particular—thus setting the psychic stage for later anxieties and aberrations concerning sex.

It is significant to note that the "villain" in nearly all of Freud's psychological soap operas was Mother. Freud's mothers were the archetype of dysfunctionality. They traumatized their male children by being implicitly seductive; their female children by insisting upon excessive attention to cleanliness and refusing to adequately explain why girls lack penises. My own mother's reaction to this psycho-babble was typical. Suddenly, after rearing me in the bliss of ignorance for twelve years or so, she became afflicted with anxiety. Needing to better understand the dos and don'ts of child rearing according to Freud, she went straight to the source, reading and rereading nearly all of his arcane writings. I remember her telling me, when I was in my early adolescence, that she and I mustn't become too close lest I be unable to eventually disentangle myself from her apron strings. Thus permanently enmeshed, I would be incapacitated when it came to forming healthy relationships with women, in which case I might become a homosexual! Little did my mother realize that her well-intentioned warning was the single most traumatic event of my childhood. She couldn't have timed it any worse. I just got over it last week.

"Helping" professionals sought not to calm, but rather capitalize on this upsurge in maternal anxiety. Child-rearing manuals, each promising to tell parents (mothers, actually) how to go about this delicate business so as not to traumatize their children, began flooding the marketplace. In the late '60s, California psychologist Thomas Gordon developed a parent-training workshop which he networked across the country using certified "trainers." His ideas and methods—which were nothing more than a "downsizing" of the theories of psychologist Carl Rogers, the progenitor of "nondirective counseling"—became the rage in professional circles.

In 1970, Gordon published one of the best-selling parenting tomes of the decade (and, therefore, ever), *Parent Effectiveness Training (P.E.T.)*. In it, he proposed that the real problem with the American family was that parents didn't so much *repress* as *suppress*. They suppressed their children's intellects and psyches by demanding obedience to rigid rules, by punishing deviations from unreasonably narrow parameters, and by not allowing their children to freely express opinion and emotion. Gordon likened these circumstances, which he said were the norm in families, to a state of subjugation. Even worse, he said parents who relied upon traditional disciplinary methods were akin to animal trainers (*P.E.T.*, pp. 168–69), and he warned that trained animals often turned on their brutal masters. In Gordon's view, power and authority were the source of many, if not most, of the world's evils. Their use, he said, was "unethical" and "immoral" (*P.E.T.*, p. 191), and it was essential for peace on the planet that parents stop using them to control children. His remedy was for families to become "democratic" rather than "autocratic." Here's a sample of Gordon's fancy concerning the ideal parent-child relationship:

> [Gordon's] No-Lose, Method III approach communicates to kids that parents think *their* needs are important, too, and that the kids can be trusted to be considerate of parental needs in return. This is treating kids much as we treat friends or a spouse. [The method] feels so good to children because they like so much to feel trusted and to be treated as an equal. (*P.E.T.*, p. 213)

Note the implication that if a child likes something adults do, they've done a good thing; whereas if the child does not like it, they've done a bad thing. This highly subversive idea was picked up and echoed by the professional community, and as a consequence parents began walking on eggshells around their children, ever wary of making them upset. For the first time in history, parents began consciously trying to maintain their children in a state of bliss.

My wife, Willie, and I were seduced by this rhetoric. We re-solved, along with thousands of parents of our generation, to "break the chain" of generations of autocratic suppression by creating a democratic family. As I detail in the Introduction, Eric ended up running our lives. We did nothing without either consulting him or anticipating how he would react. If we did something "wrong," he let us know by throwing a tantrum. He would flop backward onto the floor and begin screaming at the top of his little lungs, arms flailing, eyes rolled back in his head. Linda Blair, she of *The Exorcist,* had nothing on Eric.

We interpreted Eric's screams to mean we had made yet an-other mistake, which we immediately corrected, thus making him "happy" again. All day long Willie and I did what I call the "tan-trum dance." Eric screamed, we danced, and Eric stopped scream-ing—until the next time, that is. Naturally, the more we danced, the more he screamed, and the more we danced, and . . . you get the picture, I'm sure. It was parenting hell. And it got worse and worse and worse until one day, Willie and I came to our senses. We real-ized that the chaos in our family was a result not of two inherently bad parents, but of the inherently bad advice we were trying to fol-low. We promptly began breaking all of Gordon's rules, and just as promptly, Eric turned into a relatively civilized human being (un-derstanding that with children, a state of civility is always relative). Other parents, unfortunately, were not so bold. Traveling as I do, speaking to parents all over the country, I have the distinct impres-sion that the majority of today's parents, as was the case with Willie and myself some twenty-six years ago, are *trying to keep their chil-dren from screaming.* They are not just intimidated by their chil-dren's tantrums, they are downright *afraid* of them. They will do just about anything to prevent tantrums, and if one occurs, they will do just about anything to make it stop. Little, I'm sure, did Tom Gordon realize the havoc he was helping to unleash upon the Amer-ican family.

Your Child's Self-Esteem (YCSE), yet another million-seller by one of Gordon's disciples, family counselor Dorothy Briggs, was published in 1970. Briggs amplified Gordon's themes, especially hammering away at the fiction that traditional child-rearing methods were damaging to "self-esteem," as was the very concept of obedience. Both she and Gordon went into great detail describing democratic ways of resolving parent-child conflict, ways that recognized the basic equality of the child and therefore did not put the child in a subservient, one-down position. Within this nouveau model, parents were not to deal with disagreement or dissatisfaction on the part of children by making unilateral decisions; rather, they were to engage in "active listening," expressing respect for the child's point of view, and draw the child into negotiations that would result in compromise. Gordon and Briggs proposed that where parent-child conflict was concerned, there should be not one winner and one loser, but two winners. In Briggs's democratic family, parents and children worked things out maturely:

> Discipline is democratic when parents share power, when adults and children work together to establish rules that protect the rights of all. In democratic homes children have an equal part in working out limits. The family works as a unit to establish broad general policies while permitting flexibility within those limits. (*YCSE*, p. 244)

That's all very well and good, of course, but the problem is, children aren't mature, nor can their maturity be advanced by treating them like adults. In fact, as Willie and I and thousands of other parents discovered, treating children as equals *delays*, rather than advances, their maturity.

Child-Centered Families, Unliberated Moms

Along about this same time, "helping" professionals coined the term "child-centered family." The truly democratic family, it was said, was focused on the needs of the children. They were, after all, the most vulnerable members of the family because they were dependent upon adults when it came to getting their needs met. Inherent to this concept was the idea that the more attention parents paid to children, the better. At this juncture, professionals once again picked up on Freud's villainess, Mom, casting her in the role of "primary parent." It was the responsibility of the "primary parent," professionals said, to bond adequately with the child, give the child sufficient attention, and praise him often and lavishly, thus keeping him in a state of happy feelings about himself. In this roundabout, but extremely effective way, mothers were assigned primary responsibility for seeing to their children's self-esteem.

And then the lid on the jar of "mother bondage" was given one final turn. "Helping" professionals began referencing any and all problems children developed to undernourished "self-esteem." A sixth grader whose IQ was 125, but who was underachieving, was depressed because of not getting enough attention. A five-year-old who was throwing tantrums was angry at his parents, especially his "primary" parent, for not giving him adequate "positive reinforcement." A ten-year-old bully was "acting out" poor self-esteem. And so on and on went this psychobabble.

The oh-so-subtle implication: *Where there is a child with a problem, there is a mother who is not giving the child enough attention and praise.* As a result of (a) ignoring the child's good behavior and achievements, (b) transferring too much attention to the new baby, (c) letting the family dog sleep at the foot of her bed but requiring the child to sleep in his own, (d) failing to buy him a new bicycle for not throwing a tantrum in a shopping center, or (e) all of the above, Bad Mother had given her child no choice but to seek attention in inappropriate ways. If any mother had miraculously managed to stay guilt-free to this point, this insidious finger-pointing almost certainly pushed her over the edge.

I was in private practice from 1980 to 1990, engaged primarily in counseling with parents concerning problems with children. Halfway through my first meeting with a child's parents, I would ask what *they* thought was the root cause of their child's problems in school, with peers, or whatever. I asked the question knowing what was likely to happen, nonetheless needing it to happen so that I could make a point.

The child's father would turn toward his wife as she began to talk. I cannot recall one instance where a father—unless the only parent present was male—answered this question. A sentence or two into her answer, the mother's voice would become strained and begin to quiver. Then it would crack; then the floodgates would open. Her body would begin shaking with muffled sobs and this answer, in so many words, would burst forth: "I just know it's all my fault!" She was certain, she would sob, that she was (a) failing to give the child in question enough attention, (b) causing him, in various nebulous ways, to question her love, (c) giving him reason to believe she was partial toward a sibling, (d) yelling too much, (e) overfocusing on his bad behavior, thus giving the impression that he was nothing but a bad seed, (f) causing him to feel that he wasn't "wanted," or (g) all of the above.

The point I needed to make—which required Mom's heart-rending confession—was that *her child didn't have to take any responsibility whatsoever for his problem because Mom was appropriating every iota of responsibility for him.* Mom thought her child's problem was prima facie evidence that she needed to correct some defect in herself. She was searching the depths of her soul for the psychic cancer that caused her to be such a bad parent. Meanwhile, the child was not being corrected. By *either* parent. Every time Dad tried to correct the child, Mom would intervene protectively. From his point of view, his wife complained a lot, but refused to discipline and refused, furthermore, *to let him discipline.* When he managed to sneak in a corrective action of one sort or another, he was later raked over the coals by his wife for being overly harsh, failing to be adequately sensitive and understanding, overreacting, etc. So, unable to win for losing, Dad was usually found on the sidelines of this drama, frustrated and fuming.

Years of interaction with many other "helping" professionals have made me aware that a good number of them tend to judge the "book" of this drama by its cover. They see a mother and a father who are unable to communicate, much less be consistent, concerning a child's problems and conclude that the marriage (and by extension, the family) is "dysfunctional." They propose that the child's misbehavior is either an unconscious means of forcing his parents to resolve their dysfunctionality or a means of drawing the "heat" away from their relationship and toward himself, thus preventing them from having a complete marital meltdown. I've long thought this explanation was, more often than not, malarkey. It usually seems obvious that the child's problems are not the *result* of marital dysfunction; rather, they are the catalyst for those problems. The marriage is not the problem; rather, the problem is probably, usually, Mom's sense of inadequacy, which she hides as well as possible. But Mom is not to blame, by any means. She has simply fallen victim to forty-odd years of psychological babbling to the effect that behind every problem child there is a Bad Mother. In the late '50s and '60s, she was overly attentive. Then, around 1970, she became insufficiently attentive. Most odd, eh? Dad wants to put the onus of the child's misbehavior and/or underachievement in school on the child, but Mom can't allow that to happen because she, and only she, knows who's *really* to blame. So when Dad tries to discipline, Mom jumps in, screaming, "No! Don't do that!" because she's convinced the child "can't help it" and that Dad's discipline will only make matters worse. No, the blame doesn't belong to Mom. It belongs to a generation of "not-so-helping" professionals who have fitted today's female for the straitjacket of mother-guilt.

I spoke to a small women's group recently. I began my talk by saying, "These days, everybody's talking about family values, but the words are largely empty. We're not going to restore a proper sense of value to growing up in the typical American family as long as women like yourselves hold yourselves prisoners to the idea that the more attention you pay your children, the more you do for your children, the more *involved* you become with your children, the better mothers you are. The women of our generation have become servants to their kids. None of you, for example, feels that you have permission to say to your children what my mother said to me (before she began reading Freud) and most of your mothers said to you; namely, 'Leave me alone.'

"When I got 'underfoot,' as she termed it when I hung around her unnecessarily, my mother would fix me with her steely gaze and say, 'You can see that I'm busy. You don't need anything from me, so you're just going to have to find something of your own to do and *leave me alone*.' She didn't scream it. She said it calmly. She didn't hesitate to say it. She said it right off the bat. And she felt no guilt whatsoever at saying it.

"But you women," I continued, "you women serve and serve and serve and serve children who become increasingly demanding and petulant. And you're no different, basically, from my mother. There are many times when you wish your children would simply *leave you alone* [nervous laughter from my audience at this point].

You realize that 99 percent of their pestering is completely unnecessary. But you serve, thinking that if you do so just a little longer, they'll finally get enough of you and leave you alone of their own volition. But they don't. The more you serve, the more they expect you to serve, and the more they pester. Finally, you crack. You scream, 'Just for once, please, I beg you, *leave me alone!*' Then, you feel . . ." I left the sentence incomplete.

The women spoke in unison: "Guilty!"

"Right! Guilty. And there's only one way, isn't there, to discharge the guilt, and that's to *serve*. In fact, at this point, you must serve in double time so as to do proper penance for your sins.

"But the worst thing that's happened to you women is that in the course of trying to be the best mothers the world has ever seen, you've forgotten how to be wives."

The women, perhaps twenty in number, just sat there, stunned. Little did they think that a man could so effectively plumb the depths of their secret souls. Little did they know that men are in the best of all positions to see what's going on with women today, especially when it comes to their relationships with their children. Today's mother has a proprietary view of herself as a parent. She demands "ownership" of the child-rearing process out of fear that if she lets the control slip through her fingers, everything will fall apart. In the final analysis, however, it's herself she is protecting, not her child.

As a consequence of mother-anxiety and mother-guilt—neither of which, I hope the reader clearly understands, has anything whatsoever to do with the biological state of being female—the average American mother is, in her own mind, a single parent. She must do it all because if she relinquishes control of the process for any length of time, her carefully constructed child-rearing "house of cards" will come tumbling down and her children will turn out all wrong and it will all be her fault. So, back off, Dad, 'cause Mom's in town!

The Parenting Aide

Indeed, the average American father is nothing more than a "parenting aide." Like a teacher's aide, Dad's job is to assist Mom when she needs assistance and step in for her when she needs a break.

In either case, his involvement is peripheral, temporary, and carried out at Mom's direction only. Fathers all over America have told me that their wives want them to "get more involved" in the rearing of the kids, but when they get involved, they are often quickly told by their wives that they're doing it wrong. And not surprisingly, mothers all over America have told me that their husbands just can't be trusted to do it right. Unless they're supervised properly, that is.

A woman in San Diego once told me, for example, that she would love to leave "her" children with "their father" while she took time out for herself, but alas, she'd tried that once and "it didn't work."

"How so?" I asked.

"Well," she said, "just three months ago, I left my husband with the kids for a few days while I took a mini-vacation with my best friend from college. When I got back, I learned that my husband had let all three children stay home from school on Friday because one of them had complained in the morning of a headache." She rolled her eyes as if to say, "What am I ever going to do with that stupid man?"

"So what?" I challenged.

"So what?!" she shot back. "So what?! So, I'd have never let 'em stay home, that's what! They need to be in school, that's what!"

"Let me ask you something," I said. "Do you think if you were to come down with a disease that required a six-month hospitalization, that your husband would let the children stay home from school during that entire time?"

"Well, no," she answered, "I guess not."

"No," I said, "he certainly wouldn't. Your husband found himself in the rare position of having some time alone with the kids and decided to use the excuse of one child's headache to maximize it. What's wrong with that?"

"Nothing," she said, "except, except they need to be in school."

"We've already established that if your husband had to take over all the parenting chores, he'd send the kids to school. So, concerning that one day he didn't send them to school, is that one day going to make the difference between any of them learning to read or not, graduating from high school or not, going to college or not, making successes of their lives or not?"

"Well, no," she said, meekly, "I guess not. I guess I'm just a bit of a worrywart, aren't I?"

"I guess you are," I answered, "but I have the perfect solution."

"Which is?" she asked.

"Take more vacations with your friend."

By the way, as I was saying my good-byes to the women in the group referred to several pages ago, many of them told me that my few words had been more "liberating" than anything they'd ever experienced. And the woman in San Diego sought me out later in the day to tell me she'd given a lot of thought to what I'd said and felt, for the first time in her motherhood, "liberated." Mothers all over America, in fact, tell me that I'm lifting "burdens" off their shoulders, "freeing" them to become "real people," making them "less neurotic." Don't get me wrong. I mention this not to exalt myself, but to emphasize how stifling, confining, demeaning, degrading, and humiliating the prescriptions of nouveau parenting have been for this generation of women. The '90s woman may have access to more economic, political, and professional opportunity than did the woman of the '50s, but the '90s woman will not be *truly* liberated until she can look her children square in their eyes and with strength of purpose tell them to *leave her alone*.

I said as much to an audience in Charlotte a few years back. An older woman approached me afterward and said, "Now I understand why my daughter, who's thirty-five, single, and raising my only grandchild, will stand up to men in the workplace, but goes home in the evening and lets her five-year-old son push her around."

That little anecdote reeks with irony. Not only is the mother in the story a walking contradiction, but unbeknownst to her, she is inculcating into her son the one thing she has worked most of her adult life to overcome: *the perception that women are weak, and that their natural state is that of service to men.* After all, if this five-year-old male child is allowed to push his mother around now, how will he ever learn to treat women with dignity and respect?

CHAPTER TWO

Sounds Good,
but It Doesn't Work

*D*r. Thomas Sowell—author, columnist, economist, and brilliant cultural analyst—says that over the last three decades, social policy that worked has been replaced with social policy that sounds good, but doesn't work. The same is true concerning the rearing and education of children, where as a result of professional posturing on the subject, we have substituted the "sounds good" of self-esteem rhetoric for the lessons of citizenship and character development.

Indeed, the child-rearing language of previous generations didn't exactly sound good, replete as it was with such aphorisms as "children should be seen and not heard," "I'm going to give you as much rope as you need to hang yourself," "money doesn't grow on trees," "you made your bed, now you're going to lie in it," "you're going to have to stew in your own juices over this," and the most hated of them all, "because I said so." Each one of these terse sayings embodied an idea inherent to a common (as in commonly held) sense of child rearing, and taken together, they summed up the parenting philosophy of our forebears. Baby boomers like myself grew up hearing one or more of these things on almost a daily basis. As a result, we came to associate them with times when our parents were teaching us "lessons," which we were learning "the hard way." It was, therefore, relatively easy for "helping" professionals to convince us, as adults, that the child-rearing philosophy and methodology represented by these sayings was bogus, if not downright harmful, if not downright abusive.

And convince the majority of us they did. As a consequence, American parents have by and large distanced themselves from this bare-bones wisdom, seduced as most of us were by the idea that the emperor really *was* wearing new and wonderful clothes. Today's parents "parent" according to what sounds good, but it's becoming increasingly clear that what sounds good hasn't worked. Today's all-too-typical child is demanding, disobedient, uncooperative, disrespectful, and irresponsible. Today's all-too-typical parent is frustrated, anxious, and guilt-ridden, and the American family is in a state of crisis unrivaled in history.

For the past fifteen years I have traveled America, speaking to and talking with parents from all walks of life. With few exceptions (which I chalk up to luck), they tell me that try as hard as they can, they can't seem to get nouveau "parenting" to work. They do what the books and talk-show psychologists tell them to do: They praise their kids a lot, they try to talk through parent-child conflicts, they help their kids with their homework, they use "time-out" instead of spanking, they don't ever say "because I said so." They practice all the prescribed dos and eschew the proscribed don'ts; nonetheless, they can't get it to work.

"Helping" professionals have an explanation for this state of affairs. Where there is a parent who cannot get their advice to work, they are apt to say, there is a "dysfunctional" family. The parent in question is "resistant," "defensive," "sabotaging," "enmeshed," or "codependent." In other words, professional advice is immaculate; the problem is that some people don't have it together enough to pull it off, to make it work. This, folks, amounts to a classic double bind or, in popular parlance, a catch-22: If you ask a "helping" professional for advice, and he gives you advice that doesn't help, then *you* are sick and so, in all likelihood, is your entire family. And since the splintered baton of dysfunctionality is handed down from generation to generation, so, too, were your parents and grandparents and so on back through history to the most notorious sabotaging codependents of all time: Adam and Eve!

Well, I'm a psychologist and I'm a parent and I'm here to tell you that the failure of nouveau child rearing is due not to sick parents who rule over dysfunctional families (although there are certainly some out there), but to counterproductive, impractical, and just downright dumb professional advice. But it sure has sounded good, hasn't it?

In the sections that follow, I'm going to describe in detail the consequences of this ill-advised makeover.

Reality Then, Rhetoric Now

The child-rearing language of previous generations may not have caressed the ears, but it reflected certain realities concerning children and their upbringing, and here's a fact: *You can't rear children properly unless you are facing reality.* Today, however, those realities have been replaced by a rhetoric of child rearing that reflects a sentimental, romantic, and idealistic view of children. This nouveau rhetoric is full of maudlin gush, but because it is grounded in no actuality whatsoever, it mystifies rather than clarifies what good child rearing is all about.

The theme underlying this sentiment is that children are wonderfully pure beings who are corrupted by parents who were corrupted by their parents and so on until the beginning of civilized time. The "father" of such thinking was eighteenth-century philosopher Jean-Jacques Rousseau, who argued that humans, inherently good, were warped by society. As such, the individual was not guilty of anything; rather, society was responsible for all the depraved things people did. Rousseau's self-serving ideology (he fathered, abandoned, and refused to support three children) was subversive of the very foundation of civilization, but highly seductive, especially to pseudointellectuals then and now. In this century, the concept of collective guilt was embraced by both Lenin and Hitler and has enjoyed a resurgence of popularity since the 1960s, when it resurfaced on college campuses. You might recall, if you are old enough, that the most heinous social faux pas of the '60s and '70s was "blaming" someone for something they had done, thereby attempting to put them on a "guilt trip." The most recent mutation of this mind-set is the liberal penchant for explaining criminal behavior in terms of bad parenting, racism, poverty, and other social ills. One who suggests that criminals—unless those in question are high-achieving white males—have no excuse is likely to be accused of being narrow-minded and mean-spirited.

Following a speaking engagement in Albuquerque in 1994, one of my hosts sent me a clipping from their newspaper advertising one of the "latest things" in parenting programs. To identify the program by name would be gratuitous; suffice to say, what attracted my attention was the ad's "hook," which read, "Children Are Flowers, Not Weeds."

To say that children are flowers, not weeds, sure does sound good, doesn't it? The problem is it's completely meaningless, and the analogy is all wrong.

Children are *not* flowers. They aren't weeds either. The truth is, children are *wild things* that must be constantly pruned lest they become completely unmanageable. They are self-centered, foolish, undersocialized, undercivilized little people who, if left to their own devices, are capable of incredible selfishness and cruelty, some more than others. The author of this flowery snippet of saccharine sentiment ought to be made to do penance by hand-copying William Golding's *Lord of the Flies*.

It's not that children aren't lovable, but patronization and love are entirely different things. "Children are flowers" is patronizing, and therefore disrespectful. One is capable of loving children honestly and respectfully only if one faces facts:

Fact: Children are fraught with fault.

Fact: Their fault is inherent. It is the result of being human; of being born with free will in the head and foolishness in the heart.

Fact: It is precisely because they all share in humanity's faults—through no fault of their own—that children require unconditional love, and lots of it.

If children were flowers, we could just stand back and admire them. But flowers they aren't. They must be pruned and grafted and wired and sprayed in order that they might someday, with a little luck, become admirable adults. And all of this pruning, etc., if it's going to work, must be done with a lot of love. And a lot of hope.

A realistic, unsentimental appraisal of children is essential not only to truly loving and respecting them, but also to properly disciplining them. If, as a parent, you do not see your children with clarity, their mischevious ways are likely to throw you off balance, and you cannot discipline effectively if you have lost your center of gravity.

Once upon a time, when young parents became disillusioned and upset with their children, they went to Grandma. Entrusted with helping these young people regain their balance, Grandma said such wise things as "she's just a child" and "boys are like that sometimes, yes they are." With an economy of words, Grandma tried her best to prevent young parents from taking the things their children did personally, from being threatened by them.

Almost all young parents have their heads in the clouds where their children are concerned. As a consequence, they are prone to disillusionment and anger when their children reveal their true, imperfect selves. It was Grandma's job to help young parents get their heads out of the clouds and their feet on the ground, to help them see that their children were neither flowers nor weeds and thereby "come to grips" with them.

This is a task many, if not most, "helping" professionals and parenting "experts" have yet to master.

Solutions Then, Understanding Now

Syndicated columnist William Raspberry, who is in a league with Thomas Sowell, although they seldom are found in the same ballpark, proposes that the nouveau attempt to *understand* social problems (e.g., crime, poverty, illegitimacy) has provided certain individuals with an excuse to continue behaving in socially dysfunctional, if not downright pathological, ways. The same could be said of the nouveau attempt to *understand* why certain children seem determined to behave in self-defeating ways.

A generation or so ago, if a child misbehaved in school, the school disciplined the child, confident the child's parents would not only support their actions, but also amplify upon them at home. Misbehaving children were thus caused to "feel bad about themselves," and it was generally agreed that well they should.

There was, in those days, a sense of community participation concerning the rearing of children. Young Master Billy was to someday become a citizen of the community; therefore, the manner in which Billy behaved was of concern to everyone, and everyone agreed Billy's misbehavior needed correcting more than understanding. Occasional misbehavior was thought of as simply the result of a lack of maturity and good judgment. The way to instill that maturity and judgment was to discipline. So, when Billy misbehaved, he was penalized in some way, shape, or form. Adults asked not, "Why is Billy misbehaving?" but "What should be done about Billy's misbehavior?"

Because everyone realized that his parents could not be with Billy constantly, and that his parents' interests were synonymous with the interests of the community, Billy's discipline was a collaborative venture involving parents, teachers, shopkeepers, and neighbors. Any responsible adult in the community had implicit permission to "correct" him. As a consequence, Billy felt the pressure of one uniform set of expectations concerning his conduct. He was expected to be respectful of authority, to accept responsibility for himself, and to always "put his best foot forward." He was expected, in other words, to be a good—albeit apprentice—citizen.

That was before mental health professionals sold us on the idea that bad behavior required not correcting, but understanding. Bad behavior, they said, was the result of poor self-esteem, which was a result of grievous errors—whether intentional or otherwise—on his parents' (probably his mother's) part. Billy was suddenly and miraculously no longer personally accountable for anything he did. Any misbehavior on his part, especially if it became chronic, was merely a symptom of some underlying distress brought on by a stressful and/or inadequately nurturing home life. His parents were expecting too much, rewarding too little, using "inappropriate" (old-fashioned) discipline, not giving him enough attention, or making him feel responsible for their marital discord.

These days, therefore, when Billy misbehaves, his parents are on the community hot seat, not him. As a result, they have become rather defensive regarding any report of misbehavior on his part. When they hear such a report, their tendency is to defend him, rather than correct him. They often insist that he is incapable of the misbehavior in question. Furthermore, since Billy is not ever to feel bad about himself, any disciplinary action on the part of a teacher or other adult that causes him to feel shame or guilt is likely to be regarded by his parents as a quasi-criminal assault on his fragile psyche.

As self-esteem ideology turned the world upside down, the best interests of the community and the best interests of the child and his/her parents went from being synonymous to almost oppositional. Around each Billy there closed a protective microcommunity of parents and relatives determined to prevent anyone from making him feel bad about anything he did or failed to do.

Teachers consistently tell me they can no longer count on the support of parents when they discipline. Today's parent is all too likely to defend or rationalize a child's actions, no matter how blatantly inappropriate. Teachers discipline knowing they risk being accused of destroying the self-esteem of those they try to correct. They tell me, "We no longer have any real authority, and children know it."

Thirty-five years ago, when I was in the seventh grade, adults did not lack compassion for problem children. Nonetheless, the emphasis was on solution, not understanding. I am an authority on this subject because back then, I was a problem child. I was, in fact, more of a thorn in the side of teachers than any other child then enrolled in my suburban-Chicago elementary school. Although able to make straight A's without much study, I was inattentive, irresponsible, disruptive, distractible, immature, and infuriating.

My teachers tried everything—sitting me in the hall, keeping me in during recess and after school, making me write sentences, giving me extra assignments—but nothing worked. My parents tried everything—taking away privileges, giving me extra chores, grounding me for weeks at a time, lecturing—but nothing worked.

One February day in 1959, my parents went to the school for a conference with my teachers. They came home two hours later and summoned me into the living room, where occurred a "conversation" I will never forget.

My stepfather spoke: "This will be short. The agreement reached at the conference was that if you are reprimanded for any reason by any one of your teachers even one time between now and the end of this school year, *you will repeat the seventh grade.* In fact, your mother and I didn't agree to this; we suggested it, and your principal and teachers gladly agreed. Any questions?"

My first question was, "You're kidding, right?" to which my parents said simply, "No, but you are free to find that out for yourself."

I then asked, "But what if the teacher blames me for something I didn't do?"

My stepfather answered, "Your teachers are not, and will not be, mistaken about anything they say you do."

And that was it.

Today, it is likely that a team of "helping" professionals would descend on a similarly incorrigible child, seeking to divine the "why" of the child's problems. They would propose boredom, or attention deficit disorder, or low self-esteem due to his parents' divorce, or a neurotic need for approval from his peers and teachers due to inadequate reinforcement of positive behaviors in the home. They would investigate, speculate, theorize, temporize, label, and sublabel. Meanwhile, everyone would dance around the problem while handling the child with kid gloves and, in the process, providing the child with one or more tailor-made excuses for continuing to misbehave.

In my case, courtesy of my parents' and teachers' joint determination to simply *solve* the problem, my attention deficit disorder with massive boredom and divorce-related loss of self-esteem spawning immature social behavior was cured in but one day. For the remainder of the school year, I faced forward, locked eyes with the teacher, and said not a word unless called upon. And I passed the seventh grade.

Were my parents kidding? I asked them several years ago. They said, "You'll never know. But it worked, didn't it?"

Supervise Then, Get Involved Now

Following a speaking engagement in Omaha, a woman who identified herself as my age asked what I thought of her recent decision to retire from her career in order to . . . here's how she put it: "stay home with my young children, like my mother stayed home with my brothers and sisters and me."

I told her I thought it was always best to have a parent in the home. "But," I said, "I think you may be misrepresenting your mother."

"Why do you say that?" she asked.

"Well, I just don't think your mother stayed home *with* you when you were a child," I answered.

"Of course she did," she fired back, a bit testily. "After all, John, I was there. You weren't."

"No," I said, "I wasn't there, not in the way you mean it. But you and I are the same age; therefore, our mothers were rearing us at the same time, and I'll just bet that on nonschool mornings, your mother, like mine, made sure you'd done your chores and were properly fed and properly dressed; then she sent you outside. And she probably sent you outside with this instruction: 'Don't come back in this house until lunch or I'll keep you inside with me for the rest of the day.'"

The woman looked suddenly amazed. "I don't believe it!" she said, laughing, "That's *exactly* the way it was! I haven't thought about that in the longest time! How did you know that?"

I knew that, of course, because that's the way it was for 90 percent of the children in my generation, and the mothers of the other 10 percent were quietly referred to, by their peers, as "overprotective" and "smothering." That Omaha woman's mother—as were my mother and my friends' mothers—was home *for* her children, not *with* them. She was available to them if they needed her, but she expected them to occupy themselves, fight their own battles, do their own homework, fix their own snacks, and transport themselves around the neighborhood. Besides being generally busy, mothers weren't *supposed* to hover over their children, doing a lot of things for them. Their children, for the most part, were to do for themselves.

Supervision was the name of the parent game back then. Parents were supposed to know where their children were, what they were doing, and who they were with. They were *not*, with very few exceptions, to be involved in what their kids were doing. In the '50s, at ten o'clock on Friday and Saturday nights, nearly every television station in the country broadcast the same visual message. It read: "Parents! It's 10:00. Do you know where your children are?" Not, "What are you doing with your children?" mind you, but "Where are they?" Are you doing your job? Are you providing good supervision?

Good supervision was prerequisite to providing proper guidance. If you didn't supervise, then you wouldn't be able to guide when guidance was necessary. But the word was *guide,* not *do.* If your child needed some direction or coaching regarding an academic or social matter, you were to provide it and then let the child solve the problem on his or her own.

My mother was a single parent for most of the first seven years of my life. During that time, we lived in Charleston, South Carolina, in a walk-up apartment in what is now the historic district. My mother was a full-time student at the College of Charleston and worked many nights and weekends at the post office around the corner. Despite her busy schedule, she managed to enjoy an active social life. I remember my mother going out with her friends and on dates with the fellas in her life. She never took me on a date, and only occasionally did I accompany her and her friends on a day excursion to the beach. When she was home, she was studying, writing a paper, sewing (she made most of our clothes), cooking, cleaning, or maybe just relaxing with a book or classical music.

It was understood that I was to leave my mother alone. Don't get me wrong. If I needed her, she was unfailingly there for me. But I was not, when she was busy (which was most of the time), allowed to be "underfoot" as she called it, unless I truly had a *need.* So, she sewed or studied or whatever, and I listened to the radio or read or played with my Lincoln Logs or went outside and played with my friends. My mother believed, by the way, that children belonged outside, weather permitting, and she defined "weather permitting" very liberally. On those occasions when I happened to slip up and get "underfoot," she'd reprimand me, but not harshly. She'd say, "John Rosemond, you are underfoot. You know how I feel about that. Now, you can see that I'm very busy. You're just going to have to find something of your own to do." And with that, she would usually usher me out-of-doors, and I'd find myself on the sidewalk in front of our apartment with five or six other kids who'd also been kicked out of their houses by their mothers, and we would play. In a sense, we were "exiles," but the thought that our mothers didn't love us never even occurred to us. We didn't feel all lousy inside for hours after this banishment. We didn't even give it a second thought. We just played. We had fun!

Sometimes, your mother put you outside and told you that if

you came home, for any reason, before the next meal, you'd have to stay indoors as her helper the rest of the day. One of my friends' mothers even locked him out of the house sometimes. He must've had a rather pronounced case of "Underfoot Syndrome." Did he sit on his front stoop, his head in his hands, weeping? Not! He played with the rest of us. In fact, we all—himself included—thought the fact his mother locked him out of the house was rather funny. No "codependency" there, that's for sure. Nevertheless, his mother was definitely keeping an eye on him. One day, he fell off his bike in front of his house. Before he could yell, his mother was helping him up, checking him for broken bones. When she was certain he was okay, she walked back into her house, and "click."

Now, I'm not advocating locking children outside. I think that's a bit extreme, in fact. Risky, even. I'm saying that when it came to their relationships with their children, most of the women of my mother's generation were *truly* liberated women (pre-Freud, that is). They erected what we today term "boundaries" between themselves and their kids, and they were in complete control of when their children were allowed through those boundaries. They were not, by any means, at their children's beck and call. It was, in fact, the other way around. If you heard your mother calling, you dropped everything and came running.

Twin boys lived in the house opposite my backyard. A dinner bell had been mounted on their back porch. When their mother, a widow, rang the bell, it meant they had to go home. Immediately. In fact, she rang the bell and then counted to sixty. If they weren't home by the end of her count, they were punished. We were in the middle of a game of street baseball one day when the bell rang. One twin was up to bat, the other on third with the tying run. The game hung in the balance. Before anyone could say anything, they were gone. Baseballus interruptus.

Today's mother, by contrast, has been told she is a "good mother" to the degree she pays attention to her children, does things for them, and gets "involved" in the things they do. This is the nouveau standard to which mothers aspire, and over which they compete for the Who's the Busiest (and therefore best) Mother on the Block Award. If Mrs. Jones is driving her kids to an after-school activity every day of the week and on Saturday mornings, and Mrs. Smith is only driving her kids to activities three afternoons a week, Mrs. Smith better get on the ball. Mrs. Jones is "out-mothering" her.

Today's mother doesn't think she has permission to sternly tell her children they're "underfoot" and need to "leave her alone." She believes she is there to serve. Unfortunately, children aren't skilled at give and take. In fact, if you let them, they will do nothing but take. So, the more Mom serves, the more of her they want for reasons that are increasingly whimsical. Finally, at the end of her psychic tether, she begins ranting and raving. Then she feels guilty. And the only way to cleanse the guilt, of course, is to serve.

My mother was able to tell me to leave her alone without ever raising her voice because she had no qualms about saying it. She said it "right off the bat," calmly, but sternly. I knew, therefore, she meant business. Mom knew full well that if she gave me an inch, I'd want a mile, so she didn't give me an inch. In effect, she let me know that she was my mother, but she was much, much more than just my mother. She was a student, an employee, a friend, and a member of a church. She was a daughter, a sister, and an aunt, and she was a person who liked to sew, garden, read, and listen to classical music. She had many interests and many responsibilities, and I had to respect that. She would be my mother when I needed a mother, and sometimes when I just wanted a mother or she just wanted to be one. But more often than not, I was to get along without her attention. I was to stand on my own two feet. Because she presented herself to me as a multifaceted, interesting human being, I developed great respect for her.

Today's mother has been drained of the courage to inform her children that she's more than a mother. She's become a two-dimensional cardboard cutout with a sign around her neck that reads: I'm Your Mother. How May I Serve You? And she's so *involved!* That's the crux of the parent game today. Get involved in your children's after-school activities, today's mother is told. Get involved in your children's schoolwork. Get involved in their friendships and the things they like to do. Get involved in an exercise program with your kids. Find a hobby you and your kids can share. The more involved you are, today's mother is told, the better a mother you are.

Why, if you get involved enough, you qualify as a Miracle Mom! Today, if television stations "messaged" parents in the evening, the message would read: "Mothers! How are you spending this invaluable quality-time opportunity with your children?"

Schools have really picked up on this theme. Nearly every day, the American schoolkid comes home with a note from his teacher that starts, "Dear Parents . . ." and goes on to give his or her "parents" that day's "involvement assignment." I put "parents" in quotes because every teacher knows full well that except in cases where the only parent in the home is male, the "parents" in question will be mothers. In effect, these notes are pop tests for mothers. Those who willingly accept these assignments pass the tests and are, therefore, Good Mothers. Those who don't accept these assignments, or who do so half-heartedly, are "irresponsible." Because their reputations are on the line, most mothers take these assignments on without question. They've got something to prove, a test to pass. And so, nearly every evening in many an American family, the mother and child reunion takes place over the child's homework and drags on and on as the child tries one stalling tactic after another, hoping his mother will get fed up with his foot-dragging and do his homework herself.

Even mothers who know there's something wrong with expecting parents to help kids with homework go right ahead and accept these assignments. As one mother recently confessed, "My parents didn't do this stuff for me, and I don't think I should have to do it for my child, but if everyone else is doing it, and I'm not, then I'm afraid my child will fall behind. I'm also, quite frankly, afraid of what the teacher will think of me if she finds out."

What amazes me is that of all the supposedly smart educators in this country, none seems to have figured out that when children were expected to do their own homework and their own science projects and their own research for term papers and the like, two things were the case: First, more children did their homework and turned it in on time. Second, overall achievement levels were much, much higher. In short, when children were expected to be independently responsible for such things, they did a lot better in school! But that's not what counts, these days. These days, what counts is an educational philosophy that sounds good. Whether it works or not is irrelevant. Not secondary, mind you, but irrelevant.

I do a lot of teacher workshops. At one point, I ask for a show of hands from those who think the following is true: "A child who knows his mother is ever-ready to help him with his homework is a child who is less likely to pay good attention in class."

Invariably, every teacher in the audience raises a hand.

I then ask, "In that case, how many of you are going to immediately stop telling parents they should be involved in their children's homework?"

Very few hands go up. There is, therefore, only one explanation for the practice of expecting "parents" to get involved in their children's homework: it is "educationally correct." In other words, it is part of current educational mythology. As such, it sounds good, and that's good enough. But then, teachers tell me that even if they wanted to stop sending these notes and messages home, school administrators—who seem collectively entranced by theory—wouldn't allow it. So, teachers go on shooting themselves in their feet, day in, day out.

Like I said, whether an educational practice works or not, makes sense or not, is irrelevant as long as it sounds good.

Seen and Not Heard Then; Seen, Heard, and Deferred to Now

I begin one of the exercises I conduct with my audiences by asking for a show of hands from those folks who believe that "children should be seen and not heard." In an audience of five hundred, maybe twenty hands go up. Someone usually asks, "Do you mean always, or just sometimes?"

I answer, "Always," and their hand stays down.

I then say, "All right, now I want you to raise your hand if you believe that *when a child enters a room occupied by adults who are holding conversation, the child should pay attention, not clamor for it.*" Without hesitation, five hundred hands go up.

Then I ask, "How many of you realize I just said the same thing twice?" People begin giving one another perplexed looks as the first twenty hands go up again.

The idea that children should be seen and not heard was a centerpiece—perhaps *the* centerpiece—of traditional child rearing. Simply put, it meant that children were not allowed—except in times of emergency (which would be obvious)—to interrupt adult conversations. Actually, it meant more than that. It also meant children were not, for the most part, allowed to even participate in adult conversations or take part in adult activities.

There was, in the days of "children being seen and not heard," a distinct boundary (that word again) separating the world of adults from the world of children. Adults were supposed to be highly involved with other adults, not children. Likewise, children were to be highly involved with other children, not adults. Indeed, there were times when adults and children commingled, but these were the exception, not the rule.

I remember attending a family reunion in 1954, when I was six years old. All of the adults were gathered either on the patio or in the kitchen. They were talking about adult things, using lots of adult words that children didn't understand. The children, including myself, were playing in the yard. There were no kids, save a few infants, with the adults, and there were no adults with the kids. No benevolent uncle came out to help us organize our play. No meddlesome aunt appeared to mediate our conflicts. In fact, had a child complained to the adults that the rest of us "weren't playing fair," the complainer himself would have been told to "fight his own battles." If he continued to complain, he would have been made to sit at a distance from both the adults and the children until he decided he could get along.

The only time the two groups came together was over the meal. Even then, we children were seated at a separate table, which was fine with us. After all, separate seating meant we could flip peas at one another and do other equally mischievous things that would have been impossible if adults were looking over our shoulders, making us eat "properly." In short, adults left children pretty much alone, and it was wonderful. These were liberated adults and liberated (within limits, of course) children. Nonetheless, Thomas Gordon, Dorothy Briggs, et al., think this state of affairs was oppressive. They must've grown up in a different universe, ruled over by evil aliens.

Children being seen and not heard profited children in two important ways:

❑ *It greatly enhanced the social education of children.* Note that the first half of the aphorism clearly says that children could be *seen.* If a child entered a room where adults were holding conversation, he was not told rudely to leave (albeit he might have been told *politely* to leave if the adults were talking about something that was not for consumption by little pitchers with big ears). He was simply expected to take a seat at the periphery of the conversation and listen, pay attention. No one was going to pretend—for the sake of "making him feel good about himself"—that he was socially, intellectually, or emotionally mature enough to participate in an adult conversation. However, if he listened, he would learn! He would absorb not only a certain amount of information, but more important, he would learn *how* adults carried on conversation. He would pick up on social nuance and ritual and as a result, he would someday be ready for inclusion in these adult things. So, the idea that children should be seen and not heard did not, by any means, reflect a hostile, antichild attitude. It was, in fact, prochild! It reflected a realistic appraisal of the state of childhood as well as the potential contained within that state. It put children "in their proper place," which was the best of all possible places for them.

❑ *It enhanced the respect of children for adults.* By creating boundaries of this sort between themselves and children, adults *distinguished* themselves. They created a separate culture which excluded children, for the most part. Children, therefore, aspired to membership in adult culture. That aspiration caused them to look up to adults. Adulthood was "where it was at" for kids. By attracting the respect of children, adults provided children the opportunity to eventually acquire self-respect. Two facts are relevant to this discussion: (1) Adults cannot distinguish themselves if they are highly involved with children. In other words, the more children are included in adult activity and conversation, the less likely it is that children will "look up" to adults; (2) the less respect children have for adults, the less respect they will eventually have for themselves. Any way one looks at it, *children should be seen and not heard* was of tremendous benefit to children.

These days, children are allowed to interrupt adult conversations at will, and no one "puts them in their place" for fear of damaging their self-esteem. After a recent presentation, I found myself talking with a couple of parents who wanted to know how to set limits without stifling their children's "energy." No sooner had they asked the question than up walked a girl of seven or eight. Without missing a beat, she proceeded to address her parents as if I wasn't even there.

"When are we leaving?" she asked, plaintively. "I'm bored."

Immediately breaking off our conversation, the father said, "Now, Haroldine, what have we told you about interrupting? What are you supposed to say?"

"Excuse me," Haroldine said, mechanically, while rolling her eyes heavenward.

"That's better," the father said. "Now what is it you wanted to say?"

And right there, to my amazement and amusement, these parents demonstrated the degree to which Haroldine's "energy" is in desperate need of stifling!

But I pick on Haroldine's parents when, in truth, they are Everyparent and Haroline is Everychild. This generation of American children has, as a group, no respect for adult conversation. Which simply means they have no respect for adults. Which simply means their parents, as a group, have failed to communicate the single most important of all distinctions: That adults are not children, and children are not adults. Amen.

This generation of American children interrupts conversations epidemically because they've been included in too many adult activities (and because adults, conversely, have included themselves in too many of their children's activities); because their parents can't bring themselves to say, "Since you can't listen while we're talking, you may leave the room" for fear of stifling their "energy"; because their parents give themselves little permission to do anything without the children except go to work and the bathroom. Maybe.

Almost every day, I see more evidence of the general lack of respect on the part of children for adults. This is tragic, because a child who doesn't respect adults won't pay attention to them. And a child who isn't paying attention is a child who isn't learning. That's why, when parents ask me for ways of improving a child's IQ, I answer, "Forget improving IQ. If you want a child to be the best student he can possibly be, improve his respect for adults, beginning with yourselves."

Agents of the Community Then, Advocates for the Child Now

It's important to understand that when the "good citizenship" paradigm guided the rearing of American children, parents were not likely to lose sight of the forest—their obligations to the community—for the trees. The typical parent kept one eye on the "forest" and one eye on the individual "tree." In other words, the needs of the child were balanced against the needs of the community. In fact, they were one and the same, for everyone knew that strengthening the forest required the strengthening of each and every tree. This strengthening was not done in terms of "self-esteem," however, but in terms of *character*. Seeing to the character development of children was a matter not of "making them feel good about themselves," but a matter of instilling the "Three Rs" of Respect, Responsibility, and Resourcefulness.

Because they acted as agents of the community, parents (1) reported on the behavior of one another's children, and (2) accepted and acted upon report from other adults concerning their own children. My parents, for example, if a neighbor complained that I had ridden my bike over her lawn, did not hesitate to punish me. They took away my bike for a week and/or kept me inside for a couple of days, made me apologize to the neighbor, and acted greatly disappointed in me, which was perhaps the worst punishment of all. It didn't matter that the neighbor's "lawn" was mostly weeds. It didn't matter that my friends and I were caught up in playing "chase" on our bikes and that riding on her lawn was not intentional. It didn't matter that the neighbor in question was generally thought of by other adults in the neighborhood as a flake. All that mattered was that I had given an adult cause to complain about my behavior. It was an accident? Be more careful next time. It won't happen again? Good, and your punishment will make that more certain. She's too picky? Learn her limits, as you learn ours.

As a result of this attitude, which prevailed, the children of my (and previous) generations benefited from an increased sense of accountability concerning our behavior outside, as well as inside, our homes. This accountability helped us divest of self-centeredness, attuned us to the values of the community, taught us respect for others, even those we didn't especially "like," and in all those ways, advanced our social responsibility. Like all children, we tried to get away with certain mischief. We pulled our pranks. But we never lost sight of what adults expected, and what they would enforce.

The "self-esteem" paradigm has caused parents to lose sight of the forest and pay almost exclusive attention to the trees. The balance that once existed between the needs of the community and the needs of the individual child has been lost. Today, the needs of the child prevail. Despite whatever lip service parents might give to the issue of character, "self-esteem" rules.

That's evident in the stories teachers tell me. Generally speaking, parents no longer support discipline meted out in school. In fact, teachers are not only reluctant to discipline, but hesitate to even report misbehavior to parents. All too often, upon hearing a report of misbehavior, parents toss the "hot potato" back at the school. Suddenly, the person making the report—the teacher, principal, or whomever—is on the hot seat, being accused of lacking in sensitivity to the child's "special needs," having a "personality conflict" with the child, singling the child out unfairly, or whatever. Instead of acting as agents of the community, the parents act as advocates for—attorneys for, if you will—the child, who is as pure as the driven snow until proven, beyond a shadow of doubt, guilty.

It's not that teachers don't make mistakes, because they do. They're human. But parents of yore believed it was less important that the teacher (or neighbor, shopkeeper, etc.) be completely right than that the child in question have respect for adult authority. That respect, parents knew, would be seriously undermined if they threw the benefit of doubt to the child. They also knew that in real life, adults often have to acquiesce to authority figures whether those authority figures are right or not. If everyone knows an employer is dead wrong about something, the employees must do things his way, nonetheless. And if a policeman pulls someone over for running a stop sign, even if the someone is absolutely certain he came to a full stop, he'd better act agreeable if he knows what's good for him. Considering that the real world rewards respect for authority more than it rewards proving authority figures wrong, once-upon-a-time parents backed authority. The way they figured it, if the authority figure was wrong, so what? After all, he wasn't going to be wrong often, not if he was going to remain in a position of authority.

My daughter, Amy (also known as Famous Amos or Aimless) became embroiled in a conflict with one of her teachers during her junior year in high school. Willie and I listened patiently to daily complaints from Amy about this teacher's unfairness and bias toward certain "pets." In all honesty, prior to Amy's complaints, Willie and I had heard similar things about this teacher from other parents. Nonetheless, we kept our mouths shut. We told Amy that whether she liked the teacher or not, whether he liked her or not, she was expected to do well in his class. She had no excuse if she didn't. That, of course, made Amy even more upset. We didn't understand! she cried. No, we understood, we said. We understood that not all teachers are easy to get along with, just like not all employers are easy to get along with, but you have to learn to get along. We didn't care! she cried. No, we cared. We empathized with her plight. Nonetheless, she was going to have to grin and bear it until school was out. As I recall, Amy usually terminated these conversations abruptly, stomping off to her room.

One spring day, the teacher called. He read off a list of complaints concerning Amy, and I listened politely. Then I told him that as far as Amy was concerned, we were backing his authority. All the way. I also told him that, indeed, Amy was capable of insolence to the tenth magnitude.

Then, however, I said, "But I have to tell you something that Amy is never, ever going to know." I went on to tell him, politely but directly, that I thought he was his own worst enemy. He was going to have to decide, I said, whether he wanted to be popular with his students or whether he wanted control of his classroom. As long as he vacillated between the two, he was going to have problems with certain students and Amy was one of 'em. But, having said all that, I assured him that we would back him 100 percent. If Amy misbehaved in his class or was disrespectful toward him, he was to let us know and we would follow up appropriately at home. I hoped he would mend his ways; regardless, Amy was expected to mend hers.

I think—if you'll pardon my using a phrase from my college

days—I blew his mind. I could tell that he was prepared for me to defend Amy to the hilt, and he was ready to argue his cause. In his mind, it would have been "normal" for me to act as Amy's "agent." Little did he know that Willie and I had made a pact not to do such things. We realized, and none too late, that *if we did not support adult authority in situations such as this, our children would not only lose respect for other adults, they would lose respect for us as well.*

Because today's parents are no longer defenders of community standards, but defenders of their children, they are allowing them (unwittingly, let me assure you) to wallow in self-centeredness long past toddlerhood, when that particular pathology should be rapidly waning; to laze in various degrees of undisciplined indolence; and to have no sense of responsibility toward their families, much less communities. Sad.

I received a letter from a teacher in Albuquerque that hit the nail of this problem on the head. Responding to a column in which I bemoaned the general lack of respect today's young people have for their elders, she began by relating a conversation she had had with one of her eighth-grade students: "This young man and I have been at loggerheads for most of this year. After an unpleasant encounter, I told him we were not on an equal playing field; I am an adult, he is not, and I expect him to respect that difference. Needless to say, this did not sit well. Not surprising, however, since his parents treat him as an equal partner and have led him to believe all adults should do likewise.

"I've had numerous conversations with this student's parents. They've basically told me their son doesn't respond to my authority because he senses I don't like him. They're right, I don't like him. He has done nothing to encourage me to like him and, unfortunately, his parents have crippled him with the attitude that if you think someone doesn't like you, you are justified in treating them with disrespect.

"Some time ago, this young man wrote me a note telling me my expectations of his behavior are appropriate only to where I grew up. Here in the Southwest, he said, things are different. Isn't it interesting that respect and manners are values that don't cross state lines?"

Cut to yours truly: When the Rosemonds moved to North Carolina, we thought it rather silly that children were universally expected to address adults as "Sir" and "Ma'am." It took me a while to realize that this ritual was far from insincere; that it was not only an invaluable tool for training respect, but a fairly reliable reflection of it as well. From that day forth, both of my children were expected to address adults in that fashion. It's paid off, I assure you—for them.

"In our family," Albuquerque went on to say, "my husband and I have purposefully drawn the line between children and adults, and we insist our children respect that line. They are precious to us, but they are not the center of our lives. Their teachers frequently comment on how courteous and respectful they both are. To us, that's every bit as valuable as an A. I might add that comments such as those have done wonders for their 'self-esteem' as well."

What's truly alarming, sad, tragic, depressing, upsetting, etc., is this teacher's comments are in line with what I hear from teachers all over the country. They describe a generation of children who are to a great degree self-absorbed, yet have little true self-esteem; for as Judeo-Christian scripture tells us, self-respect and respect for others are two sides of the same coin.

Self-absorbed is what you get when you lose sight of the forest for the trees.

In the 1950s and before, when a child was reported by an adult to have made trouble in the community, the child's parents said "How dare you!" to the child and exacted penance in one way or another. Today, when a child is reported by an adult to have made trouble in the community, the child's parents are likely to say "How dare you!" to the adult and threaten retribution.

In the 1950s and before, if a child got in trouble with the law, the parents said, "You made your bed, now you're going to have to lie in it." Today, if a child runs afoul of the law, the child's parents hire a lawyer who sets out to make the child into the victim.

Case in point: Nicole Bobek, a lovely little figure skater who was crowned U.S. National Champion in 1994 and placed third at the world championships in 1995, all of which means she's probably been pampered and pushed and pressured and petted to such an extent that she'll never have memories of her childhood because she hasn't had one. But that aside, it came to light that in November

1994, Nicole, age seventeen, unlawfully entered the home of a friend from the Detroit Skating Club and was allegedly in the process of collecting money when the friend's father came home and called the police. Nicole subsequently pleaded guilty to a felony charge of home invasion and was placed on two years' probation. As is the case in juvenile matters, the records were sealed.

Someone, however, leaked information to the press. The judge then dismissed the charges and rescinded Nicole's probation on the grounds that her confidentiality had been breached. This did not, of course, mitigate the fact that she was guilty of felony home invasion.

Her lawyer, one Michael Friedman, became incensed. According to him, Nicole was not a perpetrator, but a victim. What that makes the owners of the home Nicole unlawfully entered is anyone's best guess. Friedman was reported in *USA Today* of having said that some villainous blackheart—he suspects a former coach—was trying to "sully Nicole's reputation."

Wait a second! Am I mistaken, or did Ms. Bobek not sully her own reputation by illegally entering someone else's home? This child engaged in criminal behavior that she is old enough to know is wrong, and the public is to feel sorry for her because her misdeed became public? Friedman's indignation is straight out of "Alice Through the Looking Glass."

Despite her celebrity, Nicole Bobek was a child when all this occurred. As such, and especially considering that the act was apparently uncharacteristic, she merits forgiveness. What isn't forgivable is Friedman's attempt to paint her as the victim. When the crime became public, and Nicole became humiliated, her lawyer and parents should have said, "Well, Nicole, that's the way the ball bounces. If you hadn't been where you didn't belong, none of this would be happening. We hope you've learned a valuable lesson."

Instead, she was treated like a poor, misunderstood darling. Her coach, Richard Callaghan, said the media's interest in her trespass was "unfair." Oh, really? Since when is it unfair to have to lie in a bed you have made?

Considering the positions taken by her counsel and her coach, it should come as no surprise that Nicole, when asked for a comment, flippantly replied, "I was in the wrong place at the wrong time. It was just a mistake." Is it me, or is that statement curiously devoid of shame, penitence, or even embarrassment?

America is having, we are told by the media, one crisis after another with its children: a drug crisis, a teen pregnancy crisis, a dropout crisis, an underachievement crisis, crises of crime, depression, and children rearing children . . . and the list goes on and on. There's one crisis, however, that everyone seems to be ignoring. Oprah hasn't even held one of her intellectual forums concerning it. I'm referring to the biggest of all the crises we are having with our children, and Nicole Bobek's story is an example of it: a crisis of plain old irresponsibility.

After all, doesn't it all come down to that? Whether delinquency or drugs, pregnancy, dropping out, or just coasting through school, we're talking about irresponsibility. A dearth, in other words, of character. A crisis of citizenship, values, proper moral instruction.

Everyone's talking about the symptoms and how we need to demand that schools—get that: the schools!—address these issues more effectively, as if parents don't need to do anything for eighteen years of a child's life but twiddle their thumbs and wait for the schools to take action. But nobody's talking about the disease itself. Come to think of it, maybe nobody wants to address, or even admit to, the real problem because deep down, in our secret heart, we all know the problem is us.

Consequences Then, Choices Now

In 1994, I was invited to a northern metropolis to be part of a panel of "parenting experts" slated to talk to and field questions from an audience of some eight hundred parents and professionals.

One of the other panel members was Adele Faber, coauthor (with Elaine Mazlish) of *How To Talk So Kids Will Listen and Listen So Kids Will Talk* (1980), a popular tome on how to properly communicate with children. Faber's ideas are very akin to those of Thomas Gordon and Dorothy Briggs. I think it's safe to say that Gordon and Briggs have served as primary sources of Faber's inspiration. She is fervid about her beliefs, eloquent, and dispenses highly idealistic rhetoric concerning children. At one point in her talk, she said with great passion, "Children do not like being told what to do! We must give them choices so they learn to make good decisions!"

Such choices, the audience was then told, include asking a four-year-old, "Would you rather pick up your toys now, or would you rather pick them up later?"

This sort of approach, Faber said, respects a child's need for autonomy and affirms that he is a person in his own right. The audience was left to conclude that telling a child, in no uncertain terms, what he can, cannot, and must do is disrespectful of, if not harmful to, the child.

By appealing to sentiment, Faber is able to portray herself as a completely committed friend of children. Nonetheless, I contend that her statements and advice, however well intentioned, are clearly *not* in the best interests of children. Put more bluntly, they are anti-child.

In the first place, no one *likes* being told what to do. It is, however, a sign of maturity that one *accepts* being told what to do by legitimate authority. The earlier one accepts this, the better. The first authority children encounter is that of their parents. If they do not learn to accept their parents' authority, then when and how, I ask, do we expect them to ever fully accept any authority whatsoever? In short, parents have a *moral obligation* to present themselves to their children in ways that do not obfuscate these realities.

Second, the fact that a child does not *like* something an adult does is no indication that the decision or action in question was wrong. Children will react with great distress to decisions that are clearly in their best interests, and with great glee to ones that just as clearly are not. The implication that parents must be *pleasing* to their children is subversive. The fact is, children should want to *please their parents*. Given romanticized rhetoric of Faber's sort, however, it's no wonder that by their teen years, many children don't seem to care what their parents think.

Third, children will, when the time comes, make good decisions if good decisions are made for them before that time. There is absolutely no evidence to the contrary. Children respect parents who take the bull by the horns. That respect enables them to slowly but surely internalize their parents' values, and it is a heritage of solid values—not a childhood full of "choices"—that makes for good decision making as an adult.

Fourth, the job of parent is that of shepherding children into adulthood. This requires that within the workshop of childhood, parents help children assemble the values, understandings, knowledge, and skills they will need to lead successful adult lives. In that regard, I am not aware of any workplace in the private sector where employees are given a choice concerning when projects are to be finished, reports are to be turned in, or assignments are to be carried out. Nor am I aware of any law that allows U.S. citizens the option of obeying it later if one is not inclined to obey it now. The I.R.S. has never sent me a letter saying, "Would you like to pay your taxes now, or would you rather pay them later?" A policeman, after stopping me for speeding (yes, I'm a petty criminal), has never said, "John, you can obey the speed limit now, or you can exceed it now and obey it later. It's up to you." In short, the "choice" usually facing adults is simple: Act in one clearly defined manner or suffer the consequences. If a child chooses between a jacket or a sweater in the morning, fine. But to let "choice" prevail in the child's life is irresponsible and morally reprehensible.

Fifth, children don't handle the sort of "choices" Faber recommends responsibly. My father, when I would ask if I could carry out one of his instructions "later," would always say, "Tomorrow never comes." That used to drive me nuts. I had no idea what he meant. In fact, he couldn't have explained himself clearly enough to cause me to understand and accept that from a child's point of view, if an adult grants "later" once, the adult should grant it again, and again, and again. Eventually, the adult is going to have to say, "No, not later. Now!" At that point, the child will probably resist, and the adult will have to become insistent, and a "scene" will likely ensue. Everyone will expend less energy, and there probably will not be a scene if when the child first asks for "later," the parent says, "Nope. Now."

Last, it is not responsible to treat a child like a miniature adult. It is respectful to treat a child like a child. Children cannot manage their own lives; therefore, they need good managers. Above all else, a good manager communicates clearly.

In that regard, ask yourself, which is the clearer communication: "Would you rather pick up your toys now, or later?" or, "It's time for you to pick up your toys"?

Later in the same seminar, I mentioned that the only "choice" I'd be willing to give a child concerning picking up his toys would be, "Do you want to pick up your toys, right now, or would you rather spend the rest of the day in your room and go to bed immediately after supper?" I was not baiting the audience, but I was trying to get a rise, and a rise I definitely got.

Things immediately began to deteriorate. An individual who identified herself as a psychology instructor at a local college got up and made a three-minute speech concerning her shock at hearing me recommend such things as children being seen and not heard, and "because I said so," and worst of all, that children be *punished* for misbehavior. The research was clear, she said: Punishment doesn't work. It results in all manner of social pathologies, and the practice of punishing children and adults for misdeeds is probably the reason why the world is in such dire straits. Someone else then spoke of how "concerned" she was that I was advocating child-rearing ideas that had been associated with the abuse of generations of children. She then asked Ms. Faber to share her feelings about me with the audience.

After a relatively long pause, Faber said that she too was concerned, saddened even, that I was dispensing such advice. She expressed herself diplomatically, but nonetheless made it perfectly clear that she and I are at complete opposites when it comes to our thinking about children, their rearing, and education. Indeed, to paraphrase the title of a currently popular book, Adele Faber is from Venus, while I am from Mars. She holds to what I consider sentimental ideas concerning children, while I hold to what I consider practical, realistic ideas concerning them. Her ideas sound good, while mine sometimes don't.

I think I understand the Adele Fabers of the world. There was a time when I believed as she does about children and their upbringing. I question whether she understands me, however. I say that because I think the philosophy I espouse upsets her, as it upsets people like her. In all likelihood, Adele Faber thinks everyone should be as put off by me as she is. That's fine. It's good, in fact. I think it's healthy for people to see the clear contrast between John Rosemond and Adele Faber/Thomas Gordon/Dorothy Briggs. I think it's important for people to understand that there is no middle ground between us. Like the clear, black versus white choices I think adults should give children, the choice between us is black versus white, and I am the man in black.

I believe, for example, that when children misbehave, they should be punished. No doubt some people think that's proof of my lack of compassion, sensitivity, caring, or whatever toward children. Let's take a moment and examine this one issue in depth.

One of the main tenets of social liberalism—and this goes back to Rousseau's writings—is that right and wrong, good and evil, are relative constructs. Behavior deemed wrong by one culture might be esteemed in another, liberals point out. Cannibalism, for example. And even within a particular culture, definitions of right and wrong might vary from group to group, neighborhood to neighborhood. The idea that punishment is a just response to misdeeds springs, social liberals say, from the chauvinistic idea that one culture's or one group's definitions of right and wrong are absolute. Since there are no absolutes, they further reason, punishment is not just.

Social liberalism also holds—here comes Rousseau again—that crime is an indictment of the society in which it occurs. Addressing crime requires solving the "root causes" of social disintegration. These include poverty, racism, capitalism, unequal distribution of wealth, greed, and so on. In short, the problem of crime isn't going to be solved by punishing the criminal. Rather, it is necessary to understand what social forces have caused the criminal to "act out" and devote ourselves to correcting them, not him.

Faber, Gordon, and Briggs and other similarly minded helping professionals apply this same argument to the issue of children who misbehave. Children don't choose to misbehave; rather, they are *caused* to misbehave because of pathologies within their families.

Like adult criminals, misbehaving children are merely victims of forces which they are powerless to control. They have been dictated to, abused, forced to do labor within their families, not given reasons for the limits their parents set, led to believe they are responsible for their parents' bad marriages, enticed into codependent relationships with their parents, and generally treated like second-class citizens. Punishment, say the child-rearing deconstructionists, isn't going to stop a child from misbehaving. In fact, within this context, to punish a misbehaving child is immoral.

Lest you think I'm not portraying this philosophy fairly, let's hear from Thomas Gordon, writing in *Parent Effectiveness Training:*

> One of the last strongholds for the sanction of power in human relationships is in the home—in the parent-child relationship. . . . Why are children the last ones to be protected against the potential evils of power and authority? . . . My own conviction is that as more people begin to understand power and authority more completely and accept its use as unethical, more parents will apply those understandings to adult-child relationships; will begin to feel that it is just as immoral in those relationships; and then will be forced to search for creative new nonpower methods that all adults can use with children. *(P.E.T.,* p. 191)

At the root of Gordon's polemic is the idea that parents really don't know what is best for children. Their definitions of right versus wrong are no more valid for children than society's are for the criminal. Gordon argues that because there are no child-rearing absolutes (except his own absolute that no child-rearing method but his is valid), the adult-child relationship should be democratic, with limits, privileges, and expectations subject to negotiation.

Rush Limbaugh, writing in the July 1994 issue of *The Limbaugh Letter,* says this about punishment:

> Punishment requires something anathema to liberalism: a moral certitude, and a moral authority. . . . In order to punish, society must be certain of right and wrong; it must believe that those who obey the law deserve protection and those who break the law deserve to lose their freedom.

That certitude is what Gordon, Briggs, Faber, et al. eschew. As their ideas worked their way into our culture, parents began to question their own decisions, especially those their children didn't like. And they began to question their own authority, especially when children rebelled against it. And the more they questioned themselves and hesitated when it came to the exercise of authority, the weaker they became. And the more out of control their children became. At this point, the reader just might want to refresh him- or herself concerning just how out of control many of today's children are by rereading the statistics pertaining to juvenile violence, crime, drug and alcohol use, suicide, and depression contained in the Introduction.

Supreme Court Justice Clarence Thomas, one of the most powerfully intelligent men I've ever had the pleasure of hearing speak, said: "An effective criminal justice system, one that holds people accountable for harmful conduct, simply cannot be sustained under conditions where there are boundless excuses for violent behavior and no moral authority for the state to punish."

Likewise, an effective child-rearing paradigm, one that holds children accountable for their own behavior, simply cannot be sustained under conditions where there are boundless excuses for children's misbehavior, uncertainty when it comes to limits, and no moral authority for parents to punish.

Adult-Centered Then, Child-Centered Now

Once upon a time, the typical American family was an adult-centered institution. The marriage stood center stage, meaning the husband-wife relationship was primary. It came first, and it remained first through the child-rearing years. When the kids were up and gone, people wanted to have marriages that were still viable. The marriage was the nucleus of the family, the children were satellites that revolved around the nucleus like planets to a sun. As they grew, their orbits expanded, carrying them away from their parents and, eventually, into lives of their own. Parents accepted the paradoxical job of encouraging that expansion, even pushing it when necessary, while keeping it in check so that the child did not suddenly begin spinning out of control. This regulatory function can only be done from the center of the family. The center is "mission control," and the only people qualified to command are adults.

Intuitively, parents understood that children could not emancipate themselves successfully from the center of the family. The center of the family is too comfortable, cozy to the point of being addicting. The only people who belong there are the people who are supposed to stay there forever. Knowing this, parents kept children out of the spotlight. Oh, there were times when, for brief periods, children were allowed to be center stage, but these were the exception, and therefore, they were *special* times for adults and children both, all the more enjoyable because they were rare.

The ideologues of self-esteem changed all that. The more attention children were paid, they said, the more of that miraculous psychic ether they would acquire. In the late '60s, parenting professionals coined the term *child-centered family* and proclaimed it the ideal. Self-esteem could not flourish, said the professionals, unless the child's needs came first. Nearly everything, by the way, that made children happy was defined as a "need." After all, said the professionals, self-esteem was the greatest "need" of all, and self-esteem and happiness were one and the same. Understandably, parents understood all this to mean they were to keep their children happy. What other conclusion was there to draw?

Let me, for the moment, stop right here. In 1776, Thomas Jefferson told Americans that it was impossible to make someone happy. He wrote, in the Declaration of Independence, that all men, created equal, were entitled to three inalienable rights: life, liberty, and the *pursuit* of happiness. Jefferson was a very wise man. He understood that people could be guaranteed the right to *pursue* happiness, but could not, under any circumstances, be guaranteed its attainment. In fact, reading between Jefferson's lines, it follows that if someone tries to *make* someone else happy, they unwittingly disable that person's ability to engage successfully in the pursuit. One predictable outcome, therefore, of the self-esteem paradigm is a nation of children who cannot seem to make themselves happy. And that, indeed, is what I hear and witness. Teachers tell me kids come to school expecting to be entertained, and act defeated when a problem frustrates them. Parents tell me their children can't occupy themselves, are demanding, and whine a lot. Oh, does this generation of kids whine! And contrary to what many people, including many professionals, believe, whining is not—I repeat, *not*—normal childhood behavior.

Grandparents and great-grandparents have told me children didn't use to whine much. Furthermore, they occupied themselves. Teachers who began their careers in the '50s and early '60s have told me that back then, children stuck with difficult problems until they solved them. No mystery to any of this. It's a simple fact: The more parents do for and pay attention to children, the more children whine. Likewise, when children are expected to do for themselves and be responsible members of their families, they aren't likely to be whiners. The fact that whining is not a normal part of child behavior is attested to by parents from other countries who never cease to be amazed, they tell me, at how "whiny" American children are. I spend nearly all of my vacations on a small island in the Bahamas, population sixty-five. I've never heard any of the children on the island whine. I've never heard any of them complain to adults about one another. I've never heard any of them throw a tantrum. If they aren't in school, they are playing and they require no adult direction to keep themselves occupied. I've never seen them play with what American children would consider a "toy." They fashion their playthings with the alchemy of imagination, transforming sticks into horses, leaves into plates, stones into food. That, folks, is *normal* childhood behavior. But then, people who are old enough to remember tell me American children were once that normal.

As self-esteem became the "stuff" of child rearing, the American family turned inside out, upside down, and backward. Today, children sit center stage, and parents orbit around them, tending to their "needs." Parents fuss over their children, parade their children's accomplishments in front of everyone who will listen, serve their children, and then! And then they expect their children to be well behaved and are amazed when they're not. Hah! Put a tomato in the sun for too long, it spoils. Put a child in the spotlight for too long, the child spoils. And a spoiled child, by definition, is not well behaved. A spoiled child is a nuisance, and that's unfortunate, because the child, of course, had no choice in the matter.

The consequences of child-centeredness do not begin and end

with children. One of the more insidious upshots of this inside-out-ness involves its impact on women. In the 1950s, a woman with children who worked outside of her home was called a "working wife." As the term implies, her employment was primarily a *marital* issue. As silly as it may seem today, a wife's employment outside the home was generally taken as evidence that her husband was not a sufficient provider. The fragility of male egos aside, the point to be made is that this was, first and foremost, a husband-wife matter.

Following her remarriage in 1954, my mother continued to work as a medical lab technician. One day, she and my stepfather took me aside and told me, in the most solemn of terms, that I was not to tell any of my friends that she worked. It was, they said, "none of their business." It seemed like a strange request at the time, but I now understand that the taboo against making my mother's job public was necessary to help my stepfather "save face" in the community.

Today, by contrast, a woman with children who works outside of her home is called a "working mother." The change in terminology reflects a change in our collective thinking concerning such things. Where once a woman's employment was a marital issue, today it is a child-rearing issue. Where once such things were negotiated between husbands and wives, today they are negotiated between mothers and their children. Most important, "working mother" indicates that where once a woman with a family was primarily a wife, today she is considered primarily a mother. Her most immediate relationship, and therefore her first obligation, is with and to her children. This puts a whole new spin on *everything* that happens in American families.

My mother, when she came home from work, didn't feel guilty at having "left me to my own devices" during her absence. After all, had she been at home she would have expected me to occupy myself according to my own devices anyway. She came home to be a wife first, a mother second. Actually, that's not exactly true. She came home to be a wife first, herself second, and a mother third. And let me reemphasize, *I never, ever felt shorted.*

Today's working woman, when she comes home from eight hours on the job, comes home shouldering a burden of guilt that she discharges by putting her children first, second, and third. She has no life of her own because taking time for herself only increases her guilt. Her husband, when he comes home, shifts into father, the role that complements his wife's (perhaps it's more accurate to say his *ex-wife's*) preoccupation. And with that, the child-centeredness in the family is complete.

In bygone times, a woman with children who took care of hearth and home was called a "housewife." Today, she is called (and calls herself) a "stay-at-home mom." Again, the change in terminology reflects a sea change in our perceptions of a woman's role within her family. Once wife, now mother. Where once she spent the evening with her husband while the children did their homework, she now spends the evening with her children, helping them with their homework. Meanwhile, her husband, "Dad," stands ready to help. He is, remember, nothing more than a "parenting aide."

I am convinced, by the way, that the typical father of the '50s was not, as myth would have it, "distant," "unapproachable," or "cold." The typical father of the '50s loved his children. But his role was that of provider. Therefore, he worked hard. When he was home, his marriage came first; therefore, if he wasn't relaxing (earned), or working on a fix-it project (of necessity), he was spending the majority of his time with his wife. The typical father of the '50s was busy in his work and a devoted husband/family man. Compared to his wife, who was generally at home through the day, he might have seemed less accessible, but that was a consequence of his responsibilities, not an inability to relate warmly to his kids.

Nonetheless, it's amazing how this myth has worked its way into the contemporary psyche. A father recently remarked to me, "I don't want to be like my dad. He was too busy for his kids, and when he was home, he was remote."

I asked, "When did you come to this conclusion, that your dad was remote?"

"What do you mean?" he rejoined.

"I mean," I said, "did you come to this conclusion as a child or as an adult?"

"I came to the conclusion recently," he answered.

"Then your father's 'remoteness' didn't bother you when you were young?" I asked, rhetorically.

He thought for a moment. "No," he finally said, "I guess not."

"Then what's the problem?" I asked.

He thought again. "So what you're telling me is that my dad was an okay dad and that somehow I've become lately convinced he wasn't?"

"Right," I said. "I'll just bet he was a good provider, a good husband, a paragon of masculinity, and a respected member of his community."

"Yes, he was all those things," the man replied. "So, tell me, how is it that I came to the conclusion that he wasn't a good father?"

"I'll just bet," I answered, "you've been reading too much."

Indeed, if you believe the mythology concerning the typical father of the '50s—much of it, again, the product of the "helping" professional myth-mill—when he wasn't remote, he was punitive, if not abusive. I suspect, as does David Blankenhorn, author of *Fatherless America* (1995), that this mythology serves the convenient purpose of rationalizing the "okay-ness" of single-parent families. By demonizing fathers, by making them out to be either irrelevant, abusive, or both, the father-absent family comes to be regarded as "no big deal." As we are slowly discovering, however, a father's presence in his children's lives *is* a big deal. Blankenhorn and other researchers have discovered that children who grow up without their biological (or adoptive) fathers are at greater risk for social, academic, and emotional problems. Ironically, the "remote" father of the '50s has been replaced by the absent father of the '90s, and as Blankenhorn makes clear, even being a "remote" dad is better than being a dad who's not there at all.

In the intact family, the contemporary father is likely to strive energetically to be unlike his own supposedly distant father. In so doing, he ends up being more of a father/buddy than a mate to his wife and unwittingly contributes to the most insidious family dysfunction of all—child-centeredness. (Note: Given the contemporary American female parent's proprietary attitude toward child rearing, it's actually safer for today's father to be a "buddy" to his kids. His wife, remember, is likely to take issue with actions he takes as a parent.)

People ask me, "How can someone tell if their family is child-centered or not?"

It's actually easy to determine. A family is child-centered if, when adults and children are together, the adults act primarily from within the roles of mother and father/buddy as opposed to the roles of husband and wife.

"Mom" and "Dad" are focused on children. That's child-centeredness. Husband and wife are focused primarily on one another or the responsibilities appertaining to that commitment. That's marriage-centeredness. Neither state can be exclusive, of course. There will be times in even the most marriage-centered of families when necessity or custom will dictate child-centeredness: when a child is sick, for example, or has a birthday, or is graduating from high school. And there are, and well should be, times when child-centeredness just happens rather naturally. Nonetheless, the roles of mother and father should never become "habits." When they are called for or just happen, they should be put on *over* the roles of husband and wife, not substituted for them.

Marriage-centeredness creates more security for children. Nothing makes a child more insecure, after all, than the feeling his parents are in a state of discord. Conversely, nothing makes a child feel more secure than the feeling his parents are in a state of accord, of unity. The *only* way, therefore, to properly meet a child's need for security is to put the marriage center stage.

Child-centeredness causes children to want more attention than they need. They become addicted, literally, to being in the spotlight. It's long been an observation of mine that children who seem "starved" for attention are getting entirely too much from their parents. The child who is truly not getting enough attention typically withdraws, becomes depressed. The child who is overdosed on attention clamors for ever more. He can't "get enough" because he's getting too much in the first place.

Child-centeredness makes discipline difficult. In the first place, child-centeredness retards a child's ability to give up self-centeredness. One of the primary purposes of discipline is that of helping children divest of self-centeredness. Child-centeredness in a family is counterproductive to this goal, which is necessary to proper socialization. In the second place, a parent cannot discipline effectively unless the child is paying attention, *and a child will not pay sufficient attention to a parent who is paying too much attention to the child.* In the third place, discipline will forever be a hassle unless husband and wife are unified concerning it. Unity isn't possible when the adults in a family are wearing the "habits" of father and mother. Why? Because their loyalties are divided, confused. People who get "stuck" in "Mom" and "Dad" tend to forget (and I mean this literally) that they are husband and wife. They forget that their first loyalty is to one another, not their kids. Their children, therefore, find it easy to "divide and conquer." It is for this reason that I maintain, whenever the subject is raised, that a child younger than eight or so is generally incapable of being "manipulative." The label suggests the child needs to change, when in fact the people who need to do the changing are the child's parents, who need to "get a marriage."

In a marriage-centered family, a lot is expected of children. More than anything, they are expected to stand on their own two feet. It is another general observation of mine that children from families that are obviously marriage-centered (and you can tell, if you know the difference, in a heartbeat) are more obedient, more self-reliant, more cooperative, more responsible, more independent, and are higher achievers.

In a child-centered family, parents expect a lot of themselves, and their children expect a lot of them. Child-centered parents always act as if their first order of business is to *do* for their kids. And the more they do, the more their children want them to do, demand they do, whine for them to do. And the more the parents do, the less obedient, cooperative, responsible, achieving, and self-reliant the children are. It's quite simple, really. The more parents do for kids, the less kids do for themselves and the less they do *for their families.* You want a child to be a "jewel in the crown" of your family? Don't do a lot for the child.

A couple of friends of mine recently asked my advice concerning their two daughters, ages nine and eight, both of whom were acting increasingly helpless. The older girl had been diagnosed with attention deficit disorder (ADD), and the diagnosing professional had led the mother—I'll call her Kyle—to believe that if she didn't help her daughter with homework, the child would never succeed academically. Kyle soon found herself helping not only the older daughter, but also the younger one, who wanted the same treatment. Homework consumed the major part of the evening, and when it was done, Kyle was drained.

School mornings were a major battle as well. Kyle and her husband, whom I'll call Rick, spent upward of an hour every morning lighting one fire after another under the children, who dawdled and dawdled and dawdled and drove Kyle and Rick up the wall. Every day in the Kyle and Rick household started with stress and ended with stress.

I gave them a copy of my third book, *Ending the Homework Hassle,* and directed them to the chapter on homework management. I also advised them on how to set up a morning routine that would tie getting ready for the bus on time to after-school privileges (going outside to play, having a friend over, staying up until regular bedtime). From that point on, the kids were on their own in the morning. Kyle and Rick were to simply monitor and enforce, not nag or even "help." If one of the kids failed to be out the door on time for the bus, she lost her after-school privileges.

One month later (!), Kyle and Rick reported that both girls were doing their homework independently, finishing it before bedtime, and—get this—*making better grades than ever before!* So much for a certain professional's advice. And that's not all! Every morning, the kids got up, consulted their list of responsibilities, did what they had to do, and were out the door on time for the bus without fail. Meanwhile, Kyle and Rick drank coffee, talked to one another, and read the newspaper. And that's not all! Since the kids started taking responsibility for their homework and getting ready for school, they had become more spontaneously responsible around the house. They were doing things like pulling out the vacuum cleaner and vacuuming the entire house. Without being asked! And that's not all! Willie and I visited them in their home and during the entire visit neither girl interrupted the adult conversation even one time. They said polite "hellos," then went to their area of the house and occupied themselves. Without television! These girls had, in one month's time, become "jewels in the crown" of their family simply as a result of parents who stopped doing so much for them.

When Rick and Kyle recounted all of this to me, they didn't say it was the best thing that ever happened to their kids. Oh, no. They said, "It's the best thing that ever happened to our marriage." But a good marriage, you see, *is* the best thing that can ever happen to a child.

Epilogue

Spying me mingling with the audience a few minutes before I was to make a presentation, a woman walked up and said, "Do you know what really bugs me about you?"

"No, I sure don't," I answered, amused by her boldness. "You'll have to tell me."

"You make it sound so easy, that's what."

She wasn't mad, that much I could tell, but she definitely had a bone to pick.

"You're right. I make child rearing sound easy because I believe it *is* easy. Granted, some children are more difficult than others, and there will be difficult moments with any child; nonetheless, I am convinced that child rearing is a relatively simple, commonsensical proposition. I am trying my best to put parents back in touch with the ease of the process, and for that I make no apologies."

"Well," she huffed, "my friends and I agree that if you were a *woman*, you wouldn't think it was so easy."

I thought about that for a moment, then replied, "I agree. If I was a woman living in these times, I think that I, too, would probably be experiencing the rearing of children as disproportionately difficult and demanding."

I let that sink in before continuing. "Now, since you've been fairly forward with me, may I do the same concerning some impressions I have about you?"

"Why, uh, sure," she stammered, "but you could hardly know anything about me after just two minutes."

"In a sense," I said, "I've been talking to you for the past fifteen years. Ever since I began writing and speaking, numerous women have told me they think child rearing is the hardest thing they've ever done. Interestingly enough, I've yet to hear this from a man. When a woman expresses this complaint, my experience tells me I'm talking to a woman who *can't stop being a mother*."

She stiffened. "What do you mean?! Of course I can't stop being a mother. I *am* a mother! I have three children!"

"What I mean is that you won't give yourself permission to be anything else *but* a mother," I said. "I'll just bet, for example, that the first thought on your mind when you wake up in the morning has to do with your children, and the last thought on your mind before you fall asleep at night has to do with your children, and that sandwiched between those two mental events is a lot of mental, physical, and emotional activity centered on your children.

"I'll just bet, too, that you take *mother* into nearly everything you do. Do you work outside your home?"

"Well, uh," she answered, "yes, I do."

"I'll just bet you refer to yourself as a working *mother*, and I'll just bet you spend a good amount of energy worrying about what your decision to work is *doing* to your kids, and I'll just bet your husband never, ever worries about what *his* job is doing to the kids. And I'll just bet, furthermore, that when you're in a social situation, you usually end up talking with other women about your children and theirs, and that you often introduce yourself as "so-and-so's *mother*," and that since you became a parent, you have denied yourself the right to indulge in many of the things that brought you pleasure before your parenthood. When you're not with your kids, I bet you think a lot about how they're doing without you. I bet you even have dreams about your kids, in which they always need you for one thing or another."

As I rambled on, her eyes widened, her mouth dropped slightly open, her posture relaxed ever-so-slightly. She looked speechless.

"Well?" I asked. "What about it?"

After a moment of silence, she answered, "John, I have to admit, you've got me pegged. You just described me to a T. How did you know all that about me?"

"I told you," I said, "I've been talking to 'you' for fifteen years. You're no different than 90 percent of the women I talk to day in and day out."

"So how do I stop being a mother all the time?"

"Be a wife, to begin with. Remember the vows you took? They didn't say, 'until children do us part,' now did they? Then, remember the woman you were before you had children; the things you liked doing and so on. Start doing them again! And if that means not doing so much for the kids, so be it. You have a life inside of you that has nothing to do with rearing children, and the best thing you could ever do for your kids is let that life out of its cage so they can begin to see that Mom is not just Mom, not just a servant there to do their bidding, but an interesting person, a person worth looking up to."

"Whoa!" she exclaimed. "That stung!"

"Good," I said. "That means we're getting somewhere."

Postscript

In the spring of 1995, I was in San Jose to do a talk. A woman approached me before the presentation (I usually mill around in the lobby, talking to people) and told me she'd met me prior to a presentation I'd given in that western city three years before.

She said, "I told you I couldn't stay because I had to take my daughter to her dance lesson, and you asked me why *I* wasn't the one taking the dance lessons. I didn't know what to say to you. I felt insulted, to tell you the truth. But I thought about what you said, and I finally understood, and I'm here tonight to tell you that I'm doing a lot less for my daughter these days and a lot more for myself, and we're both a lot happier, and it's all because of you."

Man! Talk about making my day! She made my whole year!

CHAPTER THREE

Why Our Schools Are Floundering

Once upon a time not so long ago, America had no permanent underclass. Our free-enterprise system extended opportunity to one and all, and the world's poor voted for American democracy "with their feet," surging in wave after wave to the land of the free, the home of the brave, where anything was possible.

Immigration, furthermore, didn't stop at Ellis Island. America was the only country in the world where if you didn't prosper in one place, you could pack up and try your fortunes in another. That freedom propelled southern blacks north where they began creating a new urban middle class that was rich in culture and slowly but surely increasing in wealth. It lured Dust Bowl sharecroppers to the promised land of California. It drew Irish, Italians, Czechs, Poles, Germans, Russians, et al. out of New York's ethnic enclaves to brighter futures in Pittsburgh, Cleveland, Chicago, Des Moines, and points west.

In America, you might arrive poor or be born poor, but you did not have to stay poor. If you had a dream and were willing to pull out the stops in its pursuit, you could become "somebody."

The sky was the limit, but the ride wasn't free. The price tag on upward mobility read "An Education." Everyone understood that although it was freely available, obtaining this currency required effort, perseverance, and sacrifice. Public schools were the portal to the American dream, and anyone willing to run the demanding academic gauntlet could succeed. It is fitting, therefore, that Ms. Liberty holds a tablet and a light by which to read it.

When, in 1952, I entered first grade, America's public schools were approaching their peak. The literacy level was rising, the dropout rate was low, achievement scores were high, and teachers were regarded with great respect. Educators dedicated themselves to the proposition that every child passing through the system would succeed at a level commensurate with his or her ability. Academic standards, therefore, were relatively high, classrooms were disciplined places, and students had to demonstrate adequate mastery in order to be promoted. At home, parents supported and followed through on the discipline meted out by teachers, expected children to do their homework independently, and made it clear that "getting by" was not the name of the game. Compromise had no place where the education of America's children was concerned; and yet, the postwar baby boom was straining educational resources to the limit.

My third-grade class picture shows forty-two students! We sat in six rows of seven each. Our teacher, Mrs. Hoy, had no aide. All forty-two of us used the same texts, including the same reader. Some children, of course, read better than others, but everyone read well enough to keep up (and the parents of a number of students couldn't even speak good English!). I can't, for the life of me, remember any unruly classmates.

Third grade was never boring. Quite the contrary, it was demanding, challenging, and exciting. Cutting the proverbial mustard required tenacity, responsibility, initiative, learning from your mistakes. And speaking of mistakes, if you made one, you heard about it. Mrs. Hoy told each and every one of her students the truth about themselves and their performance. She was warm and caring, and we all liked her, but she wasn't about to pull any punches for the purpose of making us "feel good about ourselves." If you wanted to feel good about yourself, you had to work. You had to behave yourself and do your best. That was the picture of American education in 1954, when it was thriving.

In today's typical third-grade classroom, there are no more than thirty students, and the teacher almost certainly has an aide. The children are assigned to one of three reading groups, with children in the lowest group reading as much as a year behind grade level. A handful of children—those with even lower reading levels—are given reading instruction outside of class in one of several "special education" programs. In all likelihood, several children are prone to unruliness, and a few more are chronically inattentive.

A visitor to the class might see one group of children working with the teacher, another with her aide, some children working independently, and several doing what might be described as "milling about." Talking with one another is allowed, as long as it's done quietly. Students who finish their work can fill time at one of several "enrichment centers" located around the room.

Everyone works at his own level, and no one is in danger of being retained. Students are graded according to ability rather than performance; therefore, a child reading a year behind grade level might well receive straight A's in reading. Another, although reading slightly above grade level, might be getting B's.

Today's third grade isn't hard. Nor can it be called exciting. For those children who come to school prepared to work hard, it's downright boring. Students who don't turn in assignments when they're theoretically due are probably not penalized. The teacher is required to always be positive when it comes to giving children feedback on their work, which means, of course, that she isn't always being honest. If she reprimands a student in front of the class or gives a child a bad grade on an assignment, even a test, she's likely to have a complaint lodged against her by the child's parents.

Since the mid-1960s, public school curriculums have been steadily "dumbed down." Today's expected fifth-grade reading level, for example, is on a par with a 1950 third-grade *McGuffie Reader*. Not surprisingly, illiteracy in the United States is on the rise. Today, nearly one in four seventeen-year-olds is unable to read with comprehension at a fifth-grade level (functional illiteracy). Behavior problems, learning disabilities, and a strange and controversial affliction called attention deficit disorder (ADD) have become epidemic. As one veteran third-grade teacher recently told me, "Twenty-four years ago, when I started teaching, teaching was fun. These days, I feel more like a baby-sitter or a policeman than a teacher."

America's public schools are diseased and dying, and everything we hold dear is in jeopardy as a consequence. The viruses attacking the system include legal obstacles to dismissing mediocre teachers; administratively top-heavy bureaucracies bent on perpetuating (and expanding) themselves no matter the cost to the taxpayer; school boards constituted of wannabe politicians whose primary aim is re-election (and who are therefore reluctant to rock the boat); an increasing emphasis on social-engineering experiments at the expense of academics; the introduction—and subsequent failure—of one "progressive" educational "reform" after another (no exceptions here), all of which have transformed public schools into laboratories and children into guinea pigs; the institutionalized pampering of undisciplined students; and a pseudoeducational rhetoric created from the whole cloth of "self-esteem," resulting in what I term "educational welfare," a peculiar form of affirmative action which has transformed grades—if they haven't been dispensed with altogether (they damage self-esteem, don't you know?)—into a joke.

The Failure of School Reform

For most of the past twenty-five years, one bandwagon after another has come clanking down the corridors of America's public schools. Each time one of these bandwagons made its much-heralded appearance, administrators and school boards climbed enthusiastically on board, dragging teachers behind them, some kicking and screaming. Needless to say, not one of these new technologies, philosophies, or methodologies has resulted in either enhancement of the educational process or benefit to student achievement. Hardly surprising, since the efficacy of these innovations was never determined before they were implemented.

Along came New Math, and the math achievement levels of America's kids began a long, continuing decline. Along came Open Classroom Education, and general achievement levels fell that much more precipitously. As Whole Language replaced phonics, reading problems became epidemic. Cooperative Learning proved that what works for adults in an automobile assembly plant in Kentucky doesn't necessarily work for fourth graders in Des Moines. Nonetheless, these experiments persist, their advocates unwilling to admit the obvious.

The latest nouveau methodology to invade America's schools goes under the misleading title of Outcome-Based Education (OBE). In brief, the idea is to insure that mastery, not age, determines a child's advancement from one curriculum level to the next. The emphasis is on analytic skills rather than rote memorization; on the *how* of learning as opposed to mere facts and figures. Sounds good, doesn't it? The problem, however, is that no one has a clue as to what the outcome of Outcome-Based Education will be. Administrators, legislators, and school boards across the country are buying into OBE strictly on the basis of fancy rhetoric.

Besides the lack of a track record, there's a disturbing hidden agenda at the heart of OBE. Writing in *Future Trends: Considerations in Developing Exit Outcomes,* William Spady, acknowledged as the "father of OBE," says that "despite the historical trend toward intellectual enlightenment and cultural pluralism, there has been a major rise in religious and political orthodoxy, intolerance, fundamentalism and conservatism with which young people will have to be prepared to deal." The question, then, becomes: Just how should America's children be prepared to "deal" with these apparently unenlightened points of view? In this regard, both former secretary of education William J. Bennett and Phyllis Schlafly, syndicated columnist and founder of the conservative Eagle Forum, have expressed concern that OBE can be used to indoctrinate children with liberal social values. Ms. Schlafly points to Oklahoma's OBE standards, which include that students will "identify different types of family structures, so that no single type is seen as the only possible one" and be able to talk with one another about "sexual behavior." Sounds like ideology to me.

Spady does nothing to dispel these concerns. In fact, he maintains that schools have always inculcated values: "There is no way we are going to keep values out of the educational process." It's true that teachers can't help expressing judgments and, thereby, conveying values, but:

❏ The values previously inherent to America's public schools were consensually validated. They were not a matter of controversy, much less public debate. Furthermore, they were *implicit* to the educational process. Students were not required to demonstrate "mastery" of them.

❏ The nouveau values inherent to educational reform are controversial. They are, by all accounts, not the values the majority of American parents desire for their children. Furthermore, if educational reformers have their way, they will form the basis for student evaluations. When other countries use their schools to indoctrinate children in politically correct thought, we term it "propaganda." When it happens here, America's educational reformers term it "progressive."

More than thirty states have experimented with OBE, and parents around the country are slowly discovering that despite its name, OBE has little, if anything, to do with raising academic standards. In fact, it replaces skill-based measures of academic achievement with vague "outcomes" that sound like they were written by a team of psychotherapists. In Minnesota, for example, where OBE supporters were able to establish a major toehold, proposed graduation requirements mandate that students will be able to "apply informed decision-making processes to promote healthy lifestyles." Missouri's proposed standards call for students to "plan effective verbal and nonverbal communications for a variety of purposes and audiences, anticipating the impact of the message." Ohio's standards require that a high-school graduate be able to "function as a responsible family member" and "maintain physical, emotional, and social well-being." It's impossible, of course, to measure nebulous "outcomes" of this sort, and that's the point: Outcome-Based Education neatly prevents parents and taxpayers from assessing the quality of education in their local schools. The reformers who control the rhetoric of OBE also control how its effectiveness is assessed.

For twenty-plus years, the public education establishment has been terrified that taxpayers will wake up to the fact that as per capita educational expenditures have tripled (in constant 1994 dollars), academic achievement has declined. The National Education Association (NEA) would have the taxpayer believe teachers are grossly underpaid and public education is starving for money. The truth:

❏ Considering they work nine months a year (including a two-week vacation in December), six or seven hours a day (including lunch and preparation time), teachers are very well compensated relative to other four-year college grads.

❏ A disproportionate amount of the educational dollar goes into paying administrative and administrative-support salaries and benefits. As demonstrated by the success of private and parochial schools, which conserve on administration, thus returning a greater share of their dollar to the classroom, most public school administrative positions are completely superfluous to educational quality. Public schools don't need more money; they need to trim their fat.

As the disparity between expenditure and achievement grows, public awareness of public education's excesses, wastefulness, and failures is approaching critical mass. Ironically but shrewdly, Outcome-Based Education is an attempt to co-opt the coming debate by shifting its focus from measurable outcomes to content, thus effectively concealing from the taxpayer that public education is failing to properly educate America's children. Numbers scare OBE proponents because numbers are hard to fudge. If goals are nebulous, however, then student assessment will have to be subjective, thus impossible to verify.

Along these same lines, the National Center for Outcome-Based Education asserts that "failure should be removed from our vocabulary *and thoughts*" (emphasis mine) and that "children should never have to compete for learning or grades" because "competition in the classroom is destructive." The truth is, when competition in the classroom was the name of the game, America's public schools did an exemplary job under circumstances that existed in no other country on the planet: namely, heterogeneous classrooms comprised of children from extremely diverse ethnic and socioeconomic backgrounds. The truth is, competition in the classroom causes children to rise above mediocrity. The truth is, competition in the classroom is destructive only to vested interests within America's educational establishment.

Consistent with their aversion to verifiable things, OBE advocates eschew what they term "factoids." They believe public schools should focus on "higher-order thinking skills" rather than rote memorization of facts and figures. Again, it's easy to accurately assess whether or not a student has memorized something, but nigh unto impossible to assess whether he's mastered "higher-order thinking skills." Furthermore, OBE's promotion of "active learning techniques," which include field trips, independent lab work, community volunteerism, and the like, further reduces instruction time, and *America's teachers already spend less time in classroom instruction than those of any other industrialized nation.*

In 1993 in Gaston County, North Carolina, where Willie and I live and raised our children (both attended public schools), the local school board approved a school reform plan which incorporated OBE and its stepchildren, cooperative learning and whole language. The plan, called "Odyssey," was to be funded by a twenty-million-dollar grant from the New American Schools Development Corporation, a nonprofit foundation that was created in response to President Bush's "America 2000" education initiative. Odyssey would have replaced traditional grades with "outcome-based" assessments. Cooperative learning, in which more responsible students shoulder the load for less responsible ones, would have been the modus operandi of the classroom, with teachers serving as "consultants" to the "learning process." In addition, students would have been required to attend weekly seminars that addressed national and world affairs as well as personal values(!), all with—according to one apologist—"a focus on multicultural issues to prepare them to live in a global society."

Rhetoric of that sort concealed the fact that Odyssey was nothing more than the emperor's new clothes—one more attempt on the part of the education establishment to convince the American taxpayer that its very progressive eye is fixed on the future. The fancy language and shrewd marketing of the plan concealed an undeniable fact: Once again, children would have been guinea pigs in an experiment that would have had less to do with education than social engineering.

An article in the September 1992 issue of *North Carolina* magazine said Gaston County's school system—run along fairly traditional lines to that point—was "inarguably failing to adequately educate students." Interesting. My two children were both educated in Gaston County public schools. Neither is brilliant, but both made the best of the opportunities extended them by their teachers, graduated high school, and were accepted at good universities. Ah, but then Eric and Amy were reared to respect legitimate authority, do their best at any task assigned, accept complete responsibility for their own behavior, and accept that adversity, even failure, always precedes success. Take a child reared with those traditional values, provide the child a traditional (as in old-fashioned, back-to-basics) education, and the child will learn, and learn well.

After much public debate during which hyperbole flew from the mouths of all concerned, Odyssey was defeated. Most of the school board members responsible for bringing it to the table were voted out in the next election (or declined to run), and the "visionary" superintendent whose pet project it was resigned shortly thereafter. The battle was a waste of everyone's time, but if it hadn't been fought, Odyssey would have wasted the precious time of no small number of America's children and laid the groundwork for similar social-engineering experiments in other school systems.

There was nothing badly wrong with public education until someone decided it was possible to create a perfect school system that would perfectly meet the needs of each and every student. This is as pie-in-the-sky as trying to create a perfect world, but such is the mark of undisciplined (synonymous with idealistic) thinking. At that point, a system that wasn't perfect, but surely wasn't broken either, was subjected to attempt after desperate attempt at overhaul.

Integral to the problem of educational reform is the fact that supposed innovations like OBE are never designed by teachers. Rather, they are concocted by theorists working within America's ivory towers. Certain of these academics play their politics well enough to be invited to speak at major educational conferences and published in major educational journals, following which they make themselves available as consultants to school systems wishing to purchase their "product." These purchasing decisions are made by administrators who then direct teachers to implement these nouveau programs in their classrooms. It's ironic that the very folks who know, firsthand, what works and what doesn't at the classroom level are rarely, if ever, part of these decision-making processes.

And why is this? Because America's public schools are administratively obese, that's why. And most administrators know their jobs could be dispensed with tomorrow and not one student would suffer. In this environment, decision making becomes a territorial issue. Administrators are threatened by the idea of teachers being allowed to make decisions because letting them do so might let the cat out of the bag: namely, on the whole, teachers probably make better decisions concerning curriculum and classroom management than administrators.

After I wrote a letter to our local newspaper criticizing the school board's decision to implement Odyssey, a school board member called me to complain that I'd made her job "difficult." When I told her she'd made my day by saying so, she claimed that teachers who were resisting Odyssey simply "didn't want to change."

Wrong. America's teachers would welcome change: retro-change, that is. Trust me on this. I do a workshop for teachers on an average of once a week, and I've done so in more than forty states to date. America's teachers crave for a return to a time when students were held to strict standards; when "to educate" meant teaching subject matter rather than nurturing student self-esteem; when administrators didn't tiptoe around disciplinary issues; when school boards were constituted of citizens who cared more about the preservation of traditional educational and cultural values than their own reelection.

In the Name of Self-Esteem

Revitalizing public education in America is going to require that the concept of "self-esteem" be purged from our educational vernacular. Over the last thirty years, every "progressive" step taken in American education has resulted in a lowering of standards and the steady worsening of student achievement, and every one of those steps was taken in the name of self-esteem.

Beginning in the '60s, teachers were told by educational theorists (many of whom had never taught in either an elementary or high school) that a child with positive self-esteem would *want* to learn; therefore, it would be unnecessary to *make* him learn. In fact, applying any academic pressure at all, teachers were told, might cause learning to be frustrating. This, in turn, would cause the student to develop an aversive response to education.

Included among the things that caused kids to become frustrated and "turn off" to school were grades. Grades, the reasoning went, resulted in competition, which resulted in some children being rewarded more than others, whether or not they expended more effort than the lower achievers. This inequity caused children who weren't as "competitive" to feel defeated and lose self-esteem; therefore, grades had to go. Some school systems responded to this psychological crisis by eliminating grades altogether. Instead of letter grades, they adopted a binary system involving ratings of either "mastered" or "not yet mastered." Other school systems retained grades, but began grading on the basis of ability (or, in some cases, *potential*) rather than achievement. Theoretically, this "levels the playing field" such that a child with average ability can earn grades that are just as good as those of a child with superior ability. In *fact*, it devalues the efforts of those children who come to school prepared to work hard.

Many a teacher has told me that it is no longer possible to give D's or F's unless parents give their permission (ha!). It's no longer "educationally correct" to penalize a child for turning in an assignment late. No matter what a child's achievement or level of responsibility, some excuse must be divined for awarding the child a good grade, one that doesn't damage his or her self-esteem. It should not surprise anyone, therefore, to learn that while educational achievement has dropped, grades in American schools have actually risen. In 1966, U.S. students earned twice as many C's as A's. That's consistent, by the way, with "the curve." By 1978, the number of A's exceeded the number of C's. By 1990, more than 20 percent of all entering college freshmen averaged A minus or above on their high school transcripts.

If self-reports are valid, then the goal of improving the self-esteem of U.S. students has worked! Although Korean students are among the best in the world when it comes to math and science, less than 25 percent rate themselves "good" in either subject. On the other hand, although U.S. students score below the international average in science and math, more than two-thirds claim to possess good skills in these areas. Unfortunately, to paraphrase my dad, "good self-esteem and fifty cents will buy you a cup of coffee," whereas an empty wallet but truly good math and/or science skills will get you a job. Of course, the jury is still out on whether this is really indicative of good self-esteem, or just a collective delusion of grandeur on the part of a generation of kids who've been told they're wonderful no matter what they do.

Here's a fact: *It is impossible for someone to improve his or her performance in a certain area without accurate feedback.* If, for example, every time an individual who's learning how to put together a small engine makes a mistake he's nonetheless told he's doing just fine, he'll never learn to put together small engines.

Here's another: *If a task is worth learning, the person trying to learn it will initially fail at it.* One of my graduate professors put it this way: If something's worth learning, it's worth failing at.

The obvious conclusion: *It is nothing short of immoral to not give children honest feedback on their performance in school.* If that means a child receives an F in a subject, so be it. To give the child a C when he deserves an F is to guarantee he will never truly succeed in that subject area. The educational theorists responsible for this crime against children ought to be ashamed of themselves, but they're not. They will defend what they did to the ends of the earth.

The next thing to go was rote memorization. The theorists posited that memorization fails to teach children "how to think." If a child learns *how* to think, he will learn all he needs to learn, including his multiplication tables, on his own. Besides, said the theorists, multiplication facts are meaningless to a child who doesn't have a grasp of the "cognitive processes that infuse them with validity," blah, blah, blah. Moreover, rote memorization was needlessly frustrating, they claimed. It, too, damaged self-esteem, especially that of students whose "cognitive style" did not lend itself to memorizing anything. (In previous generations, by the way, such a "cognitive style" would have been called "lazy.") Thus we now have new math and whole language, neither of which rely on memorization. And when compared with students from other industrialized nations, U.S. students score dead last in math and science. Cogitate on the following:

❑ A greater percentage of U.S. seventeen-year-olds are illiterate than in any other industrialized nation and in many "Third World" countries to boot!

❑ Today's achievement-test scores are lower than they were in 1960.

❑ Colleges expend huge amounts of money and human resources on remedial math and English courses.

❑ One-third of major U.S. corporations are teaching employees reading, writing, and arithmetic.

One must at least wonder whether any of this has to do with a de-emphasis on memorization. Speaking for myself, I don't wonder about it at all. I'm absolutely sure of it.

The next thing to go was strict standards of conduct. Punitive methods of discipline—meaning anything done before the 1960s to maintain order in classrooms—cause children to harbor "negative feelings" toward not just their punishers, but themselves as well, or so said the academics. Therefore, children could no longer be punished. Besides, children who "acted out" (the new term) were only doing so because they were frustrated (there's that word again) by something. If someone would just take the time to discover what was "bothering" them, they'd stop misbehaving. Thus were real-life consequences for misbehavior replaced with attempts to "understand" undisciplined children; and thus did all hell break loose in America's classrooms.

In 1993, the *Washington Post* ran a story in which it reported that "in classrooms and school hallways . . . many students are 'going off' on teachers and administrators, cursing them and calling them names without regret or restraint." If that, in itself, isn't amazing enough to anyone who was born before 1965, a teacher—obviously suffering from too many "self-esteem" workshops—wrote a letter to the editor of the *Post* saying, "Teachers need to seek cooperative solutions to problems. Respect cannot be dictated."

Excuse me? Cooperative solutions? Cooperation requires two adults. Adults *cooperate* with one another. Children don't cooperate with adults. They either *comply* or they don't. In too many cases today, however, they don't. They don't obey precisely because they've been expected to do no more than *cooperate* by the likes of the above hopelessly brainwashed teacher. Here's where expecting children to *cooperate* and not insisting upon respectful behavior has gotten us:

❑ The U.S. Justice Department reports an average of nearly five hundred thousand violent incidents per month in the nation's public schools.

❑ Each month, one thousand teachers require medical attention because of in-school assaults by students.

❑ Each month, another 125,000 are threatened by students.

Then there's the great retention scam. If frustration damaged self-esteem, failure devastated it, or so said the educational theorists. They argued, therefore, that children shouldn't be retained (held back a grade). In 1991, the National Association of School Psychologists (NASP) issued a position statement which held that no child should ever be retained. They based this proclamation on research which purported to prove that being retained was extremely likely to have adverse effects on a child's social development, later academic achievement, and, of course, self-esteem. The problem is that the research cited to support these contentions was so badly done as to be laughable. It would have been used as an example of stupid science in my graduate school class in experimental methods. To give an example: In one of the studies in question, the researchers determined that retention damaged self-esteem by asking children who'd been retained questions like, "How do you feel about having been retained?"

Guess what? They said things like, "Not so good," and "Well, I don't like to talk about it 'cause it's kind of embarrassing," and "I wish it hadn't of happened." Conclusion: Being retained had *caused* these children to "feel bad about themselves." Therefore, children shouldn't be retained. The further inference, of course, but one the researchers failed to mention, is that adults shouldn't do something to children if it makes them the least bit uncomfortable. Gosh, I wish self-esteem had been around when I was made to stay after school every day for a month for talking back to my fifth-grade teacher.

As a result of stupid science of this sort, many school systems around the country have adopted blanket nonretention policies. At the very least, they retain only in extreme cases. The end result of such policies is that a child who should have been retained in first grade is moved to the second grade and then the third and then the fourth, by which time he's one or more years behind in academic achievement. A school psychologist (a member of NASP, no doubt) is then called in to evaluate the child. After lengthy observation and testing, the psychologist is likely to discover that the child is "learning disabled" and qualifies for a special-education program which he attends one or more hours a day from that point on.

In all likelihood, however, receiving "special" education never brings this child up to academic speed. In the first place, by the time he's identified as having a problem, he's lost one to three years of school. In the second, it's safe to say that he's lost as much motivational as academic ground. Under the circumstances, special education simply keeps his problems from getting worse.

Had this child been retained in grade one, and had tutors started working with him to promote mastery of the curriculum, and had his parents withheld privileges whenever his achievement dropped below some reasonable level, this is a child who might well have been working near the top of his class by the fourth grade instead of being shunted into special education. As things stand, however, this child will never have to experience the devastating humiliation of telling someone that he was retained in the first grade, but he's probably not going to go on to a four-year college, either. As a consequence, his lifetime earnings will be considerably below what they might otherwise have been. He's more likely to experience periods of unemployment, and he may never settle into a career. In addition, his children are less likely to attend college. All in the name of self-esteem.

One last note: 26 percent of U.S. students attend special education classes, as compared with no more than 2 percent in other developed nations. And remember, children in other developed countries are doing better than ours in every academic area!

Economist, syndicated columnist, and author Dr. Thomas Sowell sums up the problem quite neatly. Referring to hysteria over what the so-called "religious right" is supposedly doing in America's public schools, he says: "*The issue in the schools today is not religion, but education. It is the secular messiahs who have redirected the schools away from intellectual activity and toward psychological tinkering and ideological indoctrination.*"

Hear! Hear!

The Alternatives

In contrast to public schools, private schools, both secular and religious, are flourishing. The headmaster of a new Episcopal day school recently told me, "Like most of my colleagues today, I can't build classrooms fast enough." But then, private schools don't give tenure, put most of their money back into the classroom rather than administrative bloat, have volunteer boards, eschew "reform," maintain high academic standards, insist upon proper classroom and social behavior, waste no time on political correctness, and won't let most educational reformers (or the NEA) through the front door. As a result, more and more American parents are willing to make the financial sacrifice necessary to provide private education for their children.

Don't get me wrong. Private schools aren't perfect, either:

❏ They tend to be somewhat elitist, although far less so today than in the past.

❏ They artificially inflate student achievement by starting academic instruction in kindergarten (or even, in some instances, in prekindergarten), and by delaying kindergarten enrollment for relatively large numbers of supposedly "immature" children, most of whom are simply average kids.

❏ They kowtow to those parents who are their most generous benefactors.

❏ Their faculty also make numerous references to "self-esteem" when discussing student achievement.

No, private schools aren't perfect, but they're a lot less *imperfect* than public schools these days.

When it comes to values, private schools are not free of ideology, and sometimes, as is the case with many church-related schools, their ideology is quite explicit. The difference is, private-school parents know what values their children are going to be taught. Furthermore, a parent who becomes dissatisfied with the values his or her child is exposed to at one private school can simply put the child in another. For many parents whose children attend public school, that isn't so easy. It may not even be an option.

Chester Finn, an assistant secretary of education during the Reagan years, allows that some American parents *want* their children's schools to teach values. He says that's fine, as long as no parent has to send a child to a school that teaches values to which the parent objects. The only solution to this conflict, says Finn, is school choice, which is, as we will soon see, the educational establishment's worst nightmare.

All things considered, there's almost no doubt but that the best education in America is being provided in Catholic schools. In the typical Catholic school, students receive a traditional education that is much like what public education was like in the 1950s. Academic and behavioral expectations are high, grades are not artificially inflated, discipline is a serious matter, and no time is wasted on such things as "self-esteem building." Moreover, Catholic schools are respectfully "hands-off" when it comes to such things as sex education and "AIDS awareness." Those sorts of issues are left up to parents, and rightly so.

Elitism, a nagging aspect of most private schools, is not a factor in Catholic schools. One of Catholic education's missions is and always has been to provide quality education to children from all walks of life and from all religious backgrounds, even non-Christian. In most cases, a Catholic-school student is in a classroom that looks more like the real world than do many public-school classrooms. Finally, Catholic education is far more affordable than secular private education. (Not only is tuition in the typical Catholic school much less than that of the average private school, but Catholic school parents are not expected to ante up with periodic "donations.") Best of all, the end results, academically speaking, are pretty much the same. Catholic schools have even fewer administrators per student than private schools; therefore, an even greater percentage of their educational dollar goes into the classroom.

The Slow Train Comin'

Public schools are showing no signs of waking up and smelling the coffee. The writing on the wall reads: In the near future, public schools will serve disproportionate numbers of children whose parents are poor and/or who don't put a premium on education, and private and parochial schools will serve the rest. To "the rest," therefore, will go the spoils of society—the best colleges (private, of course), the best jobs, the accumulation of private property, and a comfortable retirement. And that, folks, may be all it takes to drive the nail in the coffin of a growing, permanent underclass of undereducated, disenfranchised, restless, dependent, and undoubtedly angry people who find that picking themselves up and moving to another part of the country solves nothing.

I happen to believe in the merits of public education. Although my wife and I could have afforded private schooling for our children, they were educated in the public sector. Unlike some parents, however, we refused to let our children "get by." When we felt standards in a particular subject area were low, we established higher standards of our own which our children had to meet. I could see that neither of the kids was being taught how to write properly, so I took it upon myself to teach them. Unlike many of their peers, our children were expected to do their own homework and science projects, and study for tests independently. The grades they received, therefore, were *their* grades, and theirs alone. If we received a complaint from a teacher concerning one of the children, we did not give the source the "third degree." If there was any doubt in our minds, the teacher received benefit of it. The child in question was simply punished and made to apologize to the teacher the following day. In short, my wife and I dedicated ourselves to making public education work for our children. My point, however, is *we should not have had to bend over backward at all.* My parents didn't. Willie's parents didn't. She and I had to because the system is no longer serving America's children; rather, it is shorting them, and the numbers show it:

❏ While expenditures on elementary and secondary public education have *increased* more than 200 percent (in constant 1989 dollars) since 1960, SAT scores have declined 73 points. This belies the notion that America's educational ills can be solved by increased spending. As it turns out, there is no systematic correlation whatsoever between educational spending and student achievement. Of the top five states in SAT scores, only one, Minnesota, is ranked in the top twenty-five in educational spending, and Minnesota's rank is twenty-fifth.

❏ In 1992, only 20 percent of eighth-graders could do seventh-grade math, and only 6 percent of high school seniors possessed a grasp of math sufficient for entry-level college math courses.

❏ In a 1989 *National Geographic* survey of geographical knowledge, U.S. young adults finished last among nine countries, including Mexico.

❏ In the 1988 International Assessment of Educational Progress exams in science, U.S. students scored last.

The problem, however, is not confined to America's students. In his book *Inside American Education,* Dr. Thomas Sowell sheds alarming light on the "dumbing down" of teacher-education and teaching standards. Education majors achieve far lower SAT scores than students in other majors. Education majors also score significantly lower on the Graduate Record Exam. Syndicated columnist Walter Williams comments:

> Some of the least qualified students, taught by the least qualified professors, have been entrusted with the education of our children. We shouldn't be surprised by their falling for fads and substituting methods that work with methods that sound good.

It's Not Too Late

Abolishing the Department of Education and returning control of education to the states would be a step in the right direction; that being, in this particular case, a step backward toward the state of affairs that existed in the 1950s, when student achievement in America was at the highest postwar level. Returning control over educational matters to the states would also diminish the influence of the National Education Association, the country's largest and most politically powerful union, which vigorously resists any efforts in this direction. The NEA's handprints are also all over most, if not all, of the ill-fated educational reform efforts of the past twenty years. In an article published in its June 7, 1993, issue, *Forbes* magazine laid blame for both the increase in cost of education and the deterioration of educational quality on the NEA, calling it "the worm in the American education apple."

In *Public Education: An Autopsy* (1994), Myron Lieberman, one of this country's most distinguished professors of education, decries the "inherent futility of conventional school reform" and argues that as long as pubic schools are under the federal government's thumb, costs will continue to climb as quality declines. His solution: school choice. By activating free-market forces in the educational sector, school choice would go a long way toward putting public, private, and parochial schools on a par. Putting educational vouchers in the hands of America's parents would also invigorate parent involvement, while at the same time reducing the influence of both nouveau educational reformers and the NEA. This is exactly what the doctor is ordering for American education, but the NEA, fighting for its life, is pulling out all the stops in an effort to discredit and disarm the school-choice movement.

At least thirty-five states now have grassroots coalitions working for school choice. The education establishment had hoped that the defeat of California's Proposition 174 in November 1993 would take the air out of the school-choice movement nationally, but quite the opposite has occurred. Rather than having been demoralized by the defeat in California, school-choice proponents were energized, and school-choice proposals are proliferating, propelled by Gallup polls showing ever-increasing public support for the idea. But because laws must be changed, progress toward that end is painfully slow.

One of the most promising trends is the corporate-sponsored school voucher. Across the country, corporations and business coalitions are setting up programs that award scholarships to low-income students, allowing them to attend the secular private or parochial school of their choice. The response to and initial success of these initiatives have been so overwhelming that in 1994, a new organization, the Children's Educational Opportunity Foundation (CEO America), was formed to function as a umbrella for private voucher plans around the country. In April 1995, there were nineteen CEO America programs in operation around the country, with lots more on the drawing boards.

Says Jeanne Allen, president of the Washington-based Center for Education Reform (not to be confused with nouveau educational reform): "Private entrepreneurs are doing this because some of them are fed up, although for others it's purely philanthropic." Moreover, she says, corporate-sponsored vouchers are "not pegged to any one group." In other words, they're not associated with any particular political lobby, as is often the case with school-choice initiatives. It's far easier for the NEA to take potshots at Republicans or conservative Christian groups than at nonpartisan foundations that have no ideological investment whatsoever in school choice. Who can argue with programs targeted at improving educational opportunity for America's neediest kids?

Private scholarship programs like those organized by CEO America will undoubtedly have a trickle-down effect. As taxpayers see that more educational quality can be obtained with far less money, there's bound to be a revolt at the grassroots level against the status quo in public education. At that point, the groundswell for school choice will hopefully be uncontainable. One possible response on the part of the education establishment may be to set up what one CEO America official has called "Potemkin village schools." These are schools that have the outward appearance of being both innovative and demanding, but are actually dressed-up versions of the same old song. So-called "magnet" schools, which are really nothing more than an attempt to put Bordeaux sauce on a stale hamburger and call it filet mignon, are a prime example, no pun intended.

Coda

No entitlement program can level the playing field of opportunity as much as strong schools that embody high standards for teachers and students both. For anyone concerned about America's children, who are, after all, America's future, joining in the effort to clean public education's "house" should be a matter of utmost priority. What's needed are individuals from every walk of life who are willing to commit to the need for change in the way America's public schools have been conducting business since the 1960s: people who are willing to write letters to lawmakers, state and local superintendents of schools, and school board members; people who are willing to attend school board meetings, even run for school boards; people who are willing to campaign for school choice in their states and communities; people who are willing to stand up, be counted, and let their voices be heard.

How about you?

CHAPTER FOUR

The Politics of "Parenting"

*I*n early 1995, after I had written several newspaper columns in which I'd taken partisan political stands on several issues pertinent to families, a reader in Pittsburgh wrote me a long letter of scornful reprimand in which he said, "Politics has nothing to do with parenting." A reader in Los Angeles chided me to "stop bringing politics into child rearing." The editor of a large Midwestern daily that carries my nationally syndicated column said he was receiving increasing complaints from readers concerning my obvious political biases.

I wish Mr. Pittsburgh were correct, and I wish it were possible to separate child rearing from politics; but he isn't, it's not, and furthermore, it is imperative that people like myself—people who accept responsibility for shaping public opinion on the subject— take clear, strong stands on the growing number of child-rearing issues that have been politicized in recent years. In fact, it is accurate to say *there is not one single aspect of the rearing and education of children that has not taken on a political dimension,* the result of political scheming. It is also accurate to say that in each case, the instigators of the schemes in question have been liberals. Each scheme promises to expand the powers of government at the expense of civil liberties, and each scheme will create a new client group for the Democratic party.

To put my remarks in perspective, the reader should know that I am a recovering liberal. My mother was a Democratic precinct worker in Chicago, and during my growing years, it never occurred to me that Republicans might sometimes have a valid point of view. Democrats were friends of the common man; Republicans were bedmates of big business who sought to exploit the talents and efforts of "the people" to feed corporate greed. Given this sort of upbringing, it was logical that in the '60s I became a leader of student demonstrations against the Vietnam War at Western Illinois University. I was instrumental in having ROTC disallowed from recruiting on campus, applied for status as a conscientious objector (denied), and vowed to refuse induction if drafted (miraculously passed over). I voted for McGovern in '72, and Carter in '76 and '80. They were Democrats, and that was reason enough. By the late '70s, my political opinions were being informed by the likes of the *Charlotte Observer, Rolling Stone,* and *Time,* none of which can claim a lack of bias when it comes to editorial policy. Courtesy of those sources, I believed all liberals were good and all conservatives were evil. Everything humane about America—including welfare, pro-choice legislation, and sex education in schools (my knee-jerk dispositions at the time)—was due to the former; every social disease—racism, sexism, poverty, homelessness—was a conspiracy of the latter.

In the mid-'80s, two friends of mine—both attorneys, one of whom is now a federal judge—took interest in my intellectual and ideological error. With great and admirable patience, they caused me to begin looking closely at both sides of any political argument and stop prejudging the merits of either based on stereotypes. I became aware, for example, of the part welfare has played in the destruction of the black family, and how the government has taken over much of the role once occupied by the church in black communities, thus contributing to their destabilization. As one preconceived notion after another proved intellectually bankrupt, I came to the conclusion that contemporary liberalism and respect for civil liberties are not synonymous. Rather, contemporary liberals, most of whom (but by no means all) identify themselves as Democrats, seem dedicated to the proposition that big government is the proper arbiter of all human relationships. The liberal position implies (and is often explicit to the effect) that when it comes to social and economic transactions, the average citizen is too self-interested to conduct himself fairly, with proper respect for and consideration of the rights and dignities of others; government's proper role, therefore, is to dispassionately monitor, mediate, and manage these transactions, and the more complex these transactions become, the more influence government must have in them.

Not content with bringing a necessary halt to the most blatant evils of racial prejudice (a commendable achievement), contemporary liberals seem determined to mold society in their own idealistic image. Where once individual merit and achievement were the capital of success, now entitlement and affirmative action rule. As William A. Henry III points out in *In Defense of Elitism* (1994), nearly every domestic policy debate since World War II has "revolved around the poles of elitism and egalitarianism—and . . . egalitarianism has been winning far too thoroughly." In recent years, liberals have extended their enthusiasm for social engineering toward the family. In this regard, they have many natural allies within the mental health professions. A significant number of "helping" professionals share the belief that people cannot be trusted to conduct themselves properly in relationships with one another; rather, they generally require "help." The most logical source of such altruistic assistance is, of course, a "helping" professional.

Since the '50s, and in increasingly explicit ways, mental health professionals have been demonizing the traditional family unit, characterizing it as a pathological entity that employs intimidation, codependence, and various forms of abuse to maintain a superficial pretense of fealty among its members. From the radical feminist point of view, the traditional two-heterosexual-parent family was invented by men to keep women in a state of bondage. From the point of view of many child and family "experts," the traditional family keeps children, too, in a state of psychological downtroddenness. In his latest book, *Teaching Children Self-Discipline*, Thomas Gordon writes of the need to "free our children of control by power-based discipline," thus making for a "new species," as he puts it, "of young people who are less inclined to obey authority and make war."

This sort of deconstructionist rhetoric became "party line" in the '70s and '80s. According to the pundits of the profession, the average American child was a victim of his parents' archaic attitudes toward discipline and, in more general terms, the very role of children in society. Traditional disciplinary methods were psychologically damaging and, when it came to *spanking,* physically abusive as well.

To Spank or Not to Spank

Contrary to popular misconception, Dr. Benjamin Spock did not, at least initially, take a no-spanking position. In the 1968 edition of his *Common Sense Book of Baby and Child Care,* first published in 1946, he wrote:

> If an angry parent keeps himself from spanking, he may show his irritation in other ways; for instance, by nagging the child half the day, or trying to make him feel deeply guilty. I'm not particularly advocating spanking, but I think it's less poisonous than lengthy disapproval, because it clears the air, for parent and child.

The first child-rearing authority to tell parents, unequivocally, not to spank was Selma Fraiberg, author of *The Magic Years,* which has sold well over a million copies since its publication in 1959. Fraiberg warned that spankings caused children to fear their parents and, as a consequence, become more deceptive concerning the pursuit of mischief.

The no-spanking position was elaborated upon by both Thomas Gordon and Dorothy Briggs. Gordon defined as authoritarian any parent who believes it is right and proper to exercise authority in the rearing of children. Lest any reader think I am engaging in gross oversimplification, here's Gordon in his own words:

> The stubborn persistence of the idea that parents must and should use authority in dealing with children has, in my opinion, prevented for centuries any significant change or improvement in the way children are raised by parents and treated by adults. (*P.E.T.,* p. 164)

Gordon maintained (and continues to maintain) that parents who rely upon traditional, punitive forms of discipline, and especially those parents who spank, are employing essentially the same "obedience-training" techniques used by animal trainers, including the use of physical pain to promote compliance. His rhetoric not only reveals that he has never watched a professional trainer work with an animal, but is clear evidence of his exaggerated contempt for, and misrepresentation of, traditional discipline:

Children often become cowed, fearful, and nervous . . . often turn on their trainers with hostility and vengeance; and often break down physically or emotionally under the stress of trying to learn behavior that is either difficult or unpleasant for them. (*P.E.T.*, pp. 169–70)

To my knowledge, Gordon was never publicly challenged by any colleague to supply data to support such an outrageous contention. Hyperbole such as this was simply accepted at face value, I think because it suited the more insidious purpose of demonizing the traditional family unit, thus convincing millions of baby boomers that whether they realized it or not, their childhood experiences had rendered them especially needful of mental health services.

Briggs was equally forceful in her views on spanking. Spanking "fills a child with negative feelings" and "teaches fear, deviousness, lying, and aggression." She provided the antispanking movement with one of its code words by asserting that spanking was a form of "assault." Without a shred of proof, and while completely ignoring evidence to the contrary, Briggs maintained spankings taught children that physical violence was an acceptable means of conflict resolution. In effect, she defined spanking as child abuse.

This sort of rhetoric set an organized antispanking movement in motion. Initially, its aim was to educate parents concerning the drawbacks of spanking and provide more effective alternatives. While fewer parents spank today than did forty years ago, there is no sign that spanking is ever going to die out entirely. Frustrated by this fact, antispankers have all but abandoned educational efforts in favor of legislative ones.

Today, one of the leading spokespersons of the antispanking movement—its "guru," in fact—is sociologist Murray Straus of the University of New Hampshire Family Research Laboratory, author of *Beating the Devil Out of Them* (1994). Although Straus's "data" has been subjected to scientific scrutiny and found severely anemic, there are many mental health professionals who accept his conclusions at face value. Straus fails to prove that a typical, several-swats-to-the-rear-end spanking is likely to cause either physical or psychological damage, yet he defines even one swat to a child's buttocks as "child abuse." His rhetoric, not his science, is the most outstanding aspect of his work. "Corporal punishment teaches the morality of hitting," he says, and one aspect of what he terms spanking's "hidden curriculum" is the lesson "those who love you hit you," which he claims—in a blatant attempt to forge an alliance with radical feminists—is "almost a recipe for violence between spouses later in life." As these emotional appeals indicate, Straus is more of an ideologue than a scientist. He uses the trappings of science to advance a political argument: *spanking by parents should be proscribed by law.* He is careful to point out that parents have nothing to fear from such proposed law because offenders would not be subject to incarceration; rather, they would be ordered to receive parent reeducation from a "helping" professional. Presumably, parents who refused to submit to such reeducation would have their children taken away and kept in state care facilities until they admitted their sins and were willing to renounce them forever.

Spurred on by rhetoric such as Straus dispenses, a growing number of "helping" professionals are lending influential support to organizations such as End Physical Punishment of Children (EPOCH) and the National Committee to Prevent Child Abuse to bring about antispanking legislation. They are not so naive, however, as to think that any politician interested in reelection will sign such a bill, much less author it. Their strategy is to bring antispanking law about *indirectly,* as a consequence of legislation that is less politically suicidal.

The Children's Rights Amendment

A prohibition against spanking, should it ever come about, will probably stem from a judicial ruling. The actual sequence of events leading to such an edict is impossible to predict, but one such scenario involves a proposed children's rights amendment to the Constitution.

The National Task Force for Children's Constitutional Rights (NTFCCR)—whose advisory board includes a number of prominent individuals in the fields of law, medicine, psychology, and social work—believes that the best way to protect children from maltreatment within their families is through such an amendment (or separate amendments to individual state constitutions).

The wording of section 1 of the proposed amendment would open a judicial Pandora's box that could well lead to separate anti-spanking rulings in the courts:

> All citizens of the United States who are fifteen years of age or younger shall enjoy the right to live in a home that is safe and healthy; the right to adequate health care; the right to an adequate education and the right to the care of a loving family or a substitute thereof, which approximates as closely as possible such family.

In a 1991 article for the *Ohio Northern University Law Review*, one of NTFCCR's cofounders, Connecticut Superior Court Judge Charles Gill, equates a children's rights amendment with the Equal Rights Amendment. Conceding that ERA was defeated, Gill notes that nearly half our states have enacted an equal rights amendment and "nearly all state legislatures have passed legislation that [improves] the status of women." In other words, Gill is saying that while a children's rights amendment might not, at present, stand a chance in Congress, it might be possible to galvanize enough public support behind such a sentimental concept to more quietly implement its equivalent on a state-by-state basis. If such legislation is eventually enacted, it would only be a matter of time before an enterprising attorney acting on behalf of a child would file suit charging a parent who spanked with failing to provide a "safe, healthy, and loving" home environment, thus violating the protected rights of the child in question. (Murray Straus would almost surely be willing to lend his rhetorical talents to such a proceeding.) If a judge concurred, a de facto law prohibiting parental spanking would be on the books and enforceable.

Note that the amendment implies that "substitute" families are as good as or in some cases to be preferred over biological families. The not-so-subtle threat contained therein is that if biological parents are deemed inadequately "loving," government agencies will be obligated to find families that are psychologically "safer and healthier" in which to place their children. Given their penchant for redistributing income, it is not surprising that liberals are now considering redistributing children.

Antispanking is not the only proscription that might well fall out of a children's rights amendment. Its nebulous wording lends to all manner of liberal, activist interpretations. No one would deny that safe, healthy homes and loving families are in the best interests of children. The problem is in the eyes of judicial beholders when it comes to construing the meaning of such vague language. For example, do parents who make a child do chores when none of his peers are required to do so, thus making the child resentful, qualify as "unloving"? If two parents argue a lot in front of their children, does this qualify the family environment as "unhealthy"? If parents insist that a child do his own homework, study for his own tests, and make good grades in school (when all of his peers' parents are helping them in these areas), are they putting too much pressure on the child and in so doing creating psychologically damaging circumstances that violate the child's rights? If readers think these hypothetical questions come out of left field, I suggest they read on.

The Plot Thickens

Judge Gill and other child advocates feel that progress in the area of children's rights has been too slow. He characterizes the movement as being "splintered into thousands of largely ineffective shards of interests." Gill says that "until enough bodies and groups speak with a single, powerful, and politically intimidating voice for children, the status of children will not change."

That may well be happening. In 1991, the National Committee for the Rights of the Child (NCRC) was formed in Washington. According to Judge Gill, dozens of national groups, representing millions of members, met to initiate "The Next Great Movement in America." He describes these child advocates as "bright and angry."

Among the gathered were representatives from the Office for the Study of the Psychological Rights of the Child (OSPRC), established in 1980 as a joint project by the National Association of School Psychologists and the School of Education of Indiana University. One of OSPRC's first major projects was the International

Conference on Psychological Abuse of Children and Youth, which it organized and conducted in 1983. In 1986, OSPRC opened its first adjunct office at the University of Massachusetts at Amherst. As a result of its participation in the establishment of the National Committee on the Rights of Children, OSPRC is now part of a larger network of centers devoted to the study and facilitation of children's "psychological rights," including centers at Pace University and the Universities of Minnesota, Nebraska, Detroit, and New Hampshire.

The man behind this growing organization, which is viewed by other child-advocacy groups as being at the "cutting edge" of the children's rights movement, is Stuart Hart, a fifty-seven-year-old professor of education at the Indianapolis campus of Indiana University. In 1986, Hart received a $290,000 grant from the U.S. Department of Health and Human Services to develop operational definitions and measures of psychological abuse of children. Hart says he and his graduate students spent three years researching and creating the following six categories of such abuse: spurning; terrorizing; isolating; exploiting/corrupting; denying emotional responsiveness; and mental health, medical, and/or emotional neglect. Included are the following behaviors (numbered by me for later reference), not one of which, by the way, conforms to the requirements of an "operational" definition:

1. Belittling, denigrating, and other nonphysical forms of overtly hostile or rejecting treatment.

2. Shaming and/or ridiculing the child for showing normal emotions such as affection, grief, or sorrow.

3. Consistently singling out one child to criticize and punish, to perform most of the household chores, or to receive fewer rewards.

4. Public humiliation.

5. Placing a child in unpredictable or chaotic circumstances.

6. Placing a child in recognizably dangerous situations.

7. Setting rigid or unrealistic expectations with threat of loss, harm, or danger if they are not met.

8. Exploiting a child's fears or vulnerabilities by threatening to isolate, spurn, become emotionally unavailable, or exploit and corrupt.

9. Threatening or perpetrating violence against the child.

10. Threatening or perpetrating violence against a child's loved ones or objects.

11. Confining the child or placing unreasonable limitations on the child's freedom of movement within his/her environment.

12. Placing unreasonable limitations or restrictions on the child's social interactions within the home.

13. Placing unreasonable limitations or restrictions on social interactions with peers or adults in the community.

14. Modeling, permitting, or encouraging developmentally inappropriate behavior (e.g., parentification, infantalization, living the parent's unfulfilled dreams).

15. Being detached or uninvolved through either incapacity or lack of motivation.

16. Interacting only when absolutely necessary.

17. Failing to express affection, caring, and love for the child.

18. Ignoring the need for, or refusing to allow or provide, treatment for serious emotional/behavioral problems or needs of child.

19. Ignoring the need for, or refusing to allow or provide, treatment for serious educational problems or needs of the child.

Suffice to say, the list is sufficiently vague and all-inclusive as to incriminate just about any parent I've ever known, including my wife and myself. As I said, none of these "maltreatment forms" are defined operationally. It's fairly obvious that the "research" done to arrive at these criteria—very likely a number of brainstorming sessions—does not qualify as science. Hart cannot prove that any of the examples in his list result in lasting psychological damage; indeed, in many cases, the parental behavior in question would do no more than insult a child's feelings, and rather temporarily at that. But Hart's "research," although a mockery of the term, is no joke because this $290,000 waste of taxpayer money is in anticipation of legislation that will open the door to greatly expanded definitions of child abuse along with greatly expanded government interference in the functioning of families. Hart dreams of the passage of a children's rights amendment or its international equivalent (see below). In that event, his most unscientific compilation of "psychological maltreatment forms" would likely become the "test" of parental adequacy. In that regard, let's take a closer look at several of the items in Hart's list (numbers correspond with numbered items above):

1. Consider the possibility that "denigrating" in an "overtly hostile" manner might be taken to include severe verbal reprimands which cause a child to feel ashamed of some egregious misbehavior.

3. "Consistently singling out one child . . . to perform most of the household chores" is an interesting example of psychological abuse. In the first place, many a child thinks he or she does "everything" and that his siblings do "nothing." Would a child's complaint to that effect to a school counselor be reason enough to justify a humiliating investigation of the home? In the second place, what if one child is, indeed, being required to do most of the chores? What if, as was the case in our family, the oldest child, a son, is required to perform outside labor not being required of a younger sister? This is abuse?

4. Has a child been publicly humiliated when, after screaming at his parents in a store that he "hates them" because they refuse to buy him what he wants (my son did that once), the parents remove him from the store and spank him in sight of other people (as I did)? In Hart's mind, I am probably guilty. In my mind, and I daresay the minds of most parents, Eric was guilty of humiliating his mother and myself and deserved what he got. As testament to the effectiveness of my action, Eric never yelled at us in public again.

5. Does "placing a child in . . . chaotic circumstances" include a New York subway station during rush hour?

7. This raises the possibility that telling a child he must achieve a relatively high grade average or lose certain coveted privileges is a form of psychological abuse. If so, my parents were guilty, my wife and I are guilty, and most of our friends are guilty. So, probably, is the reader.

9. In the minds of children's rights advocates, this includes spanking.

11. Consider that many "helping" professionals contend—again without a shred of evidence to the effect—that confining a child in his or her room for any significant period of time is likely to cause the child to develop "negative feelings" toward the room and possibly give rise to the onset of sleep difficulties.

12. Presumably, this means parents should not tell a child who he can and cannot invite to their home.

13. Nor can parents tell a child he is not allowed to associate with certain children in the community.

14. Parentification: requiring that a fifteen-year-old look after a younger sibling on a regular basis. Infantilization: letting a two-year-old continue to drink from a bottle. Personally, I'd question the parents' judgment in both cases, but "bad judgment" and psychological abuse are apples and oranges. Also, I'm sure it took Hart and his graduate students months of meticulous research to arrive at the conclusion that "living the parent's unfulfilled dreams" is psychologically abusive. My wife wanted our daughter to be a debutante. Why? I don't know. I didn't care, and neither did Amy. Nonetheless, it was, for a time, important to Willie. Was she wanting Amy to live some unfulfilled dream of her own? I suppose, in which case I was negligent in not reporting her to the proper authorities. Too late now.

15. A parent who suffers from periodic bouts of depression during which he/she wants to simply be left alone.

18. In this regard, know that significant numbers of "helping" professionals believe children who misbehave should not be punished; rather, they merit "understanding"—a code word for therapy. The implication of this "psychological maltreatment form" is that if parents punish a misbehaving child instead of availing the child of professional help, they are guilty of psychological neglect.

Underlying OSPRC's criteria are two equally insidious assumptions: First, that parents are basically unpredictable, ignorant individuals who cannot be trusted to exercise "psychologically correct" judgment in the rearing of children. As such, they need "helping professionals" looking over their shoulders, telling them what to do and what not to do. Second, that the attitudes and methods which define traditional child rearing are pathological. According to Stuart Hart, most children of my generation (himself included?) were subjected to one act of psychological maltreatment after another. In short, children need to be protected from their parents. Parent education has failed, so the only recourse is for the government to step in and provide the buffer.

All of this would be laughable were it not for the fact that OSPRC is a high-profile member of the National Committee for the Rights of the Child, and Hart is currently president of both. In early 1995, NCRC—along with OSPRC, NTFCRC, NCPCA, EPOCH, the Children's Defense Fund, and Hillary Clinton—won an important victory, one that bodes ill for the future of the American family.

The Die Is Cast

The major media gave but passing mention of the fact that on February 23, 1995, President Clinton signed the United Nations Convention on the Rights of Children. This grave act deserved front-page headlines, for it represents the most blatant move yet toward big government meddling in family relationships.

Backers of the treaty, which is awaiting Senate ratification, claim its main purpose is to end economic and sexual exploitation of children in underdeveloped nations. A closer look reveals otherwise.

The treaty gives signatory nations two years and thirty days in which to comply with its articles, which require that each nation create and enforce laws pertaining to a long list of children's "rights." In the case of the United States, the federal government would oversee implementation and enforcement by states and localities.

Article 2 says it is primarily the responsibility of government to undertake whatever steps are necessary to provide for the well-being of children. Not the responsibility of parents, mind you, but the state.

Article 3 says that all "facilities responsible for the care or protection of children shall conform with the standards established by competent authorities." It is entirely conceivable that this could be construed to mean that parents must conform to child-rearing standards drawn up by "helping" professionals such as Stuart Hart and Murray Straus, enacted by lawmakers, and enforced by bureaucrats.

Article 12 grants children "the right to express (their) views freely in all matters." One can envision law which prevents parents from restricting their children from getting tattooed, wearing provocative clothing, or saying what they please to authority figures.

Article 15 guarantees "freedom of association." This implies parents would not be allowed to restrict a child's choice of friends. If your fourteen-year-old daughter wants to date an eighteen-year-old dropout with a police record, who are you to say she can't?

Article 16 establishes that children have a "right to privacy," which activist judges might well use to nullifying state laws which require parental notification and consent before minors can be given abortions. Perhaps this means a teen has a right to lock his parents out of "his" room with a deadbolt or lock himself and his girlfriend in there for the afternoon.

Article 19 no doubt excites Hart and Straus. It states that government "shall take all appropriate legislative, administrative, social, and educational measures to protect the child from all forms of physical or mental violence, injury or abuse, neglect or negligent treatment, maltreatment or exploitation. . . ." From what we've already seen, this includes spanking, confining a child to his room, restricting his association with other children, letting a toddler continue drinking from a bottle, and having a child live a parent's "unfulfilled dreams," whatever heinous imaginings those might be.

Article 27 recognizes the "right of every child to a standard of living adequate for the child's physical, mental, spiritual, moral, and social development" and directs signatory nations to take whatever steps are necessary to guarantee such a standard for every child. This sounds suspiciously like a mandate for more taxpayer-supported entitlements.

Article 28, which concerns itself with education, could be used to argue against home-schooling, which the National Education Association, a blatantly liberal lobby, vehemently opposes.

Article 43 sets up an international body of ten child and family "experts" (don't expect Dr. James Dobson to be appointed) to make recommendations to signatories regarding compliance. In January, this committee admonished the United Kingdom for insufficient welfare spending, allowing spanking by parents, and for plans to incarcerate hard-core juvenile criminals. In short, the UK is being told to raise taxes to support more socialism and to coddle kids—the worse the kid, the more the coddling.

This same committee has recommended that schools develop curricula to educate children concerning their rights under the convention. So, parents would pay taxes to support schools that would teach children when and how to challenge their parents' authority. Such a deal!

Under the terms of the treaty, governments are charged to "assist parents in performing child-rearing responsibilities" by establishing "institutions, facilities, and services for the care of children." In other words, the federal government would be "obligated" to help you make decisions concerning how you rear your children and who takes care of them. Decisions concerning health care, education, and discipline would be monitored and managed, if not made, by bureaucrats. I'm sure American parents are greatly relieved to hear that President Clinton is so willing to relieve them of these burdensome tasks.

Not surprisingly, the First Lady's hand can be seen in all this. The treaty is and has been a pet project of the Children's Defense Fund, which Mrs. Clinton chaired from 1986 to 1991. Its ratification would be not only a feather in CDF's cap, but also a guarantee of greatly increased political influence. Oh, and by the way, the president has nominated Peter Edelman, husband to Marion Edelman, CDF's executive director, to the federal bench, a step away from the Supreme Court. It would appear that Clinton's endorsement of this treaty is but one move in a far more ambitious ultraliberal scheme. Its ratification by the Senate would clear the way for a children's rights amendment to the Constitution, federal antispanking legislation, and a greatly expanded definition of child abuse.

As it stands, the treaty has been tabled by the Senate Foreign Relations Committee, which is chaired by Jesse Helms, a gentleman with pronounced disaffections for such things as UN committees that presume to know what's best for American families. If, however, the Democrats regain control of the Senate in '96, there is a strong likelihood of ratification.

Judge Gill praises the UN Convention, saying that whereas previous children's "rights" were paternalistic—in other words, whatever "rights" a child enjoyed were granted by his or her parents—"the *Convention makes the state directly responsible to the child*" (my emphasis). Gill makes it clear he and other children's rights advocates believe that when the interests of a certain child come into conflict with the rights of his or her parents, *the interests of the child should determine the outcome.*

Epilogue

At this writing, the American people are a Senate roll call away from ratification and implementation of the United Nations Convention on the Rights of the Child, in my view (and I am hardly alone in this) the most insidious document ever signed by an American president—possibly an impeachable act, for it allows the usurpation of the people's sovereignty by an international body. The language of the convention virtually mandates not only a children's rights amendment, but also greatly expanded definitions of child abuse of the sort proposed by OSPRC, and antispanking law—*federal,* no less. The treaty is a liberal's dream and a conservative's nightmare because it will allow government to insert itself between parent and child, thus effectively destroying parental choice and transforming the family into something akin to a baby-sitter for the parent-state.

The Declaration of Independence and the Constitution recognized the ultimate sovereignty of "the people." The Founding Fathers were more concerned about the threat an overweening state posed to civil liberties than they were regarding any hegemonic foreign power. For more than two centuries, the courts have upheld the idea that a man's home is his castle and, more specifically, the basic principle of parental prerogative in the rearing and education of children. Never in our nation's history has the people's sovereignty been placed in the jeopardy represented by the United Nations Convention on the Rights of Children, a proposed children's rights amendment, and proposed antispanking legislation.

Children's rights advocates are well intentioned, to be sure. They would, and do, sincerely deny that their intent is to undermine the Constitution. But as Supreme Court Justice Louis D. Brandeis (1856–1941) warned, "The greatest dangers to liberty lurk in insidious encroachment by men of zeal, well-meaning but without understanding." Notwithstanding their public and private poses, children's rights advocates are possessed of a social engineering mentality that springs from the idealistic belief that it is possible to bring about a perfect, brave new world. The logical starting point of such an effort is, of course, the family. And since a man and wife are not a family until they produce a child, the focus of their utopian zeal is the parent-child relationship. As Judge Gill makes perfectly and proudly clear, they believe government has a moral obligation to insure that parents rear children within certain narrow, perfectionist guidelines, and to further insure that where parents will not bend to its dictates, more suitable substitute parents will be found for the children in question.

Make no mistake about it, children's rights advocates have no intention of making the mistake that proved fatal to the Equal Rights Amendment. That ill-advised piece of legislation withered on the vine not because America is dominated by men who want to keep women barefoot and pregnant, but because too many ERA advocates spoke out stridently on the issue, causing too many of the common folk to take notice and begin asking the right questions. The one thing children's rights advocates don't want is for the common folk to begin asking the right questions about such things as the UN Convention and the children's rights amendment. The common folk are the problem, remember? Therefore, the approach being taken is one of stealth. President Clinton signed the UN Convention on the Rights of Children without fanfare, without the ceremony that usually attends such momentous acts of international diplomacy. He left it to the First Lady to make the announcement, and she did so in such a way that none of the major media felt it merited enough import to take up even a few seconds of airtime or a few inches of newsprint. Neither *Time* nor *Newsweek* reported it. National Public Radio indulged in a minor amount of low-key commentary, but the average NPR listener isn't likely to raise as much as one eyebrow at the idea that children should have rights, especially if the children in question are ostensibly Third World. And so, the common folk ask no questions.

Now that the treaty has been signed, it sits in a stack marked "Later, maybe never" on the corner of Senator Jesse Helms's desk.

As I said earlier, as long as he chairs the Senate Foreign Relations Committee, the convention will gather dust. But the important thing is, it's signed. The children's rights crowd is pinning its hopes on Clinton's reelection and the Democrats regaining control of the Senate in '96, in which case Jesse is out and you can bet someone will be in who understands the importance of bringing the treaty out of committee to a quick floor debate and equally quick ratification. And if not in '96, then in '98, or 2000, or whenever. Patience is not a virtue of any individual children's rights advocate I've ever met, but together, organized, they exercise admirable restraint.

If the Senate someday ratifies the convention, the United States will have two years and thirty days in which to comply with the treaty's articles, and the dominoes will begin to fall: the children's rights amendment, greatly expanded definitions of child abuse and neglect, antispanking law, possibly even parent licensing. And just like that, big government will become a de facto member of the family.

Guess who wants to come to dinner?

PART TWO

A Family of Value:
Rearing "Three Rs" Children

CHAPTER FIVE

The Respectful Child: Good Beginnings

*T*he rearing of children is not difficult. Having said this many times to many audiences, I know that some of you are already rolling your eyes and saying to yourselves, "Well, John Rosemond obviously doesn't know *my* children!" or "This guy's totally out of touch with reality!" Bear with me, please. Granted, some children are more difficult than others, and there will be difficult moments with any child, but the rearing of children per se is not more difficult than it was for our grandparents and great-grandparents; which is to say, it shouldn't be difficult at all.

Nonetheless, the idea that rearing children is an inherently difficult, demanding, emotionally draining task is deeply embedded in the consciousness of today's parent. I get the feeling, in fact, that some parents wear this burden with pride. There seems to be a general feeling that parents who are *not* constantly exhausted must not be putting enough effort into child rearing. Conclusion: The most exhausted parents are the best parents!

The belief that rearing children is difficult is self-fulfilling. If you think it's hard, you will make it so. I'm talking about parents who churn themselves into child-rearing frenzies by driving their children from one largely irrelevant after-school activity to another, sitting down nightly to "help" with homework, and generally paying so much attention to children that they have little energy left to pay to themselves or their marriages. Then they complain that rearing children is unbelievably hard.

Speaking for the present generation of parents, a woman in St. Paul once chastised me for making child rearing sound easy, then

121

said: "I wish it were so, but parenting is the hardest thing I've ever attempted, and I have never felt completely successful at it." Well, how sad. The fact is, if you believe child rearing is incredibly difficult, *you are not ever going to feel successful at it.* Parents who think it's difficult constantly worry whether they're doing the "right" thing. Thinking it's difficult and worrying and self-doubt go hand in hand.

All this agonizing is totally unnecessary. Several years ago, on a flight back to Charlotte from a speaking engagement in Miami, I sat next to an older couple who told me they were going home after having visited one of their sons and his family. During our conversation, I learned they had reared five children, the youngest of whom was several years older than myself. Their children were all married, and those unions had blessed these folks with thirteen grandchildren, several of whom were married, and one of whom was expecting the first great-grandchild!

The woman proceeded to tell me that she had been, in effect, a single parent during much of World War II while her husband had served two tours of duty in the Pacific theater. While he was overseas, she had worked in a munitions factory and her children—two, at the time—had spent their days in a government-funded day-care center that was part of the factory complex. It dawned on me that the trials and tribulations of many of today's parents are nothing new. Throughout history, fathers have been required to be away from hearth and home for long stretches of time, mothers have had to support or help support their families, significant numbers of single female parents have reared children, and children have been cared for by persons other than their parents or close relatives. And while all of this may have been problematic, none of it has ever been cause for great complaint. Until now, that is.

Intrigued, I asked the woman if she had ever felt that child rearing was disproportionately difficult, or if that had been a general feeling among her peers.

"Oh, no," she immediately answered, "it wasn't something the women of my generation felt was difficult at all. It was just something you did."

Something you did. No big deal. One of many responsibilities parents accepted and carried out as well as they could. Nothing to take lightly, mind you, but nothing to get all bent out of shape over, either. Isn't that refreshing?

At this point, someone out there in Readerland is saying, "Yes, but John, *times have changed.* We're not living in the '50s anymore."

But times, dear reader, have always changed. My paternal grandmother was born in 1890. During the first thirty years of her life, she witnessed more startling, disruptive changes—economically, technologically, politically, demographically, etc.—than I witnessed in the first thirty years of mine. And the same was the case with my parents, born in the early '20s, who during the first thirty years of their lives witnessed worldwide economic and political upheavals that my generation cannot begin to appreciate. In fact, in every thirty-year period since the American Revolution, times have changed, and radically so. But amidst all this change, one thing stood fast: to wit, the precepts and practices people brought to the formation and functioning of families and, more specifically, the rearing of children. Technology changed, politics changed, America's economy and social fabric changed, styles came and went, but family values remained constant. A set of timeless traditions and understandings concerning family life anchored our culture, enabling it to withstand the winds of change. When these traditions fell to the professional ax, there was nothing to buffer the winds, and chaos was loosed.

Containing this chaos requires reviving the family values and traditions that once stabilized America's ever-dynamic culture. That revival is what this book is all about. Activating that revival requires, above all else, that America's parents take back from the professional community the reins of child rearing and tell those professionals, "You told us to walk in lockstep with you, and we did, and everything is worse. Now, if you cannot walk in lockstep with us, we invite you to take a hike."

The Revival of Common Sense

Dr. Benjamin Spock, writing in the first (1946) edition *of The Common Sense Book of Baby and Child Care,* said, "Don't be overawed by what the experts say. Don't be afraid to trust your own common sense. Bringing up your child won't be a complicated job if you take it easy, trust your own instincts, and follow the instructions your doctor gives you." The "doctor" Spock was referring to, by the way, wasn't a doctor of psychology, but a pediatrician or general practitioner who had his feet on solid ground.

There is obvious irony in my criticisms of so-called "helping" professionals because I am one. In fact, I am one of a select group of "helping" professionals who are considered "experts" on child rearing, or "parenting"—the nouveau term. Nonetheless, I don't want the reader to be overawed by anything I have to say if for no other reason than from this point on, I'm not going to say anything new. I'm simply going to describe the common sense of rearing children, the same sense our grandparents and their parents before them brought to the task. If you had asked "Grandma" to tell you about child rearing, she would have said, "Well, it's not all that complicated. First off, you need to love 'em a lot, and along with that, you need to see to it they understand three things. . . ."

Warning!

Before I tell you what "Grandma" was about to say, let me warn those of you who have been seduced by the sentimental, romantic child-rearing rhetoric of the last four decades that what follows will not be sentimental or romantic. It will be grounded in fundamental, unshakable realities. As such, it will not, to some of you, sound good, and I will make no attempt to make it so. In fact, we are going to exit the Land of What Sounds Good in child rearing and return from long exile to the land of our forefathers and foremothers: the Land of What Works. I know, from much experience, that some readers may be shocked by the lack of "aren't children just the most adorable, wonderful of all beings?" platitudes in what follows. Some readers may be moved beyond shock to anger. Don't say I didn't warn you.

Three Rules No Child Can Do Without

The successful rearing of a child, as Grandma started to say, is a matter of three simple rules, or understandings. These rules, as will become readily apparent, cannot be communicated to infants or young toddlers. Properly timed, the communication begins when a child is around eighteen months of age, give or take a few months. The introduction of these rules into a child's life almost invariably cause great consternation, to the point sometimes of rage. The reason for this is quite simple: There have been no rules at all to speak of before this time. Well, that's not exactly accurate. For eighteen months, the child has been led to believe that he rules. When he wants to be fed, he is fed. When he wants to be held, he is held. And so on. No one with good sense and a basic understanding of early-childhood development challenges the authority of an infant or young toddler. These three rules are not just new, however, they contradict the child's understanding of how the world works. They upset the child's applecart, so to speak, because the child had every reason to believe *he* ran the show, and would do so forever.

So, the child screams in protest of the rules, denies that his parents are capable of enforcing them, and does many destructive things to demonstrate his defiance. This upheaval goes by the popular term "The Terrible Twos." I have written an entire book, *Making the "Terrible" Twos Terrific!* (1993), concerning this upheaval, so I won't dwell upon it herein. Suffice to say, it is the most precedent-setting of times in the parent-child relationship. If parents "stay the course" through this much-maligned stage, then by his or her third birthday, the child will have accepted that the rules are fixed, as in permanent.

The First Rule (from parent to child): "From this point on in our relationship, child of mine, you will pay much more attention to me than I will ever again, as a general rule, give to you."

The parent continues: "I will always give you the attention that you need, understanding that you will need less and less as time goes on. You, however, will give me all the attention I *want*, regardless of when or why I want it, and by the way, I am under no obligation to justify any request for your attention. I will also continue to give you all the supervision you require. When you are as tall as I am, and are in possession of a driver's license, I will still expect you to inform me as to your whereabouts, your companions, and your doings. Nonetheless, when it comes to who gives to whom the greater share of undivided attention in this relationship, let me assure you that from this point on, you will give that greater share to me."

In other words, whereas the child, for reasons having to do with absolute necessity, was the center of his parents' attention for the first two years or so of life, now his parents will be the center of *his* attention. The family, child-centered to this time, will become parent-centered, or better yet, marriage-centered.

If that first rule causes dismay, it's only because today's parents have been told that the more attention they pay their children, the more they do for them, the more "involved" they become in their lives, the better parents they are. Having been inundated with this rhetoric, many of today's parents are nothing short of shocked upon hearing this first rule. "Huh?" is the typical response.

Knowing that shock is the present state of many a reader, I'm going to share several facts. That's right, *facts*. Psychologists usually talk strictly in terms of theories which are supported by this or that study, blah, blah, blah, but not me! I'm going to give you the facts. And you will be convinced, I guar-an-tee it!

Fact: In the parent-child relationship, the *parent* is the teacher, primarily responsible for the child's social and spiritual education. If you don't think that's a fact, you are a hopeless case. Put this book down and go join a New Age cult. Don't even pass "Go."

Fact: A teacher cannot effectively teach unless the student is giving the teacher his or her undivided attention. If you have any doubts as to whether this is a fact, just ask a teacher.

Fact: A child will not pay sufficient attention to a parent who is acting as if it is his or her most pressing obligation to pay as much attention to and do as much for the child as possible. Please read that again, slowly and out loud. I'll wait.

By age three, a child has arrived at one of two intuitive conclusions concerning his or her parents:

Conclusion A: "My parents are here, primarily speaking, to be paid attention to *by me.*"

Conclusion B: "My parents are here, quite obviously, to pay attention to me."

In the mind of a child, it is either the one or the other. It cannot be both. A child cannot hold Conclusion A one minute, and Conclusion B the next. And let me assure you, if the child arrives at Conclusion B, *discipline will be a major hassle.*

Discipline is the process by which parents make *disciples* of their children. A disciple is one who will follow the lead of the teacher, a source of legitimate authority. The fact is, you cannot expect your child to follow your lead if you have not first convinced your child that you, his parent or parents, are in his life to be paid attention to *by* him rather than the other way around.

Furthermore, *the conclusion the child arrives at has nothing whatsoever to do with the child.* In other words, whether or not your child pays adequate attention to you is 100 percent up to you. Granted, some children seem more temperamentally inclined to pay better attention than others, but any child, regardless of temperament, will pay adequate attention to his or her parents if properly convinced to do so. Unfortunately, too many of today's parents seem determined to rationalize their own failure to command their children's attention by blaming the problem on some aspect of those same children. Their children don't pay attention to them, they claim, because they are "strong-willed" or "argumentative" or because they are "learning disabled" or have "attention deficit disorder." What these parents don't understand is that until they themselves take full, 100 percent responsibility for the fact their children don't pay attention to them, the problem will never be solved.

Allow me to use a personal example to illustrate my meaning: In addition to being an author, I am a public speaker, and a darned good one, at that. I know, as do all darned good public speakers, that whether or not an audience pays attention to me has nothing whatsoever to do with the audience. If the audience pays attention, it is because I have *commanded* their attention. If they don't, it's because I have failed to command. I've actually heard some public speakers rationalize their own failures in this regard by saying things like "It was the end of a long day and the audience was tired" or "A lot of people got up and left because the air conditioning system in the auditorium wasn't working properly." Those public speakers will *never* be able to hold the attention of an audience because they refuse to accept full responsibility for doing so. Likewise, parents who persist in blaming their children's lack of attention on their children's temperament or faulty "switches" inside their children will never succeed at getting their children to pay attention to them.

Note, in the above two paragraphs, my use of the word *command*. Please understand that you cannot, as many frustrated parents seem to think, *demand* a child's attention. I should say, you can demand it and get it for a few minutes maybe, but no longer; in which case, you must demand it again, and again, and again. If you want a child to pay adequate attention to you, whenever, you must *command* the child's attention. If you find yourself frequently demanding it, that is simply irrefutable evidence that you have failed to command.

"So, John, keep us in suspense no longer," the reader may ask. "What is the secret to *commanding* a child's attention?"

Good question! The answer: Always pretend that you know exactly what you are doing.

"Oh, ha, ha, ha, John. You've got to be kidding! Pretend?"

That's right, *pretend*. After all, you cannot always know what you are doing. In fact, you can only know exactly what you are doing if you possess the ability to tell the future with unerring accuracy, which you don't, so what else can you do but pretend? This same pose must be adopted by none other than the president of the United States—if he wants to effectively lead, that is. The job of president is far too complex for any one individual to completely master it. A staff of advisers makes it easier, but still the variables are overwhelming. Being merely human, the president cannot know all there is to know about any given issue, nor can he predict the future. He must, therefore, often fly by the seat of his pants. He must hope that he is making, if not the best decision possible, then one that is good enough. Regardless, he must always *pretend* that he is making any given decision with complete, unwavering confidence in its outcome.

If the president succeeds at so pretending, then the majority of American people will have confidence in his decisions and will, more often than not, follow his lead *even if they do not completely agree with him.* When he stops acting as if he knows that what he's doing is the only sensible way to do it, when he vacillates back and forth on an issue, when his bark proves worse than his bite, when he is all show and no go, then the American people lose confidence in him, and he loses the ability to effectively lead. Some recent presidents have blamed this failure to inspire the confidence of the American people on the media. They are like parents who blame their failure to inspire the confidence of their children on "attention deficit disorder" or public speakers who blame their failure to command an audience's attention on the air conditioning system. These presidents have had difficulty leading, not because of the media, but because they don't understand the first thing about true leadership. They will not accept full, complete responsibility for whether the American people have confidence in them or not.

All this is true of parents and their relationships with their children. Parents cannot always know exactly what they are doing, so they must *pretend* to know. Parenting, in short, is an act, and good parents are good actors. Those parents who succeed at being good actors inspire their children's confidence. Because they *command* their children's attention, their children follow their lead. We say about these children that they are "well disciplined." Like good disciples, they "look up" to their parents. Likewise, parents who vacillate, hedge, or are otherwise indecisive fail to command, and their child ends up not following their lead. There is, after all, no real *leader* for their children to follow. The next thing I'm going to say is extremely important, so listen up: *A child who has not been properly taught to not follow his or her parents' lead has no choice other than to misbehave.* What else can anyone expect of a child who is not receiving clear direction? And so, dear reader, the bottom line is this: The misbehavior of a child has less to do with the child—much less!—than with the child's parents.

"But, John," a parent might say, "I'm not always sure I'm making the right decision."

So? That's what I mean about parenting being an act. As any CEO of any large company will tell you, it is *impossible* for leaders, however good, to always, in every situation, make the best decision possible. Furthermore, it's not necessary. What is necessary, however, is that a CEO—whether the president of the United States or the president of Ford Motor Company—always be *decisive*, that he or she always act as if there is but one decision, in any given situation, that makes any sense. The president of a major corporation will not last long if every time he makes a decision, he says, "Well, uh, I'm not so sure this is the best course to take, but I think maybe it is. That is, I hope it is. If anyone has a better idea, please let me know." That's not a leader talking. That's a vacillator. That's a wimp. His company's stockholders aren't expecting his decisions to be im-

peccable; they are, however, expecting his *leadership* to be impeccable. In short, how one makes and communicates decisions in a business environment is often more important than the "rightness" of
the decisions themselves.

Again, the same is true of being a parent. As a parent, you cannot always be absolutely certain of the decisions you must make.
But understand this: *Parents will almost always make better decisions
for their children than their children would make for themselves* (and
the exceptions to that rule are so few as to be insignificant). That is
not to say that children shouldn't be allowed to make decisions,
even bad ones, and learn from their successes as well as their mistakes. Indeed, they should. But when you, the parent, decide that
you are the person better qualified to make a certain important decision, then make it! And once you've taken your stand, don't waver!
Pretend! Carry it off! If your children see that you know where you
stand, and that you stand firm, they will abide (for the most part, of
course, for such is the nature of children) by your decisions even if
they don't always like them. You'll see.

The Second Rule: "You will do as I say."

And the parent goes on to say (note: I use *say* figuratively, because these rules are *implicit* to a functional parent-child relationship—therefore, it is not really necessary to actually say them out
loud; in fact, the frequent need to say any one of them out loud is
probably indication that the parent has failed to make it implicit),
"Indeed, we can talk about some, and only some, of the decisions I
make, and I will always take your point of view into consideration,
even if you can't express it very well. But the talks we have will be
brief, and when all is said and done, I will make the decision. And I
am not at all sorry to say that I my decisions will not be driven by
consideration of what will make you temporarily happy. If you are
happy with a decision I make, fine. If not, you'll just have to get over
it. In fact, I know full well that if I make good decisions, you will
not be happy with the majority of them, and that is fine with me."

My, my, this is shock treatment, isn't it? Some of you, I know,
are sitting there wondering if you read me right. Psychologists aren't
supposed to be so, so old-fashioned, right? That's exactly right, in
fact. Psychologists were at the vanguard of nouveau parenting. Psychologists and other "helping" professionals have for three decades

been preaching that a child cannot develop adequate self-esteem if the child's parents don't "democratize" the relationship and treat him, more or less, like an equal whose opinions and feelings count! "Experts" such as Thomas Gordon and Dorothy Briggs and Adele Faber contended that generations of American parents have treated children as if their feelings and opinions didn't count, resulting in generations of psychologically stunted children who grew up to be psychologically stunted adults who passed on this psychological stunting to their children who grew up . . . and so on.

Well, I have news for the architects of nouveau parenting and all their disciples. The opinions and feelings of children do not count for much. The Bible tells us that "Foolishness is bound up in the heart of a child" (Proverbs 20:23). It takes children the majority of eighteen years to release an amount of foolishness from their hearts sufficient to become constructive members of society. In the meantime, their opinions and feelings do not count for much.

Don't get me wrong, please! It's not that adults shouldn't listen to children, because we should. We should listen with tolerance for their foolishness and an ear to whatever opportunities we might have to gently pry it loose from their hearts. It's not that adults should treat children as if they aren't important, because children are very important. Their opinions and feelings aren't that important, but they themselves are very important, indeed. They are the future. As such, it is vital that adults not give them the impression that their foolish opinions and foolish feelings are the stuff of importance, lest they not let that foolishness go and instead carry it with them into their adult lives. And it's not that *none* of their opinions and feelings are relatively unimportant; just most of them. Every once in a while, a child comes forth with a truly valid opinion or feeling, and those, dear reader, must be carefully cultivated. It's all part of separating wheat from chaff.

Paradoxically, the best way to dislodge foolishness from the heart of a child is to never call it what it truly is. For example, if a child is convinced that monsters reside in his closet, the very worst thing his parents can say is "There's no such thing as monsters, you foolish child!" Rather, it behooves them to go into his room and do loud battle with the monsters, finally emerging to announce that they, the most powerful parents on the face of the planet, have sent the monster packing forever. For another example, if a child expresses a really off-the-wall opinion concerning a current event, his parents shouldn't exclaim, "Why, that's the most foolish thing we've ever heard!" Rather, they should simply smile and say, "In just a few years, you will think differently about that. In the meantime, you would do well to listen carefully to what grown-ups have to say about such things." Expert teachers do not belittle their students' foolish opinions. They accept those opinions for what they are and gently coax their students toward a state of less foolishness.

What Gordon, Briggs, and other nouveau parenting "experts" don't understand is that if adults treat children as if their opinions and feelings are equal in importance to the opinions and feelings of adults, children will have no basis upon which to build respect for adults. In order for children to respect adults, adults must act wiser than children. That shouldn't be difficult. After all, with relatively few exceptions, adults *are* wiser than children. Not superior to children. Not *better* than children. Wiser. Less foolish. Hopefully.

So, being wiser, parents make the decisions; and being foolish, children should obey their parents. As children grow, their parents should allow them to make more and more decisions on their own. But who, pray tell, decides what decisions a child can make on his or her own? Why, the child's parents, that's who!

As I said, a child's parents, if they understand and accept the responsibility of parenthood, do not try to make the child happy with their decisions. They realize that if they make good decisions, their child will not be happy with the majority of them. Why? Because children want their bread buttered on both sides.

My parents used to say that about me. I didn't understand what they meant, and it was frustrating, if not infuriating, to not understand. It took becoming a parent for me to understand what my parents meant with that "bread buttered on both sides" stuff. It's something all parents should know, so here it is:

For the first eighteen months or so of a child's life, his parents treat him as if he is the most special being to ever assume human form. He yells, and they show up at his side, ready to serve. When he is uncomfortable, they make him comfortable. When he is hungry, they feed him. If he is having difficulty falling asleep, they rock him. If he is tired, they pick him up and carry him. If he cannot reach something, they get it for him. They push him through shopping centers and other crowded places in a portable throne, and people come and kneel before his throne seeking his blessing in the form of a smile. By the time a child is eighteen months old, he has been given every reason to believe that he is the One the world has been waiting for. Now, it takes eighteen months to create this impression in the mind of a child; it takes eighteen *years* to rub it out, during most of which the child clings to the belief that he really is the One and should, therefore, be treated accordingly. Quite simply, children want their bread buttered on both sides, the way it was during the first eighteen months of their lives. This, in fact, is the essence of the foolishness that's bound up in every child's heart.

Parents are given the task of buttering a child's bread on both sides and then teaching him he can't get it buttered on both sides. If that sounds a bit confusing, think of what it must feel like to a young child! Do you now have a better understanding of why toddlers have a reputation for being so "difficult"? I mean, this is a bitter pill for a toddler to swallow. His parents must slowly but surely lead him to accept that he can only get his bread buttered on one side. And that's not the whole of it, because his parents must also teach him that there will even be times when *he can't get his bread buttered on either side.* And that's not even the whole of it because his parents must also teach him that there will even be times when he won't have a scrap of bread! This simply means that life within a family should reflect certain realities, among which are the following:

❏ Each of us is nothing more than a small fish in a big pond.

❏ You can't get something for nothing.

❏ You can't always get what you want, but if you try real hard, you just might find you get what you need. (First articulated by that preeminent twentieth-century philosopher, Mick Jagger.)

❏ You can't have your cake and eat it, too.

❏ The best things in life *aren't* free. (Alternative version: There's a price to be paid for everything.)

❏ Bad things happen to good people.

Typically, children have a difficult time letting go of their foolishness and adjusting to these realities. As a consequence, when their parents reflect these realities in the decisions they make, children often react by screaming. Like my daughter is prone to saying, "Reality bites." They scream things like, "I hate you!" and "I wish you weren't my parents!" and "You're dumb and stupid and your feet stink!"

Unfortunately, many parents take this screaming seriously. Their overly serious reaction takes one of two forms:

(1) Some parents think their children's screams are indication that the parent-child relationship is falling apart and that their children are going to grow up not to like them.

(2) Other parents think their children's screams constitute flagrant disrespect which must be squelched.

Both reactions are foolish, which just goes to show that foolishness is not exclusive to children. In the first place, this screaming has nothing to do with a child growing up not to like his or her parents. It takes much, much more than parents making unpopular decisions for a child to grow up with bitter memories of childhood. I know this, because at this writing, my children, Eric and Amy, are twenty-six and twenty-three. When they were young, Willie and I made many decisions that they did not like. No, that's not correct. Children don't have moderate emotional reactions to too many things. When they dislike something, they usually report that they "hate" it. Also, children being foolish, they cannot separate the doer from the deed. If they don't like something someone does, they "hate" the someone and everything he stands for. So, when we made decisions they didn't like, it's accurate to say that our children *hated* us. And one way or another, they usually let us know just how much they hated us for our loathsome deeds. Today, when Willie and I reflect upon these same vile deeds with Eric and Amy, they laugh uproariously. I ask you: If we had not made decisions that they hated, what memories would they have to laugh about today? The answer: Very few, if any. Parents! I implore you! Give your children things to laugh about when they become adults!

In the second place, this screaming is not how children come to disrespect their parents. I cannot stress it enough: This screaming is a by-product of the foolishness that is bound up in the heart of every child. It merits no credence whatsoever. Now, if the child is so caught up in foolishness that he cannot seem to stop screaming on his own within a reasonable time, he might need to be sent to his room until he regains control of himself. In fact, since most children get "on a roll" fairly easily, it's probably a good idea to banish them to their rooms if the screaming lasts any longer than five seconds. And if a child, in the course of screaming because reality is biting him all over his little psyche, lets loose with some "choice" words, then banishment, preceded perhaps by a swat or two to the "spank absorber," is certainly in order. But banishing a child to his room—with or without a spanking—and getting all bent out of shape are two different things. A child's screams do not merit getting bent out of shape, believe me. Remember, screaming is a natural reaction to being bitten by reality. After all, reality has very sharp teeth.

When your child screams "I hate you!" or "Your feet stink!" or whatever, all you have to say is, "If I was your age, I'd feel exactly the same way." Then, having said all there is to say, you should turn around and walk away, leaving the child to *stew in his own juices*. This is the same advice Dr. Spock gave to America's parents in 1946:

> [Concerning temper tantrums] . . . don't give in . . . don't argue with him. . . . Getting angry yourself only forces him to keep up his end of the row. . . . [Instead] fade away and go about [your] own business, matter-of-factly, as if [you] couldn't be bothered.

See? Once again, I'm not saying anything new. Grandma knew all this stuff. And she never read a book, much less wrote one!

Before we leave this second rule and go on to the third, please understand that Rule Number One is prerequisite to Rule Number Two. Quite simply, a child will not do what his parents tell him to do unless he is paying attention to them in the first place. A lot of parents get this backward. They seem to think they can command without having their children's attention. As a consequence, they put the cart in front of the horse. They seem to think—this is sort of funny, really—that *children* should, as a matter of course, recognize their parents' authority and pay attention to them. When their children don't pay attention, they blame their children. These parents say things like, "What do I have to do to get you to pay attention to me?" and "I don't like yelling, but if you're not going to pay attention to me, then yelling it is."

These parents don't realize that (1) complaining to the child because he isn't paying attention is like me complaining to an audience of mine if I bored them to tears; and (2) yelling at the child is a symptom, not a solution. The fact is, yelling may get a child's attention temporarily, but it's not going to win it permanently. Nonetheless, a lot of parents these days seem resigned to fighting battle after battle with their children, not realizing that with every battle fought—whether won or not—they take one giant step closer to losing the war.

The Third Rule: "You will do what I say not because of bribe, brutality, threat, or persuasive explanation. You will do as I say because I say so. Period."

Hearing this from me, some people, it never fails, will say, "But John, that's nothing but a cop-out." It also never fails that people who challenge me thusly have spent too many years of their lives in school. As a consequence, they think too much and too analytically. And because they obsess about small details, they generally miss the big picture.

Knowing this, and therefore knowing exactly how they're going to answer, I ask, "Why is 'because I said so' a cop-out?"

And these highly educated folks always, every single time, answer, "Because *children need reasons.*"

Children need reasons. These well-meaning folks truly believe that. They think it's self-evident. Now, before I prove, beyond a shadow of doubt, that children do *not* need reasons, please understand that I'm talking here only about reasons concerning decisions adults make. I'm not—I would hope it's obvious—talking about reasons for such things as the sun appearing to "rise" in the morning, or trees losing their leaves in the fall, or water running downhill. Indeed, children need explanations for how the natural world works, but they do not need "reasons" for the decisions adults make. Well, that's not exactly true, either. They need but one reason: Because the adult in question "said so."

Here's irrefutable, incontrovertible, indubitable proof that children don't need reasons: If children, as pseudointellectuals insist, truly *need* reasons for the decisions adults make, they would express this need *every single time an adult made a decision.* But they don't. They only ask—demand, actually—to know the reason or reasons behind an adult decision *when they don't like the decision.* They never, ever ask/demand a reason when an adult decision is to their liking.

If, for example, a parent tells a thirteen-year-old child that yes, she may go with older teenagers the parent doesn't know to a Grateful Dead concert in a town fifty miles away and spend the night at the home of a friend of one of the teens the parent doesn't know, the child is not going to roll her eyes, stomp her feet, and in a demanding tone, ask, "Why?!"

Right? Of course I'm right. The child is only going to demand an explanation if the parent says, "You must be kidding. The answer is 'no.'"

Since children don't express this supposed "need" across the entire spectrum of adult decisions, but only concerning a certain class of decisions, we're obviously not talking about a need. Needs are not that selective. No, children don't *need* reasons; the truth is, they *want* them. They want them because they've learned that adults who are foolish enough to try to explain themselves to children can be lured into argument. And an adult who can be lured into an argument is an adult who can be defeated. Maybe. And children are gamblers when it comes to such matters. If a child manages to lure a foolish parent into ten arguments and only "wins"—gets his way—one out of the ten times, the child is certain to keep on trying to lure the parent into arguments.

Several years ago, a San Francisco–bound plane I was on made an unscheduled stop in Las Vegas to take on fuel. Along with everyone else, I went into the terminal to pass the time and was surprised to discover row upon row of slot machines. Fascinated, I began watching an older woman play a quarter machine. She put in ten quarters before she "won," and five quarters came back out. She got all excited and kept shoving quarters in and pulling the handle. About ten quarters after that first "win," she "won" again. Five quarters came out. She got all excited, and so on. Now, it didn't take a genius to figure out she'd put in twenty quarters and gotten ten back. She was, in short, losing. She, however, seemed blissfully oblivious to the fact that the machine was slowly making her broke. The machine's program let her win just often enough to keep her playing.

When it comes to arguments with adults, children are very much like that slot-machine lady in Las Vegas. A child who puts ten "quarters" into the "argument machine" may only get one "quarter" back. Nevertheless, that one "win" is enough to keep the child at the argument machine, hammering away.

At this point, the person who's had too much schooling is smart enough to realize I've proven my point: Children don't need reasons. So, this very smart person now says, "Well, okay, John, it may not be a complete cop-out, but 'because I said so' is still dishonest."

Again, I know what's coming next, but I love to hear it, so I ask, "Pray tell, why is it dishonest?"

And the smart person says, "Well, because there's always a reason for any decision a parent makes. A real reason! And a child has a right to know what it is."

It is now necessary that I prove beyond a shadow of doubt that the one and only *real*, true reason for any limit-setting decision a parent makes is 'because I (the parent, that is) said so." Here's the proof, and once again, it's incontestable: All limit-setting decisions are what judges would term "arbitrary and capricious." They are not based on fact, but rather parents' beliefs, values, fears, anxieties, quirks, and preferences.

Example: Your second-grade son polls his classmates and discovers his bedtime—8:30—is the earliest in the class. He comes home and demands to know why he must go to bed so early. If you're like most parents, you will try at this point to *sell* your son on the idea that an 8:30 bedtime is to his benefit. As salespeople know, if you want to sell something to someone, you must describe the benefit to them of buying the something in question. In effect, you become a salesperson. You say, "Well, I know you think it's early, but when you stay up later than 8:30, it's hard to get you up and going in the morning, and you're generally too groggy to eat your breakfast, and you go to school without proper nourishment, and that's when I'm most likely to get a note from your teacher saying you didn't finish your work, or you weren't paying attention, or something. So, most precious light of my life, I put you to bed at 8:30 *for your own good.*"

Get real! You don't put your most precious to bed at 8:30 because *he* needs his sleep. You put him to bed at 8:30 *because you need for him to sleep.* You *desperately* need for him to sleep. You are over being a parent at 8:30. There is every reason to believe that if you changed his bedtime to 9:30, he would make the adjustment in less than a week, and his schoolwork, in the long run, would not suffer. So what?! You want him in bed at 8:30, so 8:30 it is. The truth, therefore, is your son's bedtime is for *your* benefit. It's because *you* say so! Period.

Second Example: Several days later, this same son demands to know why he is the only child in the neighborhood who cannot ride his bicycle off the block. All the other kids can ride their bikes not just off the block, but to a distance of several blocks away. Why not him? Again, if you're like most parents, you will try to *sell* your son on the total fiction that this decision was made out of consideration for him, and him only. You will say something along the lines of, "I'm concerned that if I let you ride your bike off the block, you might get hurt."

Slight digression: Children are not astute. They're creative, clever, intelligent, and imaginative, but they're not astute. If children *were* astute, however, then your son, being likewise, would respond, "Mom, you are predicating your decision on probability—I *might* get hurt. That's fine. In fact, I'd prefer to discuss this issue in terms of probability because the probability is that if you allow me to ride my bike off the block, I'll never get hurt. Now, Mom, when all is said and done, and I'm no longer riding a bicycle around the neighborhood, whose probability statement is more likely to have been proven correct, your's or mine?"

He's got you, doesn't he? He's absolutely right! The overwhelming likelihood is he'll never get seriously hurt if you allow him to ride his bike off the block. So, you're going to have to swallow your pride and tell him the truth, aren't you?

"Okay, okay," you're going to have to say, "you're right. The truth is, I won't let you ride your bike off the block—and I still won't—because I am a raging, incurable neurotic. I am a sicko, and I can control my sickness as long as you stay on the block. When you ride your bike off the block, my sickness becomes uncontrollable. So, you cannot ride your bike off the block, and that's that!"

Again, the bottom line has to do more with *you*—in this case, a fear of yours—than with any fact outside of you. It is *not* a fact that he couldn't make a good adjustment—maybe even a better one—to a 9:30 bedtime. It is, however, a fact that at 8:30, you need peace. It is *not* a fact that if you let your son ride his bike off the block, he will get hurt. It is, however, a fact that if he rides his bike off the block, you will get anxious. You will worry. You will obsess. You will experience a sense of dread. You will sweat profusely and develop a facial tic. So, because of *you,* your son cannot ride his bike off the block. Because *you* say so.

No, "because I said so" isn't dishonest. It's honest. And there are no other reasons. It's the only one. Well, that's not exactly true. There are a handful of limits that are, indeed, based on fact, but they are few and far between. For example, it's a fact that if a child touches a hot burner on the stove, he will get burned. It's a fact that if he inhales underwater, he will drown. But these sorts of few-and-far-between things are not the stuff of everyday parental decisions. Concerning 99.9 percent of all everyday limit-setting decisions made by parents, "because I said so" is the truth, the whole truth, and nothing but the truth.

I know there are still some skeptics out there, so let's approach this "because I said so" business with a true story from the "lost manuscripts" of the Three Little Pigs:

As children, the three little pigs lived side-by-side-by-side in three houses in the same neighborhood. It just so happens they were born on the same day, attended the same grade in the same school, and made pretty much the same grades. A lot of people, not knowing otherwise, thought they were siblings. Their parents, in fact, all worked for the same company, and their family incomes were equivalent. The three families attended the same church and even went on vacations together.

Ah, but that's where the similarities between the three little pigs' lives ends, because the first little pig's parents insist that he cannot leave their backyard without adult supervision. The second little pig's parents let him out of their backyard without adult supervision, but not off the block. The third little pig's parents let him off the block, but not out of the neighborhood.

Everything else being fairly equal, there is only one way to explain the fact that each of the little pig's parents draw this particular "line" in three entirely different places: Each set of parents draws the line where their comfort ends and their anxiety begins. For each set of parents, that line is in a different place. It cannot be said that one line is better than either of the others or, by extension, that one set of parents is doing the best job. They are all, in fact, doing the job of setting limits, and they are all doing good jobs. Yet they are setting limits in three different places. Each set of pig-parents draws the line where they want it to be, not where it *should* be (no one really knows where it should be), or where scientists say it ought to be, or where psychologists deem best for self-esteem enhancement. They don't draw the line where "experts" say it should be drawn. In each case, it's drawn where the parents say it should be drawn. Because they say so, that's why.

Give 'Em Reasons, But Don't Reason

So, having proven that children really don't need reasons, and "because I said so" is the one, true reason, I must now tell you that I think it's right and proper, in most cases, to give a child at least one reason other than "because I said so" whenever the child so demands. That's right. Actually, it's kind of obnoxious to say nothing but "because I said so" every time a child demands a reason. You begin to sound like a broken record. So, give children reasons. But, please, understand one thing: *If a child doesn't like a limit you've set or an expectation you've described, the child is not going to like any reason you use in defense of your decision, either.*

Let's face it, you have never, after making a decision one of your children didn't like, been able to "reason" the child in question into saying, "Oh, now I get it, Mom! I see the light! I understand perfectly! This is amazing! A minute ago, I disagreed with you and thought you were the stupidest person on the face of the earth and that your feet stank, and with just a few words you've been able to prove to me how foolish I was! Oh, thank you, Mom! You're the greatest and I love the smell of your feet!"

That has never happened, and it will not ever happen as long as your child is a child. Why? Because *children cannot understand adults.* Period. It's not that children have difficulty understanding adults, or that they need to have things clearly and patiently explained in order to understand adults. Read my lips: Children *cannot* understand adults. Period. This is paradoxical, for sure, because children can understand algebra and chemistry and physics and meteorology, but they cannot understand adults. A child will understand adults when the child is an adult. Furthermore, that child will not understand his or her parents until the child is a parent of a child his present age, whatever that might be. No sooner. No matter what.

So, give a reason for any limit-setting decision you make, but don't expect the child to agree. When he doesn't, don't try to help him understand, because he can't, and the attempt will only result in an argument. Just say, "Oh, I know you don't agree with me. Why, if I were you, I wouldn't agree with me either." And turn around and walk away. Make your decision, communicate it, give a reason, acknowledge that you didn't expect the child to agree, and walk away. Disengage, leaving the child to "stew in his/her own juices." This is the difference between giving a child reasons and trying to *reason* with the child. Trying to reason is the ill-fated attempt to make the child *understand* (and therefore agree with) the parent. Not!

Most parents have very bad timing. They don't know when they've reached the point of 'nuff said. So they don't disengage at the proper moments, and as a result, they get into arguments that are pointless, counterproductive, frustrating, maddening, produce temporary insanity . . . you get my drift.

There is, you see, no such thing as an "argumentative child." There are only parents who don't know when to walk away. I myself learned how and when to walk away somewhat belatedly, but not too late. It was, I must tell you, the best thing I ever learned. An illustrative tale:

When Eric was fifteen he came to me one day and asked if we could talk about getting him a motorcycle.

"This will be the shortest conversation we've ever had, Eric," I said.

"Uh, why's that, Dad?"

"Because your mother and I will never, ever buy you a motorcycle, son."

"Why not?!" he screeched. "All my friends are getting motorcycles!"

"Then you are going to be the most special child in your peer group, son," I said. "Congratulations!"

"Ah, Dad, c'mon," he pleaded, "why won't you buy me a motorcycle?"

"Because they're dangerous, and you won't be old enough to appreciate the danger for many years to come," I answered.

"No, Dad," he cried, "you're wrong! I do know they're dangerous and Dad, I promise, if you buy me a motorcycle, I'll be careful. I won't get hurt!"

Short digression: Notice, I gave Eric a reason. Notice, too, that he didn't agree with it. I ask, is there anything I can say to Eric at this point in the conversation that will cause him to see the error of his thinking and agree with me? There's nothing I can say, is there? So, back to the story. . . .

I smiled and said, "Eric, if I was fifteen today, I'd want a motorcycle, too. And if I asked my parents if they'd get me a motorcycle, they'd tell me the same thing I just told you. And I'd say the same thing you just said to me. So, I understand you, son. I really do. Now, I don't mean to be rude, but I've got some other things to do." And with that, I turned around and began walking out of the room.

Another short digression: Did I belittle Eric? Did I put him down? Did I get mad at him? Have I left something unsaid? "No" to all of the above, right? So, I'm walking away. I've reached the "point of 'nuff said."

Eric immediately calls after me, saying, "Dad? Dad! Hey, Dad! Where are you going? I want to talk about this some more! Hey, Dad, we're not done!"

I turned around at the door to the next room and said, "Eric, I forgot to tell you something."

"What?" he asked.

"We're done." And with nary another word, I disappeared.

Eric wouldn't speak to me for three days. He hated me. I didn't care. I was determined to let him "stew in his own juices" as long as need be. He'd mumble things under his breath when we passed one another in the house. He'd sit at the dinner table stone-faced, not participating in the family discussion. It took three days.

You see, this business of children hating their parents never lasts long. A few days at most, because within a few days, the child in question has got to come and ask his parents for permission to do something. And in order to elevate the likelihood that the permission will be granted, he must pretend to like his parents again!

When parents of old said "you're going to stew in your own juices over this" to their children, they also meant "and we're not going to get in the pot with you, so you can cook all you want." Subscribing to this dictum kept parents out of argument with their children.

I talk a lot with people who reared children before World War II. They consistently tell me that they didn't have arguments with their children. Furthermore, their children, for the most part, never even asked "Why?" and "Why not?" concerning parental decisions. They simply accepted whatever decisions were made, whether they liked them or not. This means one of two things: Either there is not, as I said before, any such thing as an "argumentative child"; or, the "argumentative" gene was introduced into our gene pool by evil aliens sometime around 1955 and has been spreading like a virulent bacteria ever since.

By the way, Eric and I talked about the "motorcycle" incident a couple of years ago, shortly after his marriage to the lovely and most wonderful Nancy, the daughter-in-law of my dreams. He laughed at the memory, and a good time was had by all.

Give 'Em the Last Word

Parents often ask my advice concerning children who "want the last word."

I say, "By all means, give them the last word," to which these parents, taken aback, usually respond, "You're kidding, right?"

Au contraire. I am, for a change, being completely serious.

You have a child who wants the last word? So, what's new? All of God's children want the last word. You do, I do, our kids do. Such is the nature of being human.

The fact that adults generally "refuse" (ha!) to let children have the last word causes nothing but trouble. It is our very undoing, the virus of parental self-destruction.

The power struggle over who gets the last word begins with a parent making a decision a child doesn't like. The child responds with loud complaint, demanding reasons. The parent begins to explain. The child denounces the explanation as "stupid." The parent insists upon respect. The child, sensing that the parent is on the defensive, becomes more provocative. The parent . . . Does this sound familiar?

The end result? Nothing is accomplished except that the stage is set for further power struggles, and the level of stress in the family steadily escalates.

The child, determined to assert autonomy, but denied the right to do so, becomes ever more disrespectful, ever more "mouthy" and rebellious. As resentment builds, conflict in the family spreads from relationship to relationship like a brushfire, the child's behavior takes on risk, and the parents become angrier and angrier, all the while backing themselves further and further into the proverbial corner.

When Eric, the quintessential "strong-willed child," was in his early teens, I discovered the strategic advantage that could be gained by always giving him the last word. I realized that my infuriation over his determination to have it stemmed from the fact that I wanted it too! The last word was the prize for which we both vied in any disagreement. It occurred to me that letting him have the prize would pull the plug on his "disrespect," let the air out of the potential power struggle, and effectively contain his rebellion.

From that point on, whenever I made a decision that provoked his ire (e.g., the motorcycle incident) I'd let him express himself, then I'd say something along the lines of, "Eric, if I were your age, I'd feel exactly the same way right now, believe me. Nonetheless, I've made my decision, and I trust that you'll abide by it, whether you agree with it or not."

And he'd say, "Well, I think it's stupid," or something equally insolent, and I'd say, "Oh, I understand how you'd think so." Then I'd walk away, leaving him to—that's right—stew in his own juices.

Sometimes, he'd come back later and want to talk. We'd start to talk (not negotiate, *talk*), and he'd start getting upset because I wouldn't change my mind, and I'd again let him have the last word and walk away.

Sometimes he'd stew for hours, making nonverbal displays of disgust. But the amazing thing was, he never, to my knowledge, disobeyed. He did what he was told, albeit with a "bad attitude," of which I ask, "Who cares?"

In the early stages of my parenthood, I—like most parents—wanted my kids not only to be compliant but to have a good attitude about it as well. I belatedly realized that this was like wanting to have my cake and eat it, too. I began letting go of my insistence that they *like* what I told them to do and not do. Lo and behold, I discovered that the more free they were to express their feelings about my instructions, the more likely they were to comply.

Here's a story that illustrates this parental judo: One evening, as the Rosemonds finished dinner, I told Amy, then fifteen, to clear the table and do the dishes.

"I can't, Daddy,' she said. "I have too much homework."

"Oh, I'm sure you can do the dishes and still have plenty of time left for homework, Amy."

"No, Daddy, I have a test to study for."

"Then you'd better waste no time in doing the dishes," I said.

"Daddy! It's not my turn anyway!" she protested. "I did them yesterday, remember?"

"Amy," I rejoined, "you know there's no such thing as turn in this family. If something needs doing, someone does it, and if the same person does the same thing five days in a row, then it must have been their *turn* five days in a row."

She glared at me for several seconds, then said, "I'm not going to do the dishes, Daddy, and *that's my final word on the subject!*"

Willie and I exchanged smiles, then rose from the table together. "Amy," I said, "you may have the last word on this subject, but you know, as do your mother and I, that you *are* going to do the dishes, so there's no point in continuing this ersatz discussion."

With that, Willie and I exited the dining room as Amy continued to tell us that she *wasn't* going to do the dishes, and that was that. Willie and I retired to the living room and awaited the verdict. Several minutes later, we heard the dishwasher pop open and dishes begin rattling around. Then a cabinet door slammed shut and more dishes rattled. Remember, I didn't say she had to do the dishes with a good attitude. I just said she had to do them.

If, on the other hand, I had never discovered the advantages of letting children have the last word, I would have actually tried to intimidate a fifteen-year-old into doing the dishes. And I might have

146

succeeded, but at great cost to our relationship. Amy would have complied, but she would not have respected me, and for good reason; namely, a child cannot respect an adult who uses threat to secure compliance. Under the circumstances, I would have won the battle, but lost the war.

As it was, Amy finished the dishes, stalked off to her room, did her homework, studied for her test, and gave me the silent treatment for the rest of the evening. Ah, but I'll trade a few hours of her not liking me for a lifetime of her not really respecting me, any day.

The question arises: What would I have done if Amy had not *done* the dishes?

The answer: Why, I would have done them, of course. Cheerfully. Then, I would have waited for what I call a "strategic opportunity." I'd have waited a week or more, if need be.

I realized a number of years ago that when one of the kids misbehaved, I was often pulling the rug out from under myself by trying to come up with a consequence on the spot. This "shoot from the hip" approach to discipline rarely, if ever, worked. I became extremely flustered. I tried to intimidate the child in question into compliance. I grasped impulsively at punishments that were either irrational or unenforceable or both. I never managed to accomplish anything on these occasions except create a "scene."

One evening I was talking to a friend of mine who was complaining that his boss had that very day "written him up" for something that had happened weeks before. It occurred to me that in the real world, consequences do not always follow immediately upon misbehavior. If someone acts inappropriately at work, nothing might happen for six months, at which time he learns he's not getting the raise or promotion he had hoped for. If you fail to make a house payment on time, six months or more might pass before you learn you've been turned down for credit. I thought: If that's the way the world turns for adults, then there's nothing the matter with it turning the same way for children. So, I came up with the idea of "strategic opportunities."

A "strategic opportunity" is a delayed consequence. Instead of "shooting from the hip" when a misbehavior occurs, you wait. When the right opportunity presents itself, you take careful aim, and fire.

Another Amy story to illustrate the point: One Saturday afternoon Willie and I were leaving the house to run some errands regarding the dinner party we were throwing that evening. As we prepared to leave, I asked Amy—she was sixteen as I recall—if she'd help us out by vacuuming downstairs and cleaning the guest bathroom.

"No!" she exclaimed. "I won't! I do enough around here already! Get Eric to do it! He never does *anything,* and I'm sick and tired of being the maid and I won't, so there!"

I took a deep, relaxing breath. "Okay, Amy," I said, "if you won't, I will, but I have to tell you that I don't appreciate your tone of voice."

"Well I don't care!" she yelled, and stomped off.

Willie and I left the house and came home a few hours later to a downstairs that hadn't been vacuumed and a bathroom that hadn't been cleaned. I vacuumed. I cleaned the bathroom. I didn't say a thing to Amy. For six days, that is.

The following Friday, I came home in the early evening to find Amy and her best friend, Angie, getting ready to go out. They were all excited about their plans and couldn't wait for the night to begin.

"I'm sorry, Amy," I said, "but you can't go out tonight."

"What?!" she cried. "I've had these plans for nearly a week!"

"Well, I'm sorry it has to be this way, but you can't go out."

"Why not?!"

"Because last Saturday your mother and I asked you to do us a favor and you stood up in my face and let me have it with both barrels. You've never spoken to me more disrespectfully, Amy, and you can't do that sort of thing without paying a price. Unfortunately for you, the price has just come due."

She blew her stack. I can't print what she said, not because it isn't appropriate for a book on family values, but because it was gibberish. Very loud gibberish.

In the midst of her tirade, I said, "Sorry," and started to leave the room.

She called after me, "I'm going out anyway, and you can't stop me!"

I turned around. "Amy," I said, "I probably could stop you, in fact, but I'm not going to stop you. You are going to have to do what you feel you have to do, I guess. Understand one thing, however: Either this whole incident ends tonight, or it has a few more chapters. It's completely up to you." And with that, I exited, stage left.

She stormed. She fumed. She went outside to the driveway to see if I'd follow. I didn't. She and Angie talked for a while, then Angie got in her car and drove off. Amy sat on the steps for a while, then came in, went to her room, and stayed there the rest of the night.

The next day, she was her normal sweet self again.

Why, you might ask, did Amy stay home? Because I acted from a position of total self-control. I learned a long time ago, if you want to control your relationship with your children, you must first learn to control yourself. Whenever I had foolishly engaged in the game of "Who Gets the Last Word?" I had lost control of myself, relinquished my authority, and accomplished nothing. You want your children's respect? Then retain your authority. It's that simple. Give them the last word and get more than you ever insisted upon in return.

Give 'Em The Last Word: Part Two

A single mother in Dayton, Ohio, told me a story that illustrates the advantages of giving children the last word. Some time ago, this woman wrote me to say that she'd discovered the saving grace of this principle during her daughter's early teen years. True to form, this child had taken to expressing loud, rude contempt for any maternal decision that was not to her liking, meaning nearly all maternal decision.

The more Mom tried to explain herself, the louder and more contemptuous her daughter became. Mom finally realized that attempts to make her daughter understand the reasons behind her decisions were fruitless.

"It dawned on me," she said, "that even if Shelly listened quietly to every word I said, she still wouldn't understand me; that she would understand me when she was my age and had a daughter her age, and not a moment sooner."

Having been touched by the god of common sense, Mom

began simply telling Shelly what she could do, couldn't do, and had to do. If, as was almost inevitable concerning the latter two, Shelly protested, Mom said something along the lines of, "Oh, I understand. I'd feel the same way if I were you, sweetheart, no doubt about it. Nonetheless, that's my decision, and it's not open for discussion."

Shelly would yell something disrespectful and, getting no response, something equally insolent. Then she'd pout. But, mom told me, if left to "stew in her own juices," Shelly would eventually do as she'd been told.

"Needless to say," Mom added, "Shelly still didn't like the fact that she wasn't free to do as she pleased, but we haven't had an argument since I began letting her have the last word, and that was three years ago!

"And we get along a lot better, to boot! Oh, she gives me the silent treatment every once in a while, but that's normal, and it passes within a relatively short time."

Before leaving for her job one Saturday morning, Mom told Shelly to mow the grass. "No way," was the reply.

"Well, Shelly," Mom said, "I have company coming over this evening, and I need some help from you. So, you can either mow the grass or you can vacuum and clean the house. Whichever one you don't do, I'll do when I get home."

"I'm not doing either," she said, claiming she was entitled to a "vacation" on Saturday just like most adults got. She was, she said, "tired of being treated like a slave."

"I understand," said her mother. "I ask you to do a lot, and you're very responsible for your age. I wish there was a man around here, and I didn't have to work two jobs, and we could live more normal lives, but there isn't, I have to, and we're just going to have to live with not being normal for the time being. In any case, you can either mow the grass or clean the house, but I've got to go to work."

As Mom walked to her car, Shelly stood on the front steps, having not just the last word, but many. She tried her best to goad her mother into a confrontation, but Mom just got in her car and drove off.

Arriving home that afternoon, Mom discovered that the lawn had been mowed. And, believe it or not, the house had been vacuumed. Not a bad deal, eh? Shelly gets the last word, and Mom gets a manicured lawn and a clean house. Best of all, both enjoy a far better relationship than if Mom, like many unfortunate parents, was determined to have her cake and eat it, too.

The Rules: Redux

I cannot put enough stress on the importance of the Three Rules explained earlier in this chapter. They are the foundation of a truly successful parent-child relationship and as such, they create a context which makes it possible for a child to (1) develop true respect for his or her parents (which, in turn, enables respect for others as well as self), (2) become successfully socialized, (3) take full advantage of educational opportunities, (4) thrive emotionally, and (5) begin the journey toward spiritual fulfillment. In short, everything of importance in a child's life, both present and future, depends upon them.

The Three Rules are a "package deal," an "all or none" proposition. No one or two of them can exist by themselves. They are like the legs of a tripod. If one is missing, the structure cannot support anything. If one is weak, the structure is tenuous, and under the circumstances, will fall within a matter of time.

The First Rule—the child pays more attention to his parents than they pay to him—gradually draws the child out of infantile self-centeredness. As I have spelled out more elaborately in *Making the "Terrible" Twos Terrific!* (1993), parents who function responsibly during a child's first eighteen or so months of life ingrain in the child the belief that he or she is the One for whom the world has been waiting. The next eighteen years are spent undoing what it took those first eighteen months to do. The child, meanwhile, clings with all the tenacity he can muster to the infantile belief that the world should bend to his will. He stubbornly maintains it is his "right" to have things his way, and that his parents and teachers are being "unfair" when they deny him this right. This is the essence of the "foolishness" Proverbs 20:22 tells us is "bound in the heart of a child."

A child's socialization can proceed only as quickly as does the divestiture of his self-centeredness. In fact, self-centeredness prevents not only proper socialization, but spiritual growth as well. In order for an individual, at some point in his or her life, to accept that the center of the universe is occupied by God the All-Mighty, Creator of all things including himself, he must shift his focus, his "centeredness," first from self to other (the first "others" being his parents), then from other to God. Under optimal circumstances, this journey begins during the second year of life and is properly oriented (but by no means complete) by the end of the third.

The first step in this process of emotional/social/spiritual growth finds the child stepping down from the false throne of "I Am" and elevating his parents to the position of "You Are." During his first eighteen months, he was the center of his parents' attention; now it is of absolute necessity that they become the center of his. For eighteen months, his parents orbited around him, pleasing him; now he must learn to orbit around and please them. As the child approaches adulthood, his orbit gradually expands, and as it does so, his parents' "gravitational pull" diminishes. At some point in his young adulthood, he breaks free of his parents' "gravity" and becomes emancipated. The question now is whether or not he will choose of his own free will to be "born again" as a child of God, thus rejecting the seductions of "independence." The First Rule sets this entire sequence in motion.

The requirement that the child pay more attention to his or her parent than they pay to him is not, therefore, for his parents' benefit. The purpose behind the First Rule is *not* to elevate them, but to provide for the ultimate elevation—emotionally, socially, and spiritually—of the child. The child has no way of understanding that he must elevate his parents in order to eventually be elevated himself and will, in any case, cling to self-centeredness if allowed to do so. Therefore, parents cannot afford to be passive concerning this process. They must get actively behind it and exercise whatever force is needed to move it along and keep it on track. The child, being foolish and shortsighted, will not do so on his own.

Unfortunately, too many of today's parents are not properly executing their responsibilities in this regard. There are those who, having been smitten by idealistic, romanticized notions concerning children and child rearing, naively believe that children will grow properly if left pretty much to their own devices. These parents fail to exercise sufficient force. They are lackadaisical, permissive, wishy-washy. Then there are those who exercise *too much* force, who push rather than guide. These parents mistakenly think the Three Rules are for their *own* convenience and benefit. They are addicted to the ego-satisfaction of having "respectful," subservient children. When their children fail to satisfy their egos, they are likely to become enraged and threatening. Unfortunately, because they miss the point of the Three Rules, and especially the first one, their "rule" is nothing but superficial. Because these parents don't know how to *command* their children's attention, they wind up *constantly* demanding it (and the end results, as I will later explain, are completely different). Their children comply subserviently in order to avoid punishment, but are never genuinely *obedient* in the sense of wanting, out of love, to please. This is nothing short of tragic, for a child who is not properly guided by his parents toward wanting to please them arrives at adulthood without precedent for wanting to please God. It's not that he will never be able to make that choice, but the decision, difficult to begin with, will be considerably more arduous.

The Second Rule—*the child will do as his parents tell him*—depends upon the first. A child will not do what his parents (or any other adult, for that matter) tell him to do unless he is paying attention to them. Conversely, if he's paying attention, it follows that he will do as he is told.

The Second Rule teaches obedience to higher authority, which sets the stage for (1) good citizenship (where the higher authority is the community), (2) a valid work ethic (where the higher authority is an employer), (3) a family ethic (which prescribes self-sacrifice to the needs of one's spouse and children), and (4) a satisfying spiritual life (where the higher authority is God).

The First Rule is the foundation upon which the Second Rule is established. The Third Rule—*the "because I said so" rule*—secures the Second Rule in place. Quite simply, a child will not do what he is told if he is led to believe that he does not have to obey unless he is given a "good" reason.

Unfortunately, many of today's parents have unwittingly led their children to believe that in the absence of sufficiently good "reasons," they don't have to obey. This is perfectly understandable, given that nouveau "parenting experts" told parents that "because I said so" not only wasn't good enough, it was also psychologically damaging. Children didn't like it (true); therefore, said the "experts," it was bad for them (false). The fact is, children don't like the majority of things adults do that are good for them.

Sadly, some parents actually take pride in the fact that their children are able to "best" them in games of intellectual one-upmanship concerning rules and expectations. A mother recently related to me, for example, that her five-year-old had demanded to know why he couldn't stay up as late as his eight-year-old sister. She told him he was younger; therefore, he had to go to bed earlier. He said, "That's not a good enough reason, Mom."

At this point in the story, the woman said to me, "And you know, I had to admit, he was absolutely right. It wasn't a good enough reason. So, what could I do but start letting him stay up as late as his sister?"

It seemed to me that this mother was using this story to make the point that her child is uncommonly intelligent. Unfortunately, the story only serves to prove that she is uncommonly gullible. Of course "your sister is older; therefore, she can stay up later" is a good enough reason. "You go to bed first because I say so" is a good enough reason. Little does this woman realize that her uncommonly intelligent son is apt to be an uncommon pain in the neck by the time he is a teenager, and through no fault of his own.

One of the myths circulating about "because I said so" says it stifles curiosity and prevents children from learning to question authority. There is, let me assure you, no evidence whatsoever that might lend even a shred of credence to this ludicrous contention. I am reasonably certain that George Washington, Thomas Jefferson, Martin Luther King, Mahatma Gandhi, Rosa Parks, Marie Curie, Booker T. Washington, Louis Pasteur, Chuck Yeager, and Albert Einstein were all reared by parents who insisted they obey for no other reason than "because I said so." Yet they were all extremely curious, and they all questioned established authority (and/or challenged previously established limits of one sort or another). There exists, furthermore, a body of evidence which strongly suggests that curiosity and risk taking (both involved in questioning established authority) are inborn, rather than learned. It would appear that if a child is genetically predisposed toward such activity, it will emerge irrespective (relatively speaking) of the child's early learning. The question then becomes, Will the child's natural tendencies toward curiosity and risk taking be well disciplined (as was obviously the case with the individuals cited above) or not? In the latter instance, those same traits may drive highly dangerous, even self-destructive, "rebel without a cause" behavior. Early learning, which is primarily a matter of upbringing, would *definitely* influence this outcome. I would contend that highly curious children require the discipline inherent to the Three Rules as much, if not slightly more, than children who might not be so inclined.

But in nouveau "parenting," rhetoric prevails, not logic. Dorothy Briggs, writing in *Your Child's Self-Esteem,* says, "We adults enjoy living in a democracy, but we may overlook that children are equally as eager for a voice in the issues that touch their lives. Democracy in government has little meaning to a child unless he feels the daily benefits of it at home." Here, Briggs fails to separate the fact that although America is a political democracy, its institutions are hardly democratic in terms of their day-to-day operations. Rather, they are hierarchical, involving relationships between persons in positions of legitimate authority (those who give orders) and persons in positions of support (those who take orders). This is true of schools, places of employment, even government. Consider that once "the people" elect public officials by democratic means, they must abide by the decisions made by those same officials. Decisions made by government officials may be discussed and debated by those various officials, but they are not discussed and debated with those who vested them with legitimate authority. If the people don't like the decisions (laws) being made, they are free to elect new officials, but they are not free to break the law in the meantime.

The Three Rules are operative in every well-managed place of employment. Employees must pay attention to those who manage, and do as they are told, because they are told. Personnel policies are not submitted to employees for approval. If a certain employer issues a directive that every employee feels is counterproductive, and the employer states that the directive is not open to general discussion (which is almost always the case), the employees are bound to comply with the directive.

Good teachers establish the Three Rules in their classrooms. Every good teacher communicates to her students that (1) each and every one of them will have to pay more attention to her than she will be able to pay to any one of them, (2) they will all have to do as she tells them to do, and (3) they will follow her directions whether they agree with them or not. If a teacher doesn't establish the Three Rules, she won't be able to teach because her classroom will be in a state of relative chaos. Well, folks, parents are teachers, too. The Three Rules, therefore, are as important to carrying out the job of parent as they are to carrying out the job of classroom teacher.

If, in the above-quoted passage, Briggs is arguing that the circumstances of a child's upbringing should, as much as possible, reflect realities that exist in general society, I agree wholeheartedly. The Three Rules permeate the organizational realities that exist outside the home; therefore, the Three Rules should be implicit to the parent-child relationship. In effect, although she would protest the contention, Briggs has made a perfect case for creating families that are not democratic, but rather *benevolent dictatorships;* families, in other words, in which parents recognize and respond responsibly to children's needs for love and clear, authoritative direction. Parents who are both lovingly authoritative and authoritatively loving provide for their children's security as well as is possible. The secure child is free to explore (within limits), test limits (within limits), question his or her parents' decisions (within limits), disagree with his/her parents (within limits), experiment with new behaviors (within limits), be curious and creative (within limits), and so on. The insecure child is a child who is lacking in either love, limits, or both. In any case, insecurity prevents the child from exploring, testing, questioning, experimenting, creating. Insecurity drives behavior which is chaotic, impulsive, counterproductive, even self-destructive. In short, if you want your child to become all he or she is capable of becoming, then understand, please, that benevolent dictation (loving authority) releases that potential as well as disciplines (and therefore optimizes) it. Don't be fooled by nouveau rhetoric to the contrary.

Thomas Gordon thinks I'm wrong about all this, of course. In his latest book, *Teaching Children Self-Discipline* (1989), he says,

"Nowhere have I found more examples of using words imprecisely or without proper definition than in *Parent Power!*, a book written by child psychologist and newspaper columnist John Rosemond."

After a recent talk in Jacksonville, North Carolina, a minister and his wife approached me and told me that reading Gordon's books and attending his seminars had greatly improved their marriage. Right! Gordon's advice (and that of Briggs and Faber as well) is well suited to spousal relationships, where it is absolutely necessary that power be shared in some mutually agreed-upon manner. Gordon borrowed most of his ideas from Carl Rogers, a truly great teacher who pioneered what he termed "client-centered (or person-centered) psychotherapy." In the early 1940s, Gordon spent several years as one of Rogers's psychology graduate students at Ohio State University. As a result of that experience, he became a "Rogerian" for life. Rogers eventually extended his ideas concerning therapist-client relationships to other adult-adult dyads, including marriages, doctor-patient relationships, and business partnerships. Gordon made the mistake, however, of thinking that Rogers's communication strategies were as valid for parent-child relationships as they were for husbands and wives, etc. Then, to obfuscate the fact that he was talking about oranges when Rogers had clearly been talking about apples, Gordon invented out of whole cloth the notion that parent and child were equals, as equal, in fact, as were spouses. In short, that oranges were really apples! Dr. Thomas Sowell writes that Rogers was a man of impeccable self-control who eventually became appalled at the license people with considerably less intellectual discipline were taking with his ideas. "I started this damn thing," he is quoted as saying, "and look where it's taking us; I don't even know where it's taking me."

Another of Rogers's disciples, psychologist William Coulson, was a major player in the drive to persuade schools to adopt "Rogerian" teaching methods, the end result of which was that public schools began substituting ideological agendas for traditional academic curricula. Coulson has since come to his senses and is currently waging a one-penitent-man campaign to get people to realize what tragic mistakes his zeal brought about.

Gordon, however, is every bit as adamant today as he was in

1970. In *Parent Effectiveness Training*, he criticizes parents who "believe in restricting, setting limits, demanding certain behaviors, giving commands, and expecting obedience," and goes on to say:

> Children hate to be denied, restricted or prohibited by their parents, no matter what sort of explanation accompanies the use of such authority and power. "Setting limits" has a high probability of backfiring on parents in the form of resistance, rebellion, lying, and resentment. (p. 27)

This is exactly the sort of nouveau rhetoric I referred to above. I cite these quotes from Gordon because I want the reader to clearly understand that there is no middle ground between Gordon (or Briggs, or Faber, or any other nouveau "expert" for that matter) and myself. He (they) and I are poles apart. What Gordon thinks is bad for children, I feel is absolutely necessary. He cites the fact that children "hate to be denied, restricted, or prohibited by their parents" as evidence that parents should not do these things. I, by contrast, say the fact that a child "hates" something his parents do is nothing more than evidence of the "foolishness" Proverbs tells us is bound in the heart of a child. To ascribe significance to the fact that children "hate" certain things their parents do is tantamount to proposing that children know what is best for themselves. That point of view, I maintain, is patently disrespectful of children because it distorts what they are and are capable of. It causes parents who believe in it to behave in ways that are completely inconsistent with their children's actual needs. It causes parents to negotiate when they should stand firm, to say "yes" when they should say "no," to say one thing one minute and another the next. And these all-too-typical parent behaviors cause children to become annoying, petulant, self-centered, intrusive brats.

I can honestly say I've never known a child whose parents had effectively established the Three Rules who even approached being a pain in the neck. Invariably, these children are delightful to be around. They are polite, deferential, outgoing, and socially mature. They relate extremely well to adults but do not crave the center of attention. In short, they "know their place" and are not the least bit uncomfortable with the limits and expectations implicit to that place. When I remark to their parents how pleasantly unusual it is to encounter such children, their parents never fail to attribute their success to good old-fashioned discipline. That's validation enough for me. These children are living proof that the Three Rules are the best thing that can ever happened to a child. They provide a medium within which respect for parents can take root and grow, and respect for parents, as I've already said, is the first step toward self-respect.

By activating the Three Rules in your relationship with your child, you create a disciple, someone who will follow your lead. Having accomplished that, it then becomes necessary that you provide good leadership, which we will talk about in the chapters that follow.

On Intimidation

A parent recently asked, "But isn't there a risk that the Three Rules will cause a child to become intimidated by his parents and, by extension, other adult authority figures?"

Of course the Three Rules cause children to become intimidated by adult authority figures! That's the idea! In the same sense that adults *should* be intimidated by God, children *should* be intimidated by adults. One of the major problems in today's society, as educators, juvenile judges, police, shopkeepers, and retirees will affirm, is that too many children are *not* intimidated by adults. Intimidation, in this context, is nothing more than an immature form of respect. In fact, children are not capable of truly respecting someone. They are too self-centered. As they mature, they replace self-centeredness with respect for authority. Meanwhile, authority figures—parents, teachers, coaches—must intimidate in order to effectively teach the children the social and academic skills they must have in order to someday function as responsible adults. The child who is not intimidated by adults has no reason to pay attention and do as he/she is told. Intimidation, therefore, serves a positive purpose, and adults capitalize upon it *for the child's own benefit.*

Several years ago, I arrived at a North Carolina elementary school to talk to a group of teachers just as the afternoon dismissal bell rang. As I started up the stairs to the second-floor meeting room, the doors at the top of the stairwell flew open and a horde of young children came thundering through. As they came pouring down the stairs toward me, I realized they were oblivious to my presence. If I had not backed up against the wall to let them pass, I'm sure they would have run into, and possibly over, me.

I began my talk to the teachers by recounting this episode and asked, "Am I dreaming up a childhood that never existed, or would we, as children in a similar situation, have immediately slowed to a walk, quieted down, and moved to the side in order that the adult might continue up the stairs without interference?"

"That's exactly what we would have done," answered a teacher, "but *today's children are not intimidated by adults*" (emphasis mine).

The other teachers nodded their heads and confirmed what she had said. "That's an example of what we have to deal with every day," another said, "day in and day out."

That lack of intimidation regarding adults is the source of the discipline problems that encumber America's schools today. It's why teachers must discipline as much as they teach, but with a difference: Forty years ago, when I was in the third grade, a teacher disciplined a child once, perhaps twice for a given misbehavior and that was that. The child learned his lesson. Today's teachers tell me they must fight the same disciplinary battles day after day. Today's children, by and large, don't learn these disciplinary lessons. The problem, as these teachers know, is that today's parents don't intimidate their children; therefore, it is impossible for any other adults to intimidate them. But that's not where the problem ends. Forty years ago, when a teacher saw fit to discipline me, I was disciplined further at home. Today, when a teacher disciplines a child, she'd better watch out, because the child's parents are all too apt to file a complaint against her. Forty years ago, when a teacher retired, she did so with tears of affection for her students in her eyes. Today, if a retiring teacher sheds tears, they are probably tears of sadness for the time she saw being wasted in the lives she touched.

And, yes, there is a difference between fear and intimidation. Some adults rule by causing their children to fear them personally. These are adults who do not know how to command. Because they fail to establish the Three Rules, which are prerequisite to commanding, they must constantly *demand* obedience from their children. Those demands always involve threat, whether explicit or implicit. Parents who succeed at establishing the Three Rules do not have to invest their instructions to their children with threat. They *command* by means of the matter-of-fact exercise of legitimate natural authority. Their children have no reason to fear them personally; yet, their children are indeed *intimidated* by them.

There's nothing wrong with being intimidated, even as an adult, by legitimate authority. In my lifetime, I've had the pleasure of meeting a number of highly accomplished individuals who command almost universal respect. On each occasion, I've been intimidated by the intellectual and/or spiritual power these individuals effortlessly project, yet I have felt no fear of them whatsoever. These people *command* attention, allegiance, and respect. Likewise, a parent who knows how to command, and knows that his or her ability to do so is grounded in the Three Rules, is able to command in a relatively effortless manner.

On Love

After a talk I gave in Tallahassee, a woman approached me and after identifying herself as a clinical social worker, indicated that she was more than a bit annoyed by the fact that I had not once during a two-hour presentation made even passing mention of how important it is for parents to love their children.

"What," I asked, "does that omission mean to you?"

"In all honesty," she shot back, "I think it means that you aren't sensitive to children's emotional needs. As exemplified by your Three Rules, you see everything in terms of discipline, which is fine, but that's only a small part of the picture."

I felt that any attempt to persuade her that she was in error concerning her assessment of me would be fruitless, so I told her I respected her opinion and hoped she would always approach anything I wrote or said with an open mind. What I further hope she will someday realize (but did not tell her) is that my emphasis on discipline, to which I unabashedly admit, is not at all inconsistent with loving a child. In fact, proper discipline is *essential* to love, as love is essential to proper discipline. The problem, as I see it, is that it's impossible to improve a parent's love for his or her children. Either it's there in sufficient amount or it isn't. It is, however, possible to improve a parent's *discipline* of his or her children.

"All right, John," I've had some people say, "it may not be possible to improve how much a parent is capable of loving, but isn't it possible to improve how well he *communicates* his love to his children?"

Yes, it is, and that's precisely the point of proper discipline. Parents who command from the solid platform of the Three Rules let their children know *exactly* where they stand and where they want *them* to stand. Because their parents' expectations are unambiguous, these children engage in relatively little testing, and whatever testing they do engage in can be explained in simple terms: They are children, and even the most well-behaved child will occasionally test.

On the other hand, parents who fail to establish the Three Rules act as if they don't know where to stand and don't know, furthermore, where they want their children to stand. Because limits and expectations are uncertain, here-today-gone-tomorrow propositions, their children are forced to constantly test. For these children, testing (misbehavior) amounts to a vain attempt to pin their parents down, to get them to stand in one place, to be constant.

Unfortunately, it is inevitable that a parent who isn't clear on where she should stand is also unable to see that her child's constant testing is a symptom of her own indecisiveness. She blames the child, describing him as "strong-willed," "stubborn," "mean," "difficult," or the like. She might even say the child has "attention deficit disorder" or has an "oppositional disorder." Because she does not see the forest for the trees, her child's testing frustrates her "to no end." It induces an overload of stress into the relationship, and that stress interferes with her ability to communicate the love she genuinely feels for her child.

She complains, "It seems like I'm always yelling, but I don't know how to stop."

She doesn't realize that her yelling is a function of her failure to stand in one place. If she ever decides to stand in one place and let her child's testing run its course (which it will in relatively short order), she will stop yelling. But as long as she dances around, her child will test, she will be frustrated, and she will yell. After she yells, she will feel guilty, and she will try to assuage her guilt by doing something "special" for her child. In the process, she will relax whatever rules and limits she imposed during her tirade, and her child will again not be able to figure out where she stands, and he will start testing again, and she will begin getting frustrated again, and finally she will yell, and then feel guilty, and . . . do you get the picture? Is it you?

The bottom line is this: If you want to create circumstances within which you will be able to effectively demonstrate to your child your love for him, then you had better stand in one place. Parent, discipline thyself!

Staying Married

A journalist once asked, "John, can you boil your philosophy of child rearing down to twenty words or less?"

"Oh, sure," I said. "I can even do it in four words: Put your marriage first."

Another journalist once asked, "What is the secret to successful discipline?"

I answered, "Put your marriage first."

"What's the key to getting your children to pay attention to you?" asked yet another.

"Put your marriage first."

Those four words are "where it's at" where the rearing of children is concerned. So, someone out there is already asking, what about single parents? Good question! The simple, obvious answer: If more people put their marriages first, there wouldn't be so many single parents.

In recent years, it's become increasingly clear, and uncomfortably so for certain people, that children fare considerably better when throughout their entire growing-up years, they live with both biological parents. As David Blankenhorn says in *Fatherless America*

(1994), there is no adequate substitute for the traditional family. Single-parent families, stepfamilies, and blended families are all okay. The children who grow up in them are not doomed to failure. I should know. I lived in a single-parent family during most of the first seven years of my life, then I lived in what is today called a "stepfamily." I'm okay, I think (or is it, I think; therefore, I'm okay?). Notwithstanding my own experience, a traditional-family upbringing, even if the family in question doesn't "have it all together," offers a child the best insurance against academic problems, social problems, emotional problems, and later marital problems of his/her own. The highest achievers come from intact traditional families. The most stable marriages are constituted by people who grew up in traditional families. Furthermore, because traditional families tend to instill traditional values that enable good citizenship, traditional families strengthen our culture as well as they strengthen children.

My wonderful, tolerant wife, Willie, and I celebrated our twenty-fifth anniversary in July 1993. Given that one of every two marriages in our generation has already gone down the proverbial tube, having made it to our silver anniversary makes us somewhat of an anomaly. "What's your secret?" people will occasionally ask, as if the ongoing process of learning to live together boils down to a single kernel of wisdom that many seek but only the chosen few find. Willie and I did, however, pause to reflect upon our success as we passed this milestone in excellent repair. In addition to fidelity, learning to listen with respect, and giving one another "space" (pardon my lapse into trendiness), we came up with some counsel you aren't likely to find in any of the how-to books on marriage that have proliferated in this age of easy divorce:

Avoid how-to books on staying married. The problem with these well-meaning tomes is the problem with self-improvement books in general: They cause the reader to think too much. The more one analyzes a marriage, the more labyrinthine the relationship is likely to seem. Finding one's way through the maze of "issues" that these books identify as musts for "working through" is, we discovered, decidedly perilous. Which is not, however, to say that marriage is a really simple thing, or that the best approach to conflict is to stick one's head in the sand and wait for it to go away, because it isn't, and it won't. When it comes to conflict, Willie and I have come to rely on the visceral approach, as in, "I wish you'd stop doing that," or "Like it or not, this is the way I feel about what you did." The truth may, at times, hurt, but doing polite little intellectual dances around the truth often does a lot more damage in the long run.

Accept the Big Reality. Namely that staying married is the single most difficult challenge you will ever undertake. Why? Because both you and your spouse are highly imperfect beings, each no less so than the other. When two imperfect beings join together in an imperfect union, and their respective imperfections start to collide, imperfection begins to multiply. Here's a fact: You are never so imperfect as you are a year after you tie the knot. If you don't believe me, just ask your mate. I have to laugh whenever I hear someone accuse a spouse of being "difficult to live with." The fact is, we're all, each and every one of us, difficult to live with! Which is why, when my children were making college plans, we strongly advised them not to room with friends; not if they wanted to remain friends, that is. Now, on top of the relatively simple act of rooming together, add the complications of emotional commitment, children, shared financial responsibilities, different likes and dislikes, sexual drives that don't always mesh, and you begin to get the picture. Accept your *equal* part in all this and you will be able to retain your sense of humor, which is an outstanding feature of every truly successful marriage.

Compromise as little as possible. Yes, you read me right. Compromise is fine in certain situations and may be the only way to emerge unscathed from certain conflicts, but it's a vastly overrated "solution." In fact, compromise is often the weakest of three alternatives: (1) your stubborn way of doing things; (2) your spouse's equally stubborn ideas on the subject; and (3) the compromise, which is a point approximately midway in between. Like my grandfather used to say, "The middle of a bridge is its weakest point." Likewise, compromise is often more a means of *ending* conflict than resolving the problem at hand. Furthermore, by ending the conflict rather than resolving the problem, you often only forestall more—and more serious—problems.

Willie and I eventually realized, for example, that compromise concerning the manner in which the children were reared or the manner in which we ran our business resulted, more often than not, in further, and more weighty, problems down the road. So we agreed that when we had differences concerning the children, we would both express our opinions, but the final call, in every case, was Willie's. On the other hand, when we disagreed concerning a business matter, the final call was mine. Knowing who was going to make the final decision forced both of us to frame our arguments persuasively, rather than forcefully/emotionally. Trying to "outgun" Willie in a discussion over a child-rearing matter, for example, only made her less amenable to my point of view. If I wanted to influence *her* decision, I had to be silver-tongued, and to be silver-tongued, I had to be calm and listen better. So by dividing up decision-making "rights," we prevented our disagreements from getting heated. And lo and behold, I often found myself agreeing with Willie concerning business matters, as she found herself agreeing with me concerning the kids. Not always, mind you, but more.

Accept that neither of your personalities is ever going to change. Pretty pessimistic, eh? Perhaps, but I'm convinced that's the way it is. A few years back, I got together with several college chums I hadn't seen in over fifteen years. After a couple of days of their company, I came to the conclusion that none of them had changed a bit. They were more focused (that wasn't hard, given our favorite avocations while in college), their political views had swung to the right, their hairlines had receded, their tastes were more sophisticated, they acted generally more "mature," but their personalities were unchanged. Intrigued, I asked them if they felt I'd changed since they last knew me. The immediate, unanimous reply: "Not a bit!" Funny. I thought I had changed a lot. And they thought they had, too. I looked over and noticed Willie smiling triumphantly. "Has Willie changed?" I asked. "Not a bit!" they answered. I looked over at her again. She wasn't smiling.

Thinking, as most of us do, that we've changed over the years leads us to believe we can bring about change in our spouses. Then, when the change doesn't happen, we get frustrated, angry.

Understand that you are different people from different backgrounds, with different likes and dislikes and different opinions. It is impossible to be married without conflict. To stay married, you must accept your differences and apply no value judgments to them, as in, "That's irrational." You must not only roll with one another's differences and the natural friction they create, but learn to celebrate them! That's what learning to live together, and continuing to grow (but not change) in the process, is all about.

Don't pay too much attention to the children. Children need attention, sure, but (excepting infants and toddlers) not a lot. The more attention they get, the more they want; and the more they want, the more insufferable they become.

Despite what you may have heard, the relationship that requires the most quality time is not that of parent and child, but that of husband and wife. Over time, and after trying to always be One Big Happy Family, Willie and I came to realize that, for the most part, adults should interact with other adults, and children should interact with other children. By keeping the focus on the marriage, we allowed the children greater autonomy. In so doing, we promoted their emancipation along with our own privacy. By being husband and wife first, Mom and Dad second, Willie and I also averted the debilitating effects of "empty nest syndrome." For us, the empty nest is cause for celebration, and our young-adult children wholeheartedly agree.

Be stubborn. Huh? That's right, be stubborn, as in, "I'm going to do everything I can to make this marriage work, no matter what!" Why are so many of today's marriages failing, or doomed to fail? In large part because the people in those marriages just aren't stubborn enough. Many of them have never had to work hard for anything, never had to persevere, never had to hang in there when the going got rougher than rough, never had to make great personal sacrifice. As a result, when it comes time in their marriages to do any or all of the above, they just can't cut the mustard.

A young, about-to-be-married person recently remarked to me, "Well, we've been going together for five years, so I guess it's time to see whether we can hack it being married."

If there's one thing Willie and I discovered during our first twenty-five years together, it's that you don't stay married because your marriage, in some magical way, manages to work; rather, you stay married because you become determined to make it work. That means refusing to turn tail and run when nothing seems to be going right (and hasn't been for quite some time), never allowing "boredom" through your front door ("I'm bored" really means "I've become lazy"), and remembering always that your marriage is far more important than either of you are individually, or ever will be.

So, on our twenty-fifth anniversary, when our friends and children were proposing the typical toasts, Willie and I raised our glasses to "hard-headed stubbornness, the essence of our success!" That just about said it all.

CHAPTER SIX

The Responsible Child: Discipline That Works!

For these commands are a lamp,
this teaching a light,
and the corrections of discipline
are the way to life.

—Proverbs 6:23

When I ask teachers who've taught long enough to know, "What's different about today's kids when compared with the kids of the '50s and early '60s?" they always tell me today's kids are generally disrespectful, irresponsible, and undisciplined. *Of the hundreds of veteran teachers of whom I've asked this question over the last five years or so, not one has spoken in positive terms about the present generation of children.* Unless these folks are suffering from some mass delusion brought on by inhaling too much chalk dust, we'd better face up to the fact that we baby boomers were a far more well-disciplined bunch than are our children. This is not a matter of acid rain having damaged the gene responsible for good parenting; it's that postwar "parenting" professionals created and released into our culture a child-rearing "virus"—self-esteemus absurdicus—that's been wreaking havoc ever since.

Nouveau "parenting" professionals would have us baby boomers believe we paid a "terrible price"—they use that term a lot—for our good behavior. In the course of kowtowing to rabidly tyrannical parents, they tell us, we never learned to make choices or think for ourselves. That's a lie. This, however, is fact: The proper exercise of parental authority (and when properly exercised it is *absolute*) interferes with neither the emergence of decision-making skills nor intellectual maturity. I'm willing to bet my entire compact disc collection that Thomas Jefferson's parents told him what to do, when to do it, and how to do it. They even told him what he should think! And if young Tom ever became possessed of enough cheek to ask them *why* they insisted upon this and that and prohibited thus and so, I'm sure they answered "because we say so" or its prerevolutionary equivalent. The same, I'm equally certain, was true of Ben Franklin's parents, and Abraham Lincoln's, and Martin Luther King's, and Jonas Salk's, and Thomas Locke's, and the parents of all the other great thinkers, groundbreakers, and decision-makers of history. In short, parents who "dictate" (which *The American Heritage Dictionary of the English Language* defines as "to prescribe with authority") to their children do not—I repeat, do *not*—cripple their intellects.

Contemporary parenting professionals would also have us believe that my generation's parents' supposedly heavy-handed discipline caused our psyches to shrivel. Again, not so. All the evidence points to one inescapable conclusion: The 1950s were a better, healthier, more stable time to be an American child than any time since. Since the 1950s, every single indicator of positive childhood mental health has been in decline. As a general rule, we baby boomers were more secure, more respectful of adults, more willing to accept responsibility, more well disciplined, more resourceful, and for all these reasons, far healthier psychologically, morally, and spiritually than are the children of these "progressive" times. The question, then, becomes, How did previous generations of parents discipline children?

Answering the question requires an understanding of what the discipline of children is, and is not:

What Discipline Is: Discipline is the process by which parents make *disciples* of their children, a child-disciple being one who pays close attention to his parents and follows their lead. There are numerous aspects to this overall process, but three are of primary importance.

1. Establishing reasonable, yet challenging, expectations.
2. Setting and enforcing limits.
3. Modeling socially appropriate behavior.

Together, these three parental functions provide for a child's successful socialization, the outcome of which is responsible citizenship.

In other words, the ultimate goal of parental discipline is to produce an adult who requires minimal "management" of his or her behavior; an adult who is self-disciplining. The idea, then, is to discipline such that the child in question is enabled to eventually take the reins of his discipline into his own hands, and successfully so.

What Discipline Is Not: Discipline is not primarily a matter of punishment, although punishing inappropriate behavior is certainly part of the overall process. The goal is not to make the child passively subservient, but to make the child autonomous. The goal is not to "break" the child's will, but to "bend" it, to direct it toward rewarding ends. Discipline is not a matter of anger, although there are times when it is certainly appropriate for parents to demonstrate anger in the course of "disciplining" a child. Discipline is not a matter of spanking, although there are times when spankings are called for. Discipline has nothing to do with making children afraid of adults, although it is definitely in the long-term best interests of children that they be *intimidated* by adults. Discipline is not the sum total of a number of "disciplinary methods." It is an art, the "whole" of which is far greater than the sum of its parts.

Underlying all of the above is one basic fact: *Only self-disciplined adults can be successful at disciplining children.*

Some parents, it is obvious, discipline counterproductively. They don't understand the process, they don't understand the goal, they haven't mastered the prerequisites. But don't misunderstand me. Discipline is not something that can be mastered through intellectual rigor. When all is said and done, it's a matter of common sense, not a lot of thinking or "psychologically correct" technique.

To illustrate this, here's a story that was told to me by a woman in Lafayette, Louisiana: She'd been one of five children reared "on the bayou" by Cajun parents, neither of whom had finished high school. Her father was a carpenter; her mother a homemaker whose cooking was a matter of local legend. Miraculously, all five children went to college, graduated, and went on to successful "city" lives.

At a family reunion, she and her four siblings reminisced about their childhoods. None of them could recall having ever been spanked. Neither could any of them remember ever having been yelled at. Yet they all agreed, when either of their parents spoke, they paid immediate attention and did as they were told. The woman in question was perplexed. She was having great difficulty getting her two children to pay attention and obey. They ignored her, talked back, and were generally defiant.

She went to her parents and asked how they managed to discipline five children with such apparent ease. What was the secret behind their discipline? she wanted to know. Her parents looked at one another with puzzled expressions, then her father said, "We didn't have a secret. We just did what we had to do, that's all." Well, the daughter asked, what techniques did they use? Her mother said, "We used love." The daughter pressed for more information. What sorts of punishments did they use? She couldn't seem to remember, she told them. "There's nothing to remember, I suppose," her father replied. "We just told you kids what to do and you did it."

The woman gave up and sought me out several months later. She was obviously frustrated at the Zen-like answers she got from her folks. "What did they do to make us all turn out so well?" she asked.

"Your parents weren't playing games with you," I answered. "They can't tell you any more than they already have because they weren't rearing you and your siblings *intellectually*. They were doing it by common sense. They weren't straining their brains over it. They weren't relying on books (like this one!) to tell 'em how to do it. They weren't really even *thinking* about it all that much. They were just *doing* whatever it was they had to do, just like your dad said."

"But I try so hard," she complained, "and it sometimes seems that nothing goes right. My parents hardly seemed to try at all, and nothing went wrong."

"That was their secret," I said. "They took it one day at a time, just like everything else they did in their lives. It was part of life's rhythm. Nothing more. Nothing less."

Today, successful child rearing is regarded as a feat of intellect and effort. Today's parents think it's a matter of reading and thinking and getting hyperactively *involved* in as many aspects of their children's lives as possible. Grandma would have regarded all this straining of brain and back and budget with humor. She might have said, "Y'all never stop movin' long enough to get anything done." Or, "Don't y'all know the busiest chicken never hatches any eggs?"

In fact, Grandma's "secrets" of successful child rearing were expressed as aphorisms of that same sort. These terse, sometimes cryptic "kernels" were the sum of Grandma's child-rearing wisdom, which she had "inherited" from her parents, who had "inherited" it from theirs, and so on. The understandings represented by these sayings were the stuff of a *common* sense concerning children and their upbringing; *common* in that it was communal, shared, universally agreed upon. It was not a matter of academic controversy. Yesterday's parents understood these nonintellectual declarations of the obvious and "did what they had to do, that's all." Grandma's "parenting proverbs" included:

❑ "Children should be seen, not heard."

❑ "You can't get something for nothing." (Also expressed as "If you eat, then you work," and "You're going to earn your *keep* around here."

❑ "I'm going to give you enough rope to hang yourself."

❑ "You make your bed, you lie in it."

❑ "I'm going to let you stew in your own juices over this."

❑ "Children want their bread buttered on both sides." (Also expressed as "Children want to have their cake and eat it, too.")

❑ "You paddle your own canoe." (Or, "You fight your own battles.")

❑ "I guess it's time I lowered the boom."

❑ "A watched pot never boils."

Some of these (e.g., "Children should be seen, not heard") I've covered in previous chapters. At this point, I'm going to take the rest of these "parenting proverbs" and tell you what they meant; how, in other words, they *informed* the way Grandma disciplined her kids, thus transforming wild things into responsible citizens.

Grandma said, "You can't get something for nothing."

Yesterday's parents saw to it that by age four, children had been inducted into full, contributory participation in their families. They accomplished this by assigning their children chores. Not just occasional chores here or there, mind you, but *routines* of chores that consumed blocks of time each and every day. Shortly after his or her third birthday (if not before!), a child was given a "job description" concerning his or her role in the family. Initially, this job description was limited to helping older members of the family carry out *their* chores. Once the child had learned a job, it was transferred to him. In relatively short order, the child was "pulling his weight." As he gained weight, he pulled more and more weight until he had learned enough to be able to take over any other family member's jobs at a moment's notice.

This work was expected of the child for immediate, practical reasons, yes, but the most important reasons behind it were far-reaching.

❏ First, participation in the work of the family *confirmed the child as a valued member of the family.* The more responsibility a child accepted, the more status he had in his parents' and siblings' eyes. The child who took on the most work—usually, but not always, the oldest—was deferred to by siblings and was eventually invited by his/her parents to take part in making certain decisions.

❏ Second, *the child learned the principle of reciprocity* (or, simply stated, give-and-take), which is the centerpiece of every workable social contract. Everyone in the family relied on the child to pull his weight, and he relied on each and every one of them to pull theirs. This constituted the child's first experience with *social accountability.*

❏ Third, *chores enhanced the value of the family to the child.* They were a means, in fact, of bonding the child to the values that defined and enriched the family. The proof of this is in the proverbial pudding. Family values and traditions been passed on most reliably from generation to generation in rural, farming areas of America. And the one thing, besides the smell of manure, that most distinguishes the upbringing of a farm-reared child from that of a child reared in a city or suburb is chores. From the time a farm-reared child is "knee-high to a grasshopper," he participates as fully as he is capable in the daily work that makes the family "tick." And just as a contribution of time or effort to a local charity is evidence the contributor shares in and wants to support the values the charity represents, a child's contributions to his or her family cause the child to bond with the family's core values. Expecting children to do a meaningful amount of housework on a daily basis is essential, therefore, to creating, maintaining, and immortalizing *A Family of Value.*

Our children, Eric and Amy, were nine and six respectively before Willie and I integrated them into full membership in our family. Before that time, they were—as is typical of American children these days—*takers.* Willie and I gave, the kids took. Getting them to "lift a finger" around the house was a major hassle.

"Eric," I'd say, as Willie and I wrapped up doing the dishes, "we need someone to take out the garbage. Will you do it, please? No, Eric, not at the commercial. Right now! Did you hear me? What do you mean, we make you do everything? We hardly ask anything of you, Eric. Now look, we're asking just this one thing, then we'll leave you alone, okay? Eric? Eric? Oh, forget it, I'll do it myself."

Our only consolation was that we definitely weren't alone. Our friends couldn't get their kids to accept much, if any, responsibility around the home, either. Most felt fortunate if their kids "remembered" to make their beds in the morning. Keeping their rooms clean? Most parents we talked to rationalized having given up on that with malarkey about children having a "right" to keep their own rooms in whatever condition they please.

Willie and I finally came to our senses. We were both working long hours and the housework was being neglected. We were barely paying our bills, so a cleaning service was out of the question. One evening, we sat down to discuss the problem. Willie proposed that we shift certain chores to the kids. Which ones? She suggested we make a list of all the chores that needed to be done in the course of a week, whether daily or otherwise, and put a check next to those we felt one or the other of the kids was capable of doing. Lo and behold! When we finished, we realized we'd checked all but four: cooking, doing the laundry, ironing, and mowing the grass.

Using a legal-size sheet of plain white paper, we made a seven-day calendar such as is shown on the next page. We divided the household chores roughly equally between the kids, distributed them through the week, and posted the schedule on the refrigerator. To make things as easy as possible, we "color-coded" the chores. Chores in blue were to be done first thing in the morning. Chores in red were to be done immediately after school (or after lunch on nonschool days). Chores in green were to be done immediately after supper.

CHORE CALENDAR

	MONDAY	TUESDAY	WEDNESDAY	THURSDAY	FRIDAY	SATURDAY	SUNDAY
ERIC	MAKE YOUR BED, TIDY UP YOUR ROOM AND BATHROOM					CHANGE YOUR BEDLINENS & VACUUM YOUR ROOM	MAKE YOUR BED, ETC.
	WASH KITCHEN FLOOR & BACK HALL	VACUUM UPSTAIRS, DUST	CLEAN THE MASTER BATHROOM	EMPTY WASTEBASKETS & TAKE OUT THE TRASH	VACUUM DOWNSTAIRS, DUST	SWEEP THE WALKS, PATIO, AND DRIVEWAY	SET AND CLEAR TABLE
	SET THE TABLE, CLEAR THE TABLE, DO THE DISHES						
AMY	MAKE YOUR BED, TIDY UP YOUR ROOM AND BATHROOM					CHANGE YOUR BEDLINENS & VACUUM YOUR ROOM	MAKE YOUR BED, ETC.
	VACUUM DOWNSTAIRS, DUST	CLEAN YOUR BATHROOM	VACUUM LIVING ROOM & DEN FURNITURE	CLEAN THE DOWNSTAIRS BATHROOM	CARRY EVERYONE'S LAUNDRY DOWNSTAIRS	SET & CLEAR THE TABLE & DO THE LUNCH DISHES	DO LUNCH DISHES
	SWEEP THE FLOOR, UNLOAD THE DISHWASHER, PUT DISHES AWAY						

Job Description

Job: Clean the children's bathroom.

What You Need:

1. bucket of warm water (filled halfway)
2. liquid pine-scent cleaner (two capfuls in bucket)
3. sponge
4. tub-and-tile cleaner
5. washrag
6. toilet bowl cleaner and toilet bowl brush
7. spray bottle of window cleaner
8. several paper towels
9. vacuum cleaner

What You Do:

1. Spray the mirrors with the window cleaner and wipe them clean with the paper towels. Use the damp paper towel to wipe down the faucets in the sinks and tub.

2. Clean both sides of the glass doors on the tub with the window cleaner and paper towels.

3. Squeeze some tub-and-tile cleaner on a damp washrag and wipe the sink, the counter, and the tub, inside and out, making sure to clean all the way to the top of the tile.

4. Wipe the outside of the toilet with the tub-and-tile cleaner.

5. Squeeze some toilet bowl cleaner into the bowl and scrub the bowl with the bowl brush, then flush the toilet.

6. If the tissue dispenser is empty, put in a new box of tissues. If the toilet paper roll is empty or nearly so, replace it with a new roll.

7. Vacuum the floor.

8. Using the sponge and the pine-scent cleaner, wash the floor. Start at the toilet and work toward the door. Let the floor dry completely before going back in.

9. Put the vacuum and all of the cleaning supplies back where they belong. Be sure to rinse the sponge and washrag and wring them dry.

Each chore was described on an index card in terms of "What You Need" and "What You Do" (see example) all of which were stored in a small index-card file that was placed on the kitchen counter. This preparation took Willie and me no more than three hours. Then, we showed what we'd done to the kids, gave them a brief explanation, and asked, "Any questions?"

They both looked like they were in states of shock. They looked at the calendar, then one another, then Eric asked, "What are you guys gonna do?" Aren't kids cute?

Now, the truly amazing thing is that in the short space of one day, the Rosemond children went from being freeloaders who carped every time we asked them to do something to responsible little people. In short, they did their chores! Oh, we had to occasionally make one of them do something over again, thus teaching the "do it right the first time" principle. And we had to provide a bit more supervision initially than we had to later on (as does an employer with a new employee). But we didn't have to stand over them or even constantly remind them that they had chores to do. The secret: The expectations were "written in concrete." It occurred to me that employers give employees job descriptions because if they didn't, the average employee would come to work every day not quite sure what was expected of him. Likewise, Eric and Amy had been waking up every morning not knowing exactly what we expected, coming home from school not knowing exactly what we expected, getting up from the dinner table not knowing what we expected, and so on. Under the circumstances, our instructions to them always came "out of the blue." Suddenly, without warning (and in many cases, without precedent either), one of us would tell Eric to take out the garbage or tell Amy to sweep the kitchen floor. Nothing was routine; therefore, every time we assigned either of them a chore, the assignment interrupted something they were doing or about to do; therefore, they resented it.

Putting everything on paper made our expectations not only explicit, but *real.* Willie and I were no longer *wishing* that Eric would take out the garbage or that Amy would sweep the floor. These expectations were now the "law." Furthermore, they were organized into a routine, so there were no longer any surprises. If I said, "Eric, the calendar says it's time for you to mop the downstairs floors," his reaction was to stop what he was doing and mop. Before, I'd have said, "Eric, how about mopping the downstairs floors for us, okay?" and he would have looked at me like I'd lost all grip on reality and said something like, "Uh! You always make me do everything around here!" or "What?! I don't know how to mop floors!" or "Sure, Dad, I'll do it later."

I want to make one thing perfectly clear: Willie and I never paid either of the kids one red cent for doing any of this, nor did we threaten them with medieval tortures if they didn't. We just "put our ducks in a row," said, "Here's the new law," and provided just enough supervision and prompts to get the new routines up and running.

Whenever I tell this story to an audience, and I do so quite often, it's inevitable that someone will say, "John, what did you and Willie do if one of the kids conveniently 'forgot' to do a chore?" to which nearly everyone in the audience will begin nodding their heads and saying, "Yes, what?" The question itself says something unfortunate about the majority of American parents: namely, they *expect children to disobey.* This expectation is their undoing, in fact. It's a self-fulfilling prophecy that *will* come true, no doubt about it. Likewise, if you calmly, commandingly communicate to children in no uncertain terms that you *expect them to obey* whether they want to or not, that self-fulfilling prophecy *will* come true, too.

But don't be fooled by what I'm saying. A completely, 100 percent obedient child never has existed, doesn't exist, and never will. Parents can expect a certain amount of disobedience from even the "best" of children, but wanton disobedience is a horse of a different color. Wanton disobedience is completely unnecessary. Occasional disobedience is normal; wanton disobedience is abnormal. Furthermore, whether parents are willing to admit it or not, wanton disobedience has little, if anything, to do with the child in question. I know, because my son, Eric, was at one time what I would describe as wantonly disobedient. For several years, I deluded myself into thinking there was something "wrong" with Eric. When I finally realized that Eric's problems were largely due to failures on my part (definitely more mine than Willie's, by the way) and saw that I was going to have to set myself straight before there was any hope of setting him straight, things began to turn around. One of my most glaring failures was a "failure to communicate." I was wishing he'd obey, I was constantly surprising him with instructions that came out of the proverbial blue, and worst of all, I expected him to disobey. Every time I gave him an instruction, I expected a negative reaction, and negative reactions were just about all I ever got.

There's no magic to this, folks. If you begin expecting a disobedient child to obey—communicating clearly, straightforwardly, matter-of-factly, in calm "no uncertain" terms—the child is not going to suddenly become little Mister or Miss "How Can I Help You, Dad?" This is going to take some time, but not long, really.

"At least give us an estimate, John!"

Oh, okay. How about, let's see, three months? Actually, three months is about all it takes to get over the hump and on track with even the "worst" of kids. During that time, you have to stay the course, which requires practicing the rest of Grandma's child-rearing philosophy.

But before we hear from Grandma again, let me share the objection many parents have to assigning their children a good amount of chores: "Chores would interfere with my child's after-school activities." To that, I say, "So what?" That objection reflects a big problem with today's parents: They don't expect self-sacrifice of their children. All I have to say is, it's bad enough that children want their bread buttered on both sides. They sure as shootin' don't need parents who are actually willing to butter both sides for them, as parents who voice this objection are obviously guilty of doing.

And now, another word from Grandma.

Grandma said, "I'm going to give you enough rope to hang yourself."

I once had a conversation with a man who told me he'd reared his children "very liberally." I asked what he meant, and he replied he'd always given his kids a long rope—a lot of freedom, in other words—but always made it clear that they were in big trouble if they ever reached its end. Through most of their teen years, for example, his children set their own curfews. "But," he said, "they knew they'd be in big trouble if they didn't come in when they'd said they were coming in."

This fellow didn't realize it, but he was describing conservative, not liberal, child rearing. The defining difference between liberals and conservatives is that liberals believe in big government whereas conservatives believe that where government is concerned, the less, the better. The same applies to the governing of children.

The child-rearing style I describe in this book is conservative, and the "long rope" is an apt analogy. Just as conservatives believe government should be in the background of our lives, parents who believe in the long rope are in the background of their children's lives. They provide good supervision. They're accessible to their children (but they also define limits concerning that accessibility). Although always interested in their children and always willing to spend time with them (if they have the time), they keep their involvement in their *children's responsibilities* to a minimum.

Conservatives believe that, in the long run, attempts on the part of government to "engineer" people's lives increase their dependence on government. Likewise, parents who believe in the long rope understand that their ultimate purpose is to promote independence. As a result, they do not solve problems for children that children are capable of solving for themselves. They give their children lots of freedom and understand that their job is not to prevent errors, but to ensure that errors are contained and convey important lessons.

Here's a true story to illustrate what child rearing by the "long rope" is all about: One day during Eric's eighth-grade year, a friend of mine called to warn me about the kids with whom Eric had recently started associating. I'd met the boys, and they all seemed nice enough. I'd picked up on a slight "smart aleck" attitude, but attributed it to this age boy's unfortunate need to be regarded as "cool."

"These kids aren't cool," my friend said. "In fact, they're downright bad." He went on to open my ears with tales of property destruction, petty theft, cruelty to animals, and bullying. When he was finished, I thanked him for his concern, and told Willie what I'd just learned. We reviewed our options and arrived at a decision.

Later that day, we sat down with Eric. "You don't want us choosing your friends for you, do you?" I asked.

"Uh, no," he answered.

"Good, because we don't want to choose them either."

I then told him what I'd learned, keeping the informant's identity a secret. When he began to protest, I said, "You don't need to defend your friends, Eric, because your mother and I have no intention of interfering. The good news is you can hang out with them all you like. The bad news is we intend to hold you *completely* responsible for any problems that occur while you're in their company."

"What do you mean?" he asked.

"Well, let's just say you're with three of them and a window somehow, mysteriously, gets broken. You will pay for the entire window, Eric, not one-fourth of it. It won't matter to us how the other boys' parents handle it. And on top of that, you'll be grounded for a considerable period of time. We will make no excuses for you and accept no excuses from you. Oh, and by the way, if we even think you *might* have been involved, we will consider you guilty unless you can prove, beyond a shadow of doubt, that you weren't. These are the consequences, young man, of being able to choose your own friends."

A rather unusual approach, to be sure, taken because Willie and I had by this point in our parenthood accepted certain realities.

Reality: It's all but impossible to manipulate a teenager's social life. If a teen wants desperately enough to associate with a certain element, the teen will find a way to associate.

Reality: The more constraints parents try to put on a teen's associations, the more deceptive the teen will become. A restrictive approach often creates more problems than it solves.

Reality: All meaningful learning comes about by trial and error. A youngster learns to take responsible control of his/her life by making mistakes. It's a parent's job to make sure the child learns from those mistakes, not necessarily to prevent them.

Reality: In the end, a good, solid value system will prevail. Not always, mind you, for there are no guarantees in this business of child rearing, but far, far more often than not. When good values don't win out, there's a bigger power than parents at work.

So Willie and I took this calculated risk, knowing the earlier taken, the better. Sometimes, when I tell this story, the listener will look shocked and say, "Oh, I could *never* do something like that!" My only thought, always unspoken, is, "Then I'll pray for you."

Several weeks went by following this fateful conversation during which Eric spent all his free time with these boys. One Saturday afternoon, while working in the front yard, I looked up to see Master Eric pedaling furiously toward the house. He pulled into the drive, dropped his bike, and ran over to where I was working.

"Dad, Dad," he panted, "I gotta tell you something." He went on breathlessly to explain that he'd just been with his "friends," and they'd started planning an expensive prank. Remembering what we'd told him, Eric made excuses to leave and came straight home.

"They've probably already done it, Dad," he concluded, "but you gotta believe me, I wasn't there. And Dad, you and Mom were right about those guys, I know that now. So I'm gonna find myself some new friends, starting today."

Nice ending, eh? Now, consider for a moment what probably would have happened with a "short rope" approach:

First, Willie and I would have lectured Eric on his choice of friends and prohibited him from hanging with them ever again. Eric would have protested, but realizing he was running up against a brick wall, he would have promised compliance.

Next, he would have employed deceit to continue hanging with these boys. Our prohibition would have resulted in driving the relationship underground, where it couldn't be seen.

At some point, Eric and his friends would have been caught while in the act of committing some delinquency. We'd have grounded him, but the bond of trust between us would have been broken. Furthermore, his reputation within his peer group would have been stained. "Good" kids might have started keeping their distance from him, thus moving him to the periphery of the peer group, where you tend to find the bad element.

I'm talking about a vicious circle, which my experience, both personal and professional, tells me is more likely to be drawn by a short rope than a long one.

Oh, and by the way, our kids were also setting their own curfews by the time they were sixteen. At age fourteen, curfew was ten o'clock on nonschool nights. If no violations occurred for six months, curfew was extended to ten-thirty. No violations for six months moved it to eleven, and so on until a midnight curfew had been earned and adhered to, without violation, for six months. At that point, the child in question could set his/her own curfew.

We said, however, "This isn't freedom, however. It's responsibility. When you tell us you'll be in at two o'clock, we expect you in by two, and not a minute later. If you're late, your curfew reverts back to midnight and you'll have to have six violation-free months before being able to set your own curfew again."

The kitchen clock, and only the kitchen clock, mediated the "deal." If one of the kids came through the door one minute after the appointed or promised time, that six-month period started over again. And no excuses were accepted. None. Nada. I recall Eric had one "slip-up" when he was fifteen, and no more. And once having earned the freedom of setting their own curfews, neither abused it. In fact, the curfews they set for themselves were almost always earlier than we'd have set for them. Ain't that amazin'?!

The principle at work here is a simple one: A child will take responsibility not for things that are handed to him on a silver platter, but for things he must earn. The things he earns, the child will take care of.

Grandma said, "You make your bed, you lie in it."

One of my psychology professors, a genial, graying pedagogue with a distinct dislike for popular trends in the field, was fond of saying the Bible was "the greatest psychology text ever written." When asked to explain, he'd point out that in its parables, history, and prescriptions for living, the Bible instructs us concerning the full breadth of human emotion and motivation.

"It's all there," he'd say. "You just have to know what you're looking for."

I was reminded of the good professor several years ago when one day I realized that few, if any, of my parent-clients were answering the first "clinical" question put to them—"What brings you to my office?"—truthfully.

They'd say, "Our child has a problem," and would proceed to describe a lingering misbehavior or irresponsibility that was driving them crazy. As they told their tale of woe, the child in question would usually be sitting on the floor of my office, playing nonchalantly with a toy.

It became obvious that many, if not most, of these children

didn't have any problems at all. Their *parents* (and sometimes their teachers as well) had the problems. I then realized that all these children from all these different family backgrounds shared something in common: the biblical principles of penance and atonement were not functioning in their lives.

To simplify somewhat, penance involves the idea that when someone does something "bad," that same person, and no one else, should feel bad, or penitent, about it. The same person is also responsible for whatever atonement is appropriate, meaning he should correct the problem created by his misdeed.

In the upside-down families I was seeing, the children were doing "bad" things of one sort or another, but the *parents* were feeling bad and the *parents* were trying to solve the problems—problems which, in the final analysis, only the children could solve. The children, therefore, were off the hook.

Penance drives atonement, or so the Bible tells us. Without penance, atonement will not take place. Translate: Unless complete responsibility for a problem involving misbehavior or inadequate school performance is assigned to the child in question, the child cannot solve it. "Therapy," therefore, becomes a matter of helping the parents unload the problem from their shoulders onto the shoulders of the child. In secular terms, therapy invokes what I term the "Agony Principle": *Parents should not agonize over anything a child is doing or failing to do if the child is perfectly capable of agonizing over it himself.*

To give an example: Ted—by all accounts a capable nine-year-old—was not finishing his classwork or turning in his homework. His parents agonized and even spent lots of money having him tested and talked to by various professionals. On school nights, Ted's mother would sit with him while he did his homework. She was convinced he would not do it on his own. But the more Ted's parents tried to solve the problem, the more it appeared Ted simply didn't care.

At my suggestion, they "dropped the ball." Ted's mother stopped keeping up with his assignments and making sure he got his homework done. He was told that he had to do his homework in his room, decide himself when he was going to do it, and go to bed promptly at nine o'clock, whether it was done or not. One of his parents checked in with Ted's teacher at the end of every school day. If Ted had completed all his classwork *and* turned in all his homework *and* everything had been done properly, he was free to do pretty much as he pleased that afternoon and evening. If not (and it was an "all or nothing" proposition), he was confined to his room after school and put to bed immediately after supper (whether his homework was finished or not). Furthermore, if Ted earned more than one restriction in a week's time, he was also restricted on the weekend. What Ted did with his time after school, regardless of whether he was free or not, was completely up to him. He quickly learned, however, that his decisions in that regard affected his freedom the next day, and possibly the weekend as well. He also discovered that *his parents no longer cared!* None too miraculously, Ted suddenly started to care. He began consistently completing his classwork, doing his homework on his own, and turning everything in on time. And you know what? His grades improved dramatically! A testament to the benefits of "paddling your own canoe," another of Grandma's favorite sayings.

Once upon a time not so long ago, children were routinely assigned the consequences of their own misbehavior. If a child did something "bad," the child was made to feel bad about it, and the child had to shoulder whatever circumstances were consequent to the problem, as in *on his own.* Parents were not supposed to buffer these matters for their children. Rather, they were to support disciplinary actions taken by other authority figures and even amplify them if need be.

My parents exemplified this attitude. When I was seventeen, I was arrested, along with seven of my buddies, for making a public disturbance. Without going into details, suffice to say we had disrupted the tranquillity of the community on a summer afternoon. The police took us down to the station house and booked us. Then, because we were minors, they began calling our parents, telling them what had taken place and requesting that they retrieve us. My parents were the last to be contacted. My mother answered the phone. I listened as the desk sergeant told her what happened. Then, a most amazing thing happened: The sergeant suddenly turned, looked directly at me, and said (still talking to my mother),

"Well, maybe you should know that all the other parents are coming to get their kids. [pause] Yes, I know, but . . . [pause] Well, that's fine, I guess. How long do you want us to keep him?"

I sat there, stunned, as the realization sunk in that my parents weren't coming to take me home. They were leaving me in jail! To rot! For who knows how long!

I was fingerprinted, my pockets were emptied, and I was led, unceremoniously, to my cell, which consisted of a toilet, a sink, and a metal cot with no mattress. The other cells contained drunks, thieves, and who knows, maybe even a murderer or two! Most of these criminals were awaiting transfer to some larger, more secure facility. I couldn't sleep because I couldn't get comfortable. Besides, they never turned off the lights. I was miserable. In fact, it was the most miserable time of my life. Thirty-six hours later, just when I thought I was spending another night in a cage, my stepfather showed up to take me home. He didn't look happy. I was grounded the rest of the summer. They hired no lawyer, so when the trial came up I went to court alone. I've never been so relieved as when the judge pronounced sentence: "Considering that these boys have never before broken the law, I'm going to sentence each of them to thirty days in a juvenile detention center, suspended, with one year's probation."

My parents, meanwhile, had refused to even discuss the situation with me. The only thing I remember them saying was, "If you're old enough to break the law, then you're old enough to suffer the consequences." In short, I made my bed, I was going to have to lie in it. It was one of the hardest lessons of my life, and it was one of the best.

That's pretty much the way it was for most children of my generation. Here's an illustrative tale told to me by a number of veteran teachers, and confirmed by numerous others: In the '50s and early '60s, if a child created a problem in school, the teacher or principal called the child's home and informed his or her mother, who said, "Thank you for the information. Just send him home. I'll take care of it." The child in question walked home knowing he was "in for it." It was a long walk, spent trying to come up with an excuse that would mitigate the punishment that awaited.

I was, all too often I'm sorry to say, that child. When I got home, my mother would be waiting, eyes aflame, jaws clenched. I'd immediately start in with, "Mom, I can explain . . ." but she'd quickly cut me off with, "There'll be no ifs, ands, or buts about this, young man," and I'd "get it."

Today, however, it's a different story. A child creates a problem in school, and the teacher or principal calls home or perhaps calls one of the child's parents at work. Today's parent, however, is likely to take the "hot potato" of the child's misbehavior and toss it right back at the school. Suddenly, the person making the report is on the hot seat! The parent says, "Trinket isn't capable of such a thing," or "Angel's never had this problem with any other teacher," or "I think you [the teacher] and Rambo are simply having a personality conflict," or "It's quite obvious to me that Loquacia is simply acting out her boredom." Note that in every one of these examples, the parent blames the child's misbehavior on the teacher. The child makes his bed, the teacher must lie in it! Worse, as a good number of these teachers have told me, principals do not always support teachers in these situations! These principals, apparently, are too concerned with diplomacy to assign responsibility where it belongs. Regardless, the damage has already been done. Once the parent defends or makes excuses for the child, it no longer matters what action the school decides to take because the child's values aren't coming from school. They're coming from home.

My mother, when she heard these reports about me, might have felt the teacher wasn't the best in the world, or that she wasn't handling my behavior effectively, or even that she was making matters worse by overreacting to me, or whatever. But in my mother's mind, none of those things was as relevant as two solid facts: first, I had misbehaved; second, I required punishment. So, despite the fact that it would have been possible for her to find fault with the teacher (everyone is faulted, remember?), my mother simply punished me. I now realize that my mother felt, interestingly enough, that her first obligation was to the school, not me. When in doubt, she gave the benefit of that doubt to the teacher, not me. It's sad, indeed, that more parents do not still think as my mother did.

I remembered the lesson my mother taught me about such things when Eric, then in the seventh grade, complained to me about his history teacher.

"She doesn't like me, Dad," he said, "and I'm afraid she's not going to give me a very good grade in her class."

"She doesn't like you, eh?" I reflected. "Eric, that's a fairly serious matter. Tell me something: How many kids are in your history class?"

"I don't know, Dad," he answered. "Maybe thirty."

"And of those thirty kids, how many doesn't she like?" I asked.

He thought for a moment. "Just two. Me and one other guy."

It so happens that this conversation was taking place as Eric and I were driving somewhere. At this point, I pulled over into the next parking lot and stopped the car.

I turned to Eric. "You've just told me, Eric, that we're not talking about a teacher who dislikes children. She doesn't dislike all thirty of the kids in her history class, just two, and you're one of 'em. That tells me you and one other kid in her class are doing something she doesn't like. So, my instruction to you is this: You will go to her class tomorrow, and you will correct what you are doing that she doesn't like, and you will keep it corrected. And you'd better figure out how you're going to make a B in her class, because if your report card grade is less than a B, you're in big-time trouble with the boss, who just happens to be me. Do you have any questions?"

I wish I had a photo of Eric's expression at that moment. "Floored" is the word that comes to mind. He just stared at me, slack-jawed and speechless.

"Good," I said, "because I have a feeling any question you might ask would only make me upset, and you don't want me to get upset right now, Eric, believe me."

I put the car in gear and pulled out of the parking lot. When we were several blocks down the road, I said, "So, Eric, tell me, how was your day?"

"Uh," he answered, "it was pretty good until a few minutes ago."

Eric made a B in history that semester. He made his bed. I made him lie in it. He didn't like lying in it, so he remade his bed. He didn't mind lying in it the second time.

A Family of Value

Grandma said, "You paddle your own canoe."

Speaking at a church, I began by asking if anyone in the audience had anything in particular they wanted me to address.

A woman immediately spoke up, asking, "How do you motivate children?"

"Good question," I said, "but I'm not going to answer it until a bit later. How about the rest of you?"

"What should you do," asked another woman, "if your child waits until the last minute to start a science project?"

"Why would you do anything at all?" I asked.

You could have heard a pin drop. Everyone just stared at me, expectantly. Finally, someone said, "Well, because you care!"

"Oh, really?" I asked again. "So tell me, why would you care?"

Again, there was silence for a few moments, then someone else said, "Because you don't want them to make bad grades."

"That's an interesting concept," I said. "If your child is irresponsible, you're saying you don't want your child to suffer any negative consequences. Instead, you're going to engage in a cover-up of his or her irresponsibility, thus teaching your child that irresponsible behavior is inconsequential.

"Folks," I continued, "whether any of you realize it or not, we've answered the first question. How do you motivate children? Don't become drawn into their responsibilities. It's as simple as that. Previous generations of parents expressed that understanding by saying things like "you lie in the beds you make," and "you fight your own battles," and "you paddle your own canoe," and the like. Parents who, speaking figuratively, lay in their children's beds and fought their children's battles and paddled their children's canoes were called what?"

"Overprotective," rose a chorus of voices.

"That's right. Do any of you think being overprotective is more in a child's best interests today than it was forty years ago?"

Silence. Then one of the men said, "Of course not, John, but what would *you* have done if one of your children waited until the last minute to tell you about a science project?"

"I wouldn't have done a thing," I said. "In fact, I wouldn't have cared."

And with that, I told the story of my daughter Amy and her sixth-grade science project: One evening during the first half of that school year, Amy came to me in a panic. Her science project was due the next day, she announced, her hands flapping in front of her, and she hadn't started it and I had to take her to the store for the project materials and I had to help her. Exclamation point plus!

"This science project was assigned today?" I asked.

"No, Daddy!" she screeched. "It was assigned several weeks ago. Now hurry! We've got to get to the store!"

"Let me get this straight, Amy," I said. "Your teacher assigned a science project several weeks ago and you just decided to start it?"

"No, Daddy!" she screeched again, more exasperated this time. "I forgot!"

I thought about that for a moment. "Well, Amy," I said, "you're out of luck tonight, because I have forgotten how to drive a car."

"No you didn't!"

"Okay, you're right, Amos," I said, "I really didn't. But I'm really not going to drive you to the store, and I can assure you, neither is Mom. Sometime in the next few days, when it's convenient, one of us will take you to the store. I guess this means you're going to turn your science project in late."

"But I'll get a bad grade!"

"I trust that you will, Amy," I said. "In fact, if your teacher *doesn't* give you a bad grade, I will be the first parent in the history of that school to demand that his own child's grade be lowered."

And Amy begged, and she wailed, and she acted like she was coming apart at the seams and her self-esteem was being flushed forever down the toilet of life, but I refused to budge (so did Willie). We took Amy to the store a couple of days later but gave her no help with her project. She turned it in late, and her teacher saved me a visit to the school by giving Amy a low grade. And Amy never, ever again waited until the last minute to do a project.

That's how you motivate children. You don't paddle their canoes. Grandma said so.

Grandma said, "I guess it's time I lowered the boom!"

The favorite disciplinary method of today's "helping" professionals is "time-out." In case you just woke up from a forty-year slumber, time-out involves confining a child to a relatively isolated place (e.g., the downstairs bathroom) immediately for a short period of time (no more than ten minutes) after the child misbehaves. Let me assure you, time-out is vastly overrated. In fact, over the course of my active child-rearing years, I slowly came to the conclusion that many, if not most, of the disciplinary methods psychologists and other "helping" professionals tend to advocate are of limited usefulness. Like time-out, they work some of the time (and even with a few children *all* of the time), but they don't work with every child every time. Sometimes, quite often I think, stronger methods are called for.

When either the child or the problem seems especially resistant to correction, I generally recommend an approach my parents occasionally used with me. They called it "lowering the boom." It's very, very psychologically incorrect, so don't expect to hear many other members of my profession applauding me on this one (as if they ever do).

The "boom" refers to a consequence that, while not harsh and certainly not hurtful, is sufficient to cause the child significant, albeit harmless, discomfort. In order for the "boom" to be effective, parents should not lower it often. It should be reserved for problems that are either extremely grave, or chronic, or both. Instead of inconveniencing a misbehaving child in some *minor* way by assigning him to time-out for five minutes or by taking a privilege away for a short time, his parents impose a major inconvenience *all at once*. They lower the boom and keep it bearing down on the child for a significant period of time. Because the feeling of the lowered boom is boldly and permanently engraved into the child's memory banks, the problem is unlikely to persist. Here are several true stories that serve to illustrate the point:

Lowering the Boom, Part One: Reggie (his name has been changed to protect the guilty), nine years old and in the third grade, had a habit of dragging his feet on school mornings. Despite his mother's frenzied attempts to get him out the door on time, he was often late, thus making her late for work. But Reggie was a cool dude. None of this fazed him in the least. In fact, the more bent out of shape his mother got, the more blasé Reggie became.

Finally, at the end of her rope, Reggie's mother took him aside one night and said, "Reggie, I just want you to know that I'm never, ever going to be late for work again. Furthermore, I'm never, ever going to nag you in the morning again. Do you have any questions?"

He gave her a "you're really dumb sometimes, Mom" look and said, "Uh, no, I guess not."

The next morning, Reggie dawdled, but his mother said nothing. He finally came downstairs and announced that he was ready for his personal chauffeur to drive him to school. He and his personal chauffer got into the car and she pulled it out of the driveway.

Reggie could immediately tell that something was different. "Where are you going, Mom?" he asked. "School's the other way."

"Oh, I can't take you to school this morning, Reggie," his chauffeur answered. "If I did, I'd be late for work, and I told you I was never going to be late for work again. Didn't you hear me?"

"But Mom," Reggie protested, "I've *got* to go to school! I have a test today!"

"Sorry 'bout that, Reggie, but I'm never, ever going to be late for work again."

Reggie protested strenuously. He even managed to work himself up to a cry, but his personal chauffeur stood fast. She took him to work with her, set him up in a small conference room, and left him with instructions not to come out unless he needed to use the restroom. And that's where he stayed for nine hours, with nothing to do but invent schoolwork for himself and stare at the walls.

On one of his trips to the restroom, Reggie spotted a phone no one was using. He picked it up and called his house. When the answering machine came on, he said, "Hi, Mom. It's me, Reggie. I'm really sorry for getting you upset in the mornings, and I don't blame you for bringing me to work with you today, and it's really, really boring here, and I'm never going to make you late again, I promise."

The next morning, Reggie was ready for school thirty minutes early. And his feet haven't dragged since.

Lowering the Boom, Part Two: A mother told me her ten-year-old son came home every day from school and kicked off his shoes in the living room, threw his coat on the floor, tossed his bookbag on the sofa, and went upstairs to change his clothes. There, he left clothes all over the floor and drawers hanging open. Leaving chaos in his wake, he went outside to play with his buddies.

"I know this probably sounds trivial, John," she said, "but it's driving me crazy. I've tried everything, and nothing seems to work, not for long anyway. Got a suggestion?"

"Yes, I do," I answered, "but before I tell you what it is, I need to know one thing: Do you want all of this to stop?"

"Absolutely!" she said.

"Good! I have an idea that will not only stop the problem entirely, but will make it unnecessary that you ever again nag your son about any of these trivial things."

"Oh, happy day!" she exclaimed. "Tell!"

I told her to never again remind her son of the rules he so often broke. Nor she should warn him concerning my recommended "therapeutic delivery system."

"The next time he kicks off his shoes in the living room or does any one of the things you so deplore," I told her, "you are to say nothing. Wait until he is outside, then go put his shoes and other things where they belong and close his drawers. In other words, do *exactly* what you want your son to do."

At this point, she interrupted my explanation, objecting, "But John, I don't want him to think I'll do these things for him!"

"Hear me out, madam," I replied. "After you've been his maid, go outside and fetch him, telling him you have something very new and exciting to show him. Take him inside and show him the shoes you put away for him and the coat you hung up for him, et cetera. Then take him to his room and say, 'And look! I even straightened up your room. The good news is, any day that you don't do these things for yourself, I'm going to do them for you, without complaint. The bad news is, if I have to do even one of them for you, you are going to spend the remainder of the day in your room— even if the violation occurs on Saturday morning—and go to bed, lights out, immediately after supper. And guess what! Your punishment starts today! Right now!'"

And with that, I told her, simply turn around and exit his room, leaving him to stew in his own juices over the fact that she is finally lowering the boom by making him lie in a bed he made.

She looked positively dismayed. I asked, "Is something wrong?"

"Well, John," she said, "I, I just don't know about that idea at all. I mean, it sounds so mean and all."

"Excuse me," I said. "I must have misunderstood you. I could have sworn you told me you wanted this sloppiness to stop, as in cease and desist."

"Well, yes," she replied, "I do, but this sounds so, well, *extreme.*"

"Do you think it'll hurt him or cause him to become a criminal?"

"No, I don't guess so."

"Then what's the problem?"

"I guess it's that I've always thought a punishment should fit the crime."

"Indeed!" I said. "It should! And *the only punishment that fits a crime is one that stops the crime from happening.*"

This story is not just about a child who throws his belongings all over the house. It's about a mother who's been brainwashed by professional propaganda to the effect that old-fashioned disciplinary methods were cruel and unusual, hurtful, and even abusive. This mother looked dismayed because my recommendation no doubt reminded her of something her parents might have done to her under similar circumstances. Her reasoning, therefore, went something like this: My parents might have done something like that if I threw my belongings around the house. The "experts" say our parents' discipline was psychologically damaging; therefore, I mustn't do anything like what my parents might have done.

And that, dear reader, is one of the biggest reasons why today's parents are complaining about their children's behavior so much, much, much more than did parents of previous generations. Yesterday's parents would have *stopped* their children from throwing their belongings around the house. They would have made such a child an "offer he couldn't refuse" (a disciplinary technique first proposed by that most famous of Sicilian philosophers, Don Vito Corleone). The resulting consequence would have been *memorable,* so memorable as to insure the infraction would never, ever happen again.

By contrast, today's parents fool around interminably with their children's misbehavior. They put their children in time-out for five minutes (boring, but not memorable; therefore, seldom persuasive) or they take away their children's bicycles (so their children walk, which is no big deal, really) or they won't let their children watch television for the rest of the day (so their children go outside) or they won't let them go outside (so they watch television). They're afraid to do anything that might make their children's misbehavior simply stop, because to do so, one must almost always lower the boom, and that's old-fashioned; therefore, it simply can't be done. Better to fool around and go slowly crazy, eh?

And about this business of being *mean*, let me assure you that parents had better stand ready to be mean at a moment's notice. Let's face it, folks, "You're mean!" simply means the child in question has discovered that the parent in question *means* exactly what she says. Not sorta-kinda-maybe-but-then-again-maybe-not, but exactly! After some fancy salesmanship on my part, the mother in the story above did what I told her to do. She told me later that (1) her son's sloppiness stopped, and (2) he told her she was the meanest mother on the face of the earth. That only meant she did something memorable, as in *lasting*. She finally caused him to take her seriously. At long last, she acted like she knew where to stand and where she wanted her son to stand. Best of all, should he ever throw his belongings around the house again, she won't go crazy. He will.

Lowering the Boom, Part Three: One day, about two weeks into Eric's fifth-grade year, I got a call from one of his three teachers. She told me he wasn't doing his work. She and her colleagues knew he was capable, but he had apparently discovered his social personality and was putting most of his energy toward its exercise. I assured her Willie and I would have a serious talk with Eric.

And we did. We told him it was okay to have a little fun in school every now and then, but school wasn't for the purpose of having fun. We charged him with correcting the problem, saying, "You created it, you solve it."

To help him solve it, we promised we would stay off his back about it. In fact, we promised not to ask him even one question about school between then and the day his report card came out, which was six weeks away.

We said, "We're not going to ask you how your day was, if you have homework, if things are getting better. Nothing. And we're not going to get in touch with your teachers, either. But Eric, if you don't solve the problem, we're going to have to get very involved, and you won't like it, believe us. So do yourself a big favor and get rid of this little complication, okay?"

"Okay, okay!" he said, and that was that for the next six weeks, during which we kept our promises. When his report card came out, there were three D's on it (and I'm sure they were gifts).

Willie and I requested a conference with his teachers. We learned that after the phone call, Eric had improved slightly, but not much, and not for long. A decision was arrived at, and the conference ended.

Willie and I went home and sat Eric down. "Eric," we said, "you didn't take the bull by the horns, so we must get involved in your problem, which we don't like to do, and which you're not going to like, either.

"In four weeks, we have an appointment with your three teachers. We are not going to communicate with them until then. We will begin that conference by asking, 'How's Eric?' to which there is but one, and only one, correct answer: namely, 'Eric is doing just fine and dandy! He doesn't have a problem for us to talk about, so we can all go home!' Answers such as 'he's doing better,' or 'he's having more good days than bad days' are not acceptable.

"If all three teachers give us the correct answer, Eric, you will be allowed to come out of your room."

His eyes popped open, his jaw dropped to his waist, and he cried, "What do you mean?!"

"We mean, son, that for the next four weeks, if you're not at school, you'll be in your room. You can come out to do your chores, eat meals with us, use the bathroom, and go places with us as a family. And your bedtime, Eric, is moved back to eight-thirty, seven days a week.

"Oh, and one more thing, son. In your room, you have a record player and model-building stuff and a slot-car racing set and books and some toys. Can you guess what's happening to all that stuff?"

He hung his head. "I guess you're taking it out," he said, almost inaudibly.

"Surprise! We're leaving all that stuff in your room! You know why? Because in addition to the schoolwork assigned over the next four weeks, you have to make up most of the work you didn't do during the first grading period. That's the only way your teachers will give us the correct answer. We want you to have to constantly choose between doing your work or playing with one of the things in your room. To make sure you are always tempted to do the wrong thing, we're leaving all that stuff in there. Pretty good of us, eh?"

Of course, Eric didn't think any of this was pretty good. He begged and pleaded and threw himself upon our mercy, but we had none left. So he spent the next four weeks in his room. And when Willie and I asked his three teachers, "Hi, how's Eric doing?" all three of them said, "Oh, the day after our last conference, Eric was a totally different child. He's definitely been our best student these last four weeks."

Allow me, at this point, to address a patently ludicrous myth which originated some years back from within professional circles. I'm talking about the belief that confining a child to his room and/or sending him to bed early will cause him to develop "negative feelings" about his room and his bed, and that as a result he will start having nightmares and all sorts of low-self-esteem-related maladies. There is, let me assure, no support for this invention, which qualifies as late-twentieth-century folklore. It's an example of the highly nonscientific ideas "helping" professionals sometimes spin from whole cloth. It's also a testament to the power such professionals have attained in our culture that they can propose something that on its face is nothing but dumb and nonetheless be taken seriously by significant numbers of people.

The import of all these "lowering the boom" stories is simply that contrary to the blatant propaganda "helping" professionals have been disseminating over the last forty years or so, old-fashioned discipline still works. It's been my finding, after first using and recommending *nouveau* methods and then reembracing more traditional ones, that the latter, by and large, are considerably more effective. In the stories above and below, parents aren't laboring to *understand* the "why" of their children's problems; they aren't constructing elaborate intellectual theories that (1) can neither be proven nor disproven and (2) obstruct, more than facilitate, solution. They are taking their children's problems "at face value" and dealing with them head-on.

Now, I'm not saying that any and all attempts to understand

why certain children behave in certain counterproductive ways is never helpful, because there are times when it can be. I'm saying that modern psychologists often seem more interested in explaining the "psychodynamics" of a problem than in solving it as quickly as possible. This tendency grows out of the theory—which I was taught as a graduate student—that dealing with outward behavior is a "Band-Aid" approach to problems. Eventually, or so the theory goes, the Band-Aid will fall off. Its proponents claim that the psychodynamic approach, which usually involves months, if not years, of what I call "psychological archaeology" (digging into a person's past to uncover psychological relics), may take longer, but its results are more permanent. I have long been an outspoken critic of this orientation (so outspoken, in fact, that I came close to having my license to practice psychology taken away from me in 1988 for publicly criticizing it), especially when it's applied to children. In my estimation and experience (and there's plenty of clinical evidence to back the following heretical contention), psychodynamic approaches to children's behavior problems are, generally speaking, not only cost- and time-ineffective, but involve significant risk of making matters worse instead of better.

One of the transformational events in my professional life occurred in 1978. At the time, I was working as a consultant to public and private schools in Gaston County, North Carolina, which lies just west of Charlotte. Around the first of October, a kindergarten teacher asked my help concerning a child in her class whom she described as "wild." Indeed, Danny was the most out-of-control child I've ever seen in a regular classroom setting, before or since. He was in constant motion. He hit anyone, adult or child, who thwarted him in the slightest. He disrupted what other children were doing and destroyed what they made. He fought like a person possessed if anyone tried to contain him physically.

The teacher was at wit's end. The principal wanted Danny out of the school. The parents had a reputation for being unhelpful. They both worked as unskilled laborers in textile mills. Neither of them had finished the eighth grade. The father was functionally illiterate and possibly alcoholic. The mother was the picture of physical and emotional exhaustion. It was a bad situation.

Two weeks after I first laid eyes on Danny, everyone agreed he was well behaved enough to remain in a regular classroom. Within four weeks, his behavior was indistinguishable from that of the average kindergartner. Furthermore, he never had a relapse. Thirteen years later, he became the first child in his family's history to graduate from high school.

This amazing, permanent metamorphosis came about as a result of a teacher and a mother who joined together to call Danny's "bluff." A list of five misbehaviors—hitting, running, disobeying, yelling, and arguing with the teacher—was posted on the bulletin board. Initially, Danny was allowed ten misbehaviors a day. Every time he let loose with a targeted misbehavior, his teacher simply turned over one of ten numbered cards that were hanging above the list. When he ran out of cards, he was taken to the principle's office (kicking and screaming), his mother was called, and she came to the school, took him home, confined him to his room for the remainder of the day, and made him go to bed early. Every time he came out of his room, his mother swatted his rear end one time and put him back.

The first day, he went home fifteen minutes after school started(!). On the third, he actually made it through lunch. On the fifth day, a Friday, he used only seven of his ten cards, thus remaining in school the entire day. He went home fairly early the following Monday, *but never went home early again.* At that point, we began gradually lowering his "misbehavior quota." Within five weeks, Danny was down to four cards a day, meaning he could misbehave but three times a day and still remain in school.

But it wasn't my brilliantly creative technique that brought about Danny's rehabilitation. It came about because of a teacher who never threatened, warned, or gave him second chances. If he misbehaved, even slightly, she flipped a card. And it came about, furthermore, because of a mother who kept him in his room, against all odds. She fought the good fight, and she won. But the real winner, of course, was Danny.

I daresay that most "helping" professionals would have tried to understand Danny. They'd have talked in terms of his "dysfunctional family" and called him a "homeostatic child" who was lacking in "self-esteem." In the process, they'd have constructed a very impressive theory concerning Danny's behavior problems. Other "helping" professionals would have recommended (1) individual therapy for Danny to help him "discharge" his feelings more appropriately; (2) parent counseling to teach the parents appropriate behavior-management techniques; (3) marriage and family counseling to address the family's dysfunctionality; (4) special education for Danny outside the regular classroom, at least until the problems were solved.

Fat chance! Danny's parents wouldn't have cooperated in any of the above, unless court-ordered (which results in compliance, not cooperation). I knew that. So did the teacher, the principal, and everyone who knew the family. So we just dealt with Danny head-on. No one ever talked to him. No one ever asked him how he was feeling, or wondered aloud why he was so "angry." No one ever counseled the parents concerning "more appropriate behavior management techniques." Most "helping" professionals, I think, would have disapproved of confining Danny to his room, spanking him if he came out, and sending him to bed early. They'd have said that such methods would only have driven Danny's self-esteem even further into the ground. Well, they'd have been wrong. Dead wrong. Within four weeks, Danny was a happy, reasonably well-behaved kid, and he stayed that way.

And Danny's tale is not unique. Having seen the results of "lowering the boom" on Danny, I began recommending similar approaches with other children. Far more often than not, these approaches worked, not just temporarily, but permanently. And when they didn't, it was because parents and teachers wouldn't work at them. I've watched "lowering the boom" work to "cure" children with attention deficit disorder. I've seen it transform learning disabled kids into high achievers. I don't recommend its indiscriminate use, because there are times, indeed, when a slower, more understanding approach is needed. But I will say this: "Lowering the boom" has been a lot more helpful to me, in both my role as a parent and my role as a psychologist, than 95 percent of the "psychologically correct" disciplinary methods I learned in graduate and postgraduate study.

Exactly what, you might ask, caused Danny to turn around so quickly? Quite simply, his teacher and his mother joined forces and brought the "Godfather Principle" to bear upon him. They made

him an offer he couldn't refuse: Behave, and stay in school; misbehave, and go home. Danny didn't want to be at home. He wanted
to be where the action was. Activating the "Godfather Principle"
also activated the "Agony Principle": Danny's teacher and mother
stopped agonizing over his misbehavior and began seeing to it that
he began agonizing over it instead. Like I tell parents, your children
will not stop misbehaving because their misbehavior makes *you*
upset. They will stop when it makes *them* upset. All they need, in
other words, is parents and teachers who stop paddling their emotional canoes for them, and begin making them begin paddle them
themselves. Penance is very therapeutic, as long as the right person
is penitent.

Lowering the Boom, Part Four: Sometimes, a child who's stray-
ing off the path might need nothing more than a "wake-up call" to
get her back on the right track. Sally was just such a child.

One day, Sally's second-grade teacher called Sally's mother and
requested a conference. When Sally's mother arrived, she was surprised to find not just the teacher, but the school counselor, the
school psychologist, and the assistant principle. They solemnly informed her that Sally was not paying attention in class and wasn't
getting her work done. She was, they said, exhibiting symptoms indicative of attention deficit disorder (ADD). They recommended
testing by the school psychologist and said that Sally might need to
take medication to help her attention span.

"What is Sally doing in class if she isn't paying attention?" her
mother asked.

"Most of the time," the teacher answered, "she just sits there
twirling her hair and staring off into space. Could something be
bothering her?"

And thusly did the teacher put on the table the possibility that
Sally was experiencing psychological distress of some kind, arising,
no doubt (although no one was bold enough to actually *say* so),
from a family problem of one sort or another. The mother spent
most of the rest of the conference trying to assure everyone that the
family was okay, and that Sally had nothing to worry about. Sally's
mother later told me she was sure everyone thought she was engaging in "denial," which is psychobabble for when someone doesn't
agree with a psychologist.

Sally's mother had heard something at the conference that had piqued her attention. During the summer between first and second grades, Sally had been allowed to grow her hair long. Hair "like Barbie's" was something she had wanted for quite some time, but her parents had held off giving their permission until they were sure Sally was old enough to take care of it herself. Sally loved her long hair.

Her mother went home and cut it short. She told Sally, "If you're going to twirl it all day long, then you're not ready for long hair. When your grades improve, we'll consider it again. In the meantime, it goes, and it stays short." Snip, snip, snip.

Some of you out there in Readerland are probably aghast. You feel sorry for Sally, don't you? Your feelings about this mother are not printable in a book on family values, are they? In fact, I tell this story to disorient those among you who are inclined to think that children are fragile, that children with problems are the most fragile children of all, and, therefore that anything but a "kid gloves" approach to a problem of Sally's sort is heinous. Here's a child who may have a learning problem and is probably upset by something that's going on at home, but does her mother have compassion? No! She punishes her for something Sally can't help and makes her even *more* upset. How awful!

Sally was, indeed, upset. Better Sally than everyone else, I say. Nonetheless, Sally immediately turned over a new leaf and her grades began improving. Six weeks after the infamous haircut, her mother told me Sally was making straight A's in school. Everyone agreed she was a "totally different child."

Point: Children aren't fragile. They are resilient. In fact, they adapt better and more easily to change than adults, and even seem to get over highly traumatic experiences more quickly and successfully.

Point: Sally's mother's approach to Sally's problem was not unloving. It wasn't "kid gloves," either. It was a practical, commonsensical, "let's put our priorities in order" approach. Sally's mother didn't cut Sally's hair to *punish* her. She cut it to *help* her. This is called tough-love, folks, and there are definitely times when that's the only kind of love that will do.

Point: Sally's mother's common sense was more valid than the combined intellectual musings of four people with graduate degrees. The idea that common sense is more powerful, generally speaking, than book sense may surprise some people, but it doesn't surprise me. After all, I have a graduate degree, so I've been able to make the comparison firsthand. I vote for common sense any day.

What, pray tell, might have happened had this mother been seduced by the teacher's, counselor's, school psychologist's, and assistant principal's well-intentioned concerns? Being a psychologist, I'm fairly sure I know the answer. The mother would have given permission to have the school psychologist give Sally a bunch of tests and observe her in the classroom. There's a better-than-average chance those tests and observations would have "confirmed" the diagnosis of attention deficit disorder. Sally's doctor would have prescribed an attention-stimulating medication. Sally's teacher would have lowered academic expectations for Sally in order to compensate for her "disability" and prevent her from becoming academically frustrated and thus begin to leak copious amounts of self-esteem. Slowly but surely, Sally would have begun to think there was something "wrong" with her. Slowly but surely, she would have developed a "can't do" attitude. In short, everyone's good intentions would have created a problem, and a big one at that, where there was no problem at all. Just long hair.

Maybe someday Sally will have long hair again. Until then, as Grandma used to say, "First things first."

The Keys to Successful Discipline

To this point, this entire chapter has been devoted to making but one point: *Technique is not the key to successful discipline.* Unfortunately, most parents think it is (because "helping" professionals have made it seem so). They search "parenting" columns, magazines, and books for answers to an infinitude of "what should you do when?" questions: What should you do when your two-year-old bites the family dog? What should you do when your four-year-old throws a wild tantrum in a public place? (Answer: Hide!) What is the proper response to bad grades, disrespect, lying, or staying out past curfew?

Today's parents collect the techniques recommended by "helping" professionals and store them for future reference in the "Discipline File," located in the upper portion of the left temporal lobe. When a discipline problem occurs, they retrieve the "proper" disciplinary technique and use it. In these parents' minds, that's what successful discipline is all about: *technique.* That's the impression, certainly, that "parenting experts" have created.

While certain techniques doubtless have more merit than others, the essence of successful discipline is not technique; rather, it is self-confidence. If, as a parent, you project self-confidence in your dealings with your children, then not only will discipline problems be "small potatoes" in your family, but when such a problem arises, just about any disciplinary technique will work. If, on the other hand, you lack self-confidence, discipline is likely to be a major issue and no technique will work—not for long, anyway. At first, a new method or consequence may take a misbehaving child by surprise, resulting in temporary improvement. But sooner or later, the child will see through the "veil" of the technique and realize that *you* are not different at all. At that point, it's back to square one, because when all is said and done, it's *you* that makes the difference, not your methods.

Parents who possess self-confidence know where they stand and where they want their children to stand. They project this attitude in four typical ways:

1. *They communicate their expectations in no uncertain terms.* When it comes to communicating expectations, many, if not most, parents either beat around the bush or beat on it. They plead, bribe, cajole, and "reason." When none of this accomplishes anything, they begin screaming threats of bodily harm. Self-confident parents, on the other hand, come straight to the point. Such a parent, for example, would *not* ask, "How about doing Mommy a favor by picking up these toys?" She would say, "It's time for you to pick up these toys." Her child would hear her clearly. He would know exactly, not sorta-kinda, what was expected of him; and what parents *expect* their children to do, their children are likely to do. It's as simple as that.

2. *When the need for enforcement arises, they do so without brutality or bribery.* Self-confident parents accept that even the "best" child will misbehave; therefore, their children's misbehaviors don't

pull the proverbial rug out from under them. Keeping one's "balance" in the face of misbehavior enables an evenhanded, and therefore truly powerful, response.

A friend of mine once took her three-year-old to a shopping center. She went to one store and bought a new outfit for the child; to another for new shoes; to yet another for a new lamp for the child's room; and finally, to a toy store for some new doll clothes. As they started out of the toy store, the child asked for a toy, was told "no," and began crying loudly. My friend promptly turned around, went back to the counter, and returned the doll clothes. She then retraced her steps through the shopping center, returning the lamp, the shoes, and the outfit. She never, mind you, displayed any anger. Just *resolve*. The whole time, the child was apologizing, begging, pleading, promising to never cry in a store again. To all of this, the mother simply said, "Yes, and to help you remember your promise, I'm returning everything, and it will be a while before we try this shopping trip again."

As they got in the car to go home, she turned to her daughter and said, "From now on, that is what I will do if you cry or scream in stores." The child never threw a public tantrum again. Once again, the power of common sense.

3. They don't argue with their children. A self-confident parent knows that a child cannot, even with the best of explanations, understand an adult point of view. Therefore, he's not surprised when, after giving a child the reason behind a decision the child didn't like, the child still doesn't like it. Instead of trying to persuade the child that the adult point of view is more valid, he says something like, "If I was your age, I wouldn't like it either, but I've made the decision, and it stands," and walks away. That's nothing more, by the way, than an eighteen-word version of "Because I said so."

4. When their children misbehave, self-confident parents make sure those same children get upset. They, on the other hand, remain calm. They realize that only the penitent atone. The also understand that penance is not an inherent part of man's makeup; rather, it must be taught—first instilled, then evoked. On their own, in other words, children will not feel penitent concerning the bad things they do. On their own, children will even take a certain amount of satisfaction in doing bad things. Penance, furthermore, cannot be *talked in* to a child. It must be *forced* in (albeit there's no reason for this force to be hurtful) using enough pressure to insure that it will take root. With some children, the force can usually be slight, but it is nonetheless *force*. With other children, only the force of the "boom" will do.

Grandma said, "A watched pot never boils."

"I have to literally stand over my six-year-old to get him to do anything," said the child's mother, obviously at wit's end.

"How so?" I asked.

"Oh, I ask him to do something, usually something simple like pick up the toys he's scattered around the den, and he acts like he didn't hear me, so I raise my voice and finally get his attention, but he still won't do anything unless I stand there saying things like 'C'mon, c'mon, this shouldn't take all day' and 'Pick up that one now' and so on, and maybe five minutes later they're all picked up and I'm having heart palpitations and feel a world-class headache coming on and he's totally oblivious, as usual."

Finally pausing to take in air, she beseeched, "Can you help me? Please!"

"Well," I replied, "this sounds like a classic case of *watched-pot syndrome* to me. Although fairly common, there are no references to it in the clinical literature. What little we do know about it suggests it's probably inherited. At least, the parents of watched-pot children usually report that they, too, were watched pots."

"What on earth are you babbling about?" she asked.

"Why, I'm babbling about the fact that a watched pot never boils," I answered.

"What does that have to do with my problem?" she asked, visibly perplexed.

"It *is* your problem, madam," I said. "The simple fact is that as long as you stand over your son after you ask him to do something, he has an opportunity to get into a power struggle with you, which he does. If you wouldn't stand over him—watching his pot, so to speak—he'd be more likely to come to a boil. In other words, he'd be more likely to do what you've told him to do."

"You've obviously never met my son."

This mother is living proof that parents are their own worst enemies. Caught up in a vicious cycle with her son, she can't see that she's 80 percent (or more!) of the problem, and that the cycle will continue its downward spiral until the day she changes *her* behavior.

Watched-pot syndrome (WPS) is one of the most vicious cycles in parent-child relationships. A parent gives an instruction and then, certain that compliance will not happen otherwise, stands over the "pot," inviting noncompliance (the self-fulfilling prophecy again). The child, having someone with whom to engage in a power struggle, struggles.

Not realizing that the very act of watching the pot prevents it from boiling, the parent begins referring to the child by such epithets as "strong-willed" and "stubborn," when the fact is that the child simply knows a golden opportunity when he sees one. One of the most common arenas for WPS is the dining room table after six o'clock in the evening on school nights, where one is likely to find mother and child locked in a struggle over homework. If one asks Mom, "Why are you sitting here, night after night, obviously allowing yourself to be driven crazy?" she will answer, "Because Deuteronomy won't do her homework on her own." The "forest" Mom can't see because she's so fanatically focused on one of its trees is that her very presence at the homework table prevents little Deut from getting down to business.

The obvious solution to any and all situations of this sort: Stop watching the pot. When you want a child to do something, give the instruction and walk away. Make like a tree and leave. Give the pot a chance to boil. If, after a reasonable amount of time, the child hasn't complied, then lower the boom. If the toys aren't picked up within five minutes, for example, send the child to his room for the remainder of the day (yes, even if it's eight o'clock on Saturday morning). and put him to bed, lights out, immediately after supper. The idea is to impose a penalty that, while not painful, is nonetheless unforgettable.

Oh, and by the way, when the parent in question tells the child in question to go to his room, the child will no doubt suddenly begin to boil, saying, "I'll do it, I'll do it!" while running around picking up toys, in which case the parent should just stand there, smiling, until all the toys are picked up. Then she should say, "That was very nice, and you've done such a wonderful job! Now, go to your room for the rest of the day."

The child will look stricken and say, "But I picked 'em up!"

And the parent should say, "Not when I told you to, so you'll spend the rest of the day in your room."

The child will then say, with great sincerity, "I'll never do it again! I promise!"

The parent should then smile and say, "That's the idea. Now go to your room."

The child will then narrow his eyes, draw his lips back in a feral snarl, and scream, *"I hate you! I wish you weren't my mother! Your feet stink!"*

To which the parent should respond, "I'd feel exactly the same way if I were you. Now go to your room."

And the next time the parent in question gives an instruction to this hateful and most olfactory-sensitive child, believe me, the pot will boil. There's very little doubt about it. But just remember, Rome wasn't built in a day. Grandma said that, too.

On Foolishness and Free Will

A mother once asked me, "Is it too much to expect a ten-year-old not to lie?"

The question sounded rhetorical to me. I suspected she wanted me to simply confirm what she already believed. I hated to disappoint her, but . . .

"If you mean every once in a while, then yes, it's probably expecting too much," I answered.

She looked taken aback. "So, I mean," she stammered, "if I get angry, I'm overreacting?"

"That depends on how angry you become," I said. "The fact is, children do foolish things like lie when the truth would not have been a major problem. They do all sorts of foolish things, simply because they are children. If they never did foolish things, they wouldn't need parents, now would they?"

"But what have I done," she asked, "that would cause him to lie?"

"You gave birth to him," I answered.

This conversation brought several things to mind.

First, today's parents take children entirely too seriously. A generation or so ago, a ten-year-old who lied would have been punished, but the likelihood is no one would have thought the misdeed out of the ordinary. Almost certainly, no one would have entertained a psychological explanation. The explanation, in fact, was (and still is) scriptural: Foolishness is bound in the heart of a child (Proverbs 22:15). Not *some* children's hearts, mind you, but *all* of them. They're all foolish, every single one of 'em.

Second, today's parents take themselves entirely too seriously. The two—taking oneself and one's children too seriously—go hand in hand, of course. Today's parents give themselves entirely too much credit, in fact. They tend to think everything their children do is a product of upbringing. That little delusion borders on being grandiose. The truth is—take it from someone whose children are adults and who's now a grandpappy—that under the very best of circumstances, parents have a lot less control over their children than they think they do.

Children are human, and humans are blessed/cursed with free will. The combination of foolishness in the heart and free will in the head is extremely volatile and makes for unpredictable, incomprehensible behavior. If a certain child makes a habit of foolish behavior, his parents certainly need to take stock of themselves. But occasional foolishness—even if it's slightly outrageous—on the part of a child, says little about the child's parents.

As a consequence of taking both themselves and their children too seriously, today's parents are a paradox of overreaction and defensiveness. On the one hand, they come unglued because of their children's foolishness; on the other, they deny their children are even capable of foolishness. "My child isn't capable of (pick one: lying, stealing, cheating, cruelty, disrespect, using foul language, vandalism, blasphemy)," says today's parent, foolishly defensive out of a deep, dark fear that any flaw in his or her child reveals an even uglier flaw in him/herself.

Ha! The truth is, *any child is capable of just about anything.* Yes, your child, too. The good news is, most of your child's foolishness isn't your fault. But it is your responsibility to correct it when it occurs. Taking disciplinary responsibility for your child's misbehavior isn't the same as taking the blame. The blame, if there is any to go around, belongs to the child. Taking your proper responsibility simply means doing something that makes the child a bit less foolish than he was before.

You can begin taking this responsibility, dear parent, by never, ever denying that your child is capable of foolish mistakes. When someone informs you of a foolish mistake your child made, just say, "Thanks! I'll take care of it, believe me!" and go do your job.

In short, don't be as foolish as your child. One fool is enough.

Epilogue

During a talk I was making to high school seniors in Carroll, Iowa, a young woman raised her hand and asked if I felt teens should always be punished when they make mistakes. In fact, I don't necessarily think mistakes made during the teen years—or any other time of childhood for that matter—require punishment. Unfortunately, there are too many parents out there who think discipline and punishment are the same. Taken literally, discipline is the process of creating a disciple—one who will voluntarily (the operative word) follow your lead. This requires, as I've talked about earlier, securing your child's attention.

One natural consequence of having secured your child's attention is that your child will respect your wisdom and seek your guidance. This all but eliminates communication problems. Yet another natural consequence of having secured your child's attention is that your child will place great value on your approval. Your child will want to behave in ways that are pleasing to you (honor you!), do as well as possible in school, and accept ever-increasing amounts of responsibility for his/her life.

There is a distinct difference between a child making a mistake (fact: all children make mistakes) and a child *choosing* to misbehave when he knows better. A child who is paying attention to his parents and who values their approval will realize when he's made a mistake (be penitent) and seek to correct it (atone). If the child isn't aware of the mistake, pointing it out and making it clear that repeat performances will not be looked upon favorably will usually suffice.

Too often, parents punish when correction could, and should, have been accomplished with far less drama—a look, a word, a brief expression of disappointment. There are times, for sure, in the rearing of every child when drama is necessary in order to create a permanent memory in the child's mind, but if you lay the cornerstones properly, those times will not predominate.

CHAPTER SEVEN

The Resourceful Child:
A "Can-Do" Kid

T he glut of parenting manuals that currently floods the marketplace has created the impression that child rearing is a difficult, highly complex endeavor requiring great intellectual effort and personal sacrifice; so much so that even the most hearty and well prepared will find it emotionally and physically taxing.

Taken in by this malarkey, today's parents run themselves ragged in the service of children and then, at their Saturday night get-togethers, vie with one another for the Who's Had the Most Hectic Week with the Kids? Award.

Complaints about how difficult it is to raise children are unique to this generation of parents, who wear their moaning and groaning like a badge of honor. Implicit in all this griping is the idea that unless raising children isn't wearing you out, you must not be working hard enough at it. This is soap opera, pure and simple, starring hard-working parent in constant search of self-esteem for her child as her own slides steadily downhill from self-neglect.

In the real world, child rearing is simple; it takes more common sense than intellect, and its success is more a matter of self-confidence than sacrifice, of parents who are sufficiently self-respecting, as opposed to parents who spend all their time "self-esteeming" their tyrannical little darlings. None other than Dr. Spock said the very same thing in the 1946 edition of *The Pocket Book of Baby and Child Care:* "The desire to get along with other people happily and considerately develops within as part of the unfolding of [the child's] nature, provided he grows up with *loving, self-respecting parents*" (p. 20, emphasis added).

Today, as in Spock's day, child rearing doesn't have to be, and should not be, tremendously time-consuming and emotionally expensive. It is a practical process that can tolerate lots of error and still turn out well. Children are resilient, not fragile. They are not—I repeat, *not*—little Humpty-Dumptys perched precariously on the wall of life, needing parents circling under them with safety nets lest they lose their balance and take the One Great Final Fall.

Child rearing, as Grandma understood (but not intellectually, mind you) all too well, has three fundamental elements: function, obligation, and purpose.

The Function: A Matter of Distinction

The primary function of being a parent is that of distinguishing between what children truly need and what they simply want. This is akin to separating wheat from chaff, the necessary from the unnecessary. In this regard, it is interesting to note that the Hebrew word for "rod" as used in Proverbs 13:24 ("He who spares his rod,/ hates his son,/ but he who loves him, disciplines him diligently") is also used in Isaiah 28:27 to suggest a relatively flimsy instrument used to thresh caraway, thus separating the useful part of the grain from that part which is of no use, while insuring—now, pay attention, folks—*that the useful part will not be damaged in the process.*

Children cannot "thresh" themselves. On their own, they cannot make the distinction between need and want. To a child, a state of need and a state of want feel exactly the same. In fact, children often express *want* more urgently than they express *need*. Take, for example, the child who acts as if obtaining the latest video-game cartridge is a matter of life and death, but must be constantly reminded to drink sufficient water on a scorchingly hot day. Because need and want are virtually synonymous—and therefore indistinguishable—to children, adults must make this vital distinction for them. Adults—parents primarily—must "draw the line" between need and want in every single area of a child's life.

In so doing, parents must understand that children want ten times more attention, toys, help with homework and other tasks, freedom, and so on than they need. About the only things today's child needs more of than he or she wants are chores and consequences. So, parents must first draw the line and draw it boldly.

The Obligation: Thresh (Not Thrash) Well

The foremost obligation of parenthood is that of giving children *all* they truly need along with a *small* amount of what they want. In other words, parents should take great care with the wheat while being less concerned with the chaff.

I have often observed that today's parents seem to have no appreciation for the point of diminishing returns. They do not understand that simply because a child may indeed need a certain something, more of the same is not necessarily better. Children need food, for example, but it is not true that the more food children consume, the better off they are. In fact, too much food—as is the case with too much of any good thing—is harmful. Likewise, children need a certain amount of one-on-one attention from their parents, but too much parental attention prevents children from learning how to solve problems on their own, tolerate frustration, persevere in the face of adversity, and—in general terms—stand on their own two feet.

Today's parents need to understand not only the universality of the principle of diminishing returns, but also that where a child's wants are concerned, the point of diminishing returns *is always and in every area of the child's life* quickly reached. Beyond that point, continuing to give to the child always does more harm than good. In fact, when parents pass the point of diminishing returns, they always, in every case, do so at the expense of the child's needs. Their largesse, therefore, is a paradoxical form of neglect.

The fulfillment of this obligation gives a child a gift he can obtain in no other way, that being the gift of opportunity to figure certain things out for himself—how he's going to organize his time, occupy himself, solve academic and social problems, and so on. In the process of figuring things out for himself, the child learns to persevere and be resourceful, the two keys to success in any endeavor. When parents give excessively to a child, in whatever area, he not only doesn't have to figure anything out for himself, but is eventually rendered incapable of doing so. His parents, bless their big hearts, are figuring too much out for him.

That today's children are not learning the secrets of success is readily apparent. Thirty-seven years ago, the typical five-year-old (myself included) had perhaps five toys. That was all he *needed*. As a result of not having parents who overindulged his wants, he learned to do a lot with a little (resourcefulness). When the child of yesteryear went to school, his parents informed him that his homework was, indeed, *his* homework, not theirs. So, when he came to them for help, they might have said (as did my parents, more often than not), "You can do that on your own." As a result of parents who practiced true conservatism in every area of his life, the child learned that success was often less a matter of ability than trying and trying again and again (perseverance).

Today's child, by contrast, has consumed hundreds of toys by age five. Yet his parents will say that he frequently complains of being bored. Of course he does! He has not learned how to play independently, how to occupy his own time, how to do a lot with a little. Today's child is likely to believe play comes from Toys "R" Us. Yesterday's child understood—although he could not have articulated the understanding—that play came from right up here (I'm pointing to my head, folks). More often than not, today's child doesn't have to seek his parents out for help with homework. One of them (his mother, in all likelihood) is sitting right there at the kitchen table with him, pushing and prodding the homework to completion. This child gets good grades, but isn't learning to accept responsibility for himself, take initiative when it comes to life's little obstacles, set priorities and manage his time properly, or use trial and error when it comes to solving problems. His helpful parent is making sure he makes no errors; therefore, he has nothing to learn from.

In the process of having unwittingly abused their trust, this child's parents—unfortunately typical of today's parents—have deprived him of one invaluable opportunity after another to learn "the hard way," which is to say, the most valuable learning of all. Then they scratch their heads in wonder at how a child blessed with such generous and caring parents can be so ungrateful, so often at a loss as to what to do with himself, so whiny, so dependent.

Unbeknownst to them, their "generosity" and "caring" is the reason for all of the above. These are parents who, like many of their peers in this generation, have never drawn the line separating their child's needs from his wants. Having never drawn the line, they didn't know when they were crossing where it should have been drawn. Having crossed it, they have turned their child's world upside down by giving him too much of what he wants and not nearly enough of what he truly needs.

"But I can afford to give my child a lot," a parent recently rejoined. "And besides, like my parents wanted for me, I want my child to have more than I did as a child."

In the first place, being able to afford something is no excuse. In the second, what previous generations of parents wanted to give their children was not more *things* than they themselves had enjoyed as children, but more *opportunity*. They understood, furthermore, that you cannot open the door of opportunity for someone; you can only prepare them with the skills they will need to open it for themselves.

My parents, to cite a representative example, could have afforded a lot of the things they refused to buy. An illustrative story: My bicycle fell apart one day when I was perhaps ten years old (circa 1957). After coming home from work, my stepfather took a look at the heap that was once my bike and promised a trip to the bike shop the next day. The following afternoon, after all the chores had been done, to the bike shop we went. I immediately went over to the new ones, dreaming dreams of a new Western Flyer or Schwinn. I picked out the one I wanted and told my stepdad, who replied, "Well, that's very nice, but you're not getting a new bike."

"Why not?" I asked, dismayed.

Taking me by the hand, he said, "Come with me. I want to show you something." We walked out of the store and into the parking lot where we stopped in front of his car.

"What year car is this?" he asked.

I immediately "got" his point. "A 1951 Plymouth," I answered, my voice dropping to a dejected whisper.

He didn't say a word. We walked back into the store where he bought me a used bike, albeit a good one. My stepfather, you see, wanted to give me something far more valuable and enduring than a new bike; he wanted to help me understand that money doesn't grow on trees, that the most valuable things in life can't be bought, that you can't always get what you want, that new doesn't necessarily mean better. Indeed, my stepdad wanted me to have more than he had had as a child; but more in the form of *opportunity,* not things. When golden opportunity came knocking at my door, he wanted me to be able to open it and respond. And he knew I wouldn't be able to open the door and keep it open if I thought money grew on trees, wishes came true, etc. He drove a used car, so I was going to ride a used bike. He could have afforded a new bike. In fact, he could have probably afforded a new car. That wasn't the point. *The point: The more parents do for a child, the less the child is ultimately capable of doing for himself.* And my parents were not unique to their generation. I'll just bet that most people my age can remember similar incidents from their own childhoods.

Conservative parenting not only applies to things, but attention as well. If, for instance, you give a child all the attention he needs, but only a little bit of what he simply wants, he has to learn to do without constant "attention fixes." In the process, he begins learning the rudiments of self-sufficiency. Slowly but surely, he takes greater and greater control of his life, which brings us to the third of the three pieces of the "puzzle" of child rearing, its purpose.

The Purpose: Send Them Forth (and Rejoice!)

The ultimate purpose of rearing a child is to help the child out of your life and into a life of his or her own. You read that right, but you better read it again, slowly, or you may make the same mistake a fellow in Lincoln, Nebraska, made several years ago.

After talking to several hundred parents in that Midwestern city, I was approached by a man who said, "I liked that one about getting the child out of your life and into a life of his own."

"I didn't say that," I told him.

"You sure did!" he insisted.

"Nope. I said the ultimate purpose of rearing children is to *help* them out of our lives, not *get* them out."

"What's the difference?" he asked.

"The difference is everything," I answered. "It is every child's mission to get out of his parents' lives and into a life of his own. This mission begins asserting itself in the first year of life. After all, when a child first begins to crawl, he crawls *away from,* not toward, his parents. Later, when he learns to walk, then run, he runs *away from,* not toward, his parents. And so it goes. I'm simply saying it's our job to support this mission, to affirm its legitimacy and empower the child's ability to carry it out."

The "mission" is called emancipation, and emancipation is a process, not an event that spontaneously occurs in the late teens or early twenties. It's a parent's job to get behind the process and gently urge it along. Too many of today's parents, by contrast, are out in front of their children, sweeping the path clear of obstacle and adversity, frustration and failure. Bless their big hearts, they're only trying to make childhood a happy time for their kids.

Granted, parenthood requires that we run a bit of interference. You cannot expect children to solve every problem on their own. Parents must be ready to buffer, deflect, and even completely eliminate certain kinds of problems, especially life-threatening ones. But the facts are these:

❑ You cannot run constant interference for a child and then expect that as an adult, he will be able to successfully anticipate and deal with life's problems. (And isn't life full of them?)

❑ You cannot pursue happiness for a child for the entirety of his childhood and then expect that he will be able to successfully pursue it on his own as an adult. Child rearing may not be hard, but it does require a certain amount of hardheadedness.

Summing it all up: The opportunity to figure things out, which accrues courtesy of parents who meet all of a child's needs and deny most of his wants, endows a child with incredible self-sufficiency, which is the true essence of self-esteem, which energizes the ability to succeed where others will fail for lack of resourcefulness and purpose. It can't be any simpler.

Yes, I know, you want to get more specific, and I intend to. For starters, how about . . .

Turn Off the Television

Sit off to the side and watch your child watch television. Notice the slack jaw, the slightly dazed, mesmerized look, and ask yourself, "What's my child doing?" The answer: Nothing. Period.

Since 1979, in my books, talks, newspaper columns, and magazine articles, I've been saying we judge the book by the cover when it comes to kids and television. The programs a child watches, I've said, have less effect on development than the very process of watching. All programs, including the much-heralded *Sesame Street,* are watched the same passive way. The programs change every thirty to sixty minutes, the process remains the same.

Television watching is a deprivational experience for the formative-years child (birth through six, approximately). A preschool child who watches but twenty hours of television a week, which is well below the national average, will have spent more than four thousand hours staring at television by the time he enters first grade. Think of it! Four thousand hours! To put that in perspective, it's more time than the child has spent doing anything other than sleeping. If the child continues consuming television at this pace, then by the time he graduates high school, he will have spent more time in front of a television set than in a classroom.

Humans are nervous systems supported by various organs and systems. The brain—the human biocomputer—arrives in the world preprogrammed. During the first seven years of life, the programming continues as the child interacts with his environment. The richer the child's experiences during that time, the more the child's curiosity and imagination are fed, the better the resulting neural program, and the more competent the child.

If a young child spends thousands of hours staring at a fixed and flickering visual field, is it not reasonable to postulate that this experience will interfere with the establishment of key neural skills, including a long attention span and certain reasoning abilities? Might the fact that American children spend more time—lots more!—watching television than children in other countries go a long way toward explaining why other countries don't report significant problems with learning disabilities and attention deficit disorder and can't, furthermore, quite understand why there's such a brouhaha in the United States concerning these maladies?

Parents have, for the most part, ignored the alarm I've been sounding. Those with children who are learning disabled or have attention deficit disorder have been outraged. For obvious reasons, they prefer a genetic "it couldn't be helped" explanation over one that implies they *could* have done something about their children's problems. By and large, the professional community has dismissed my arguments, saying, "There's no evidence to support your theory."

In fact, there is. For one thing, there's anecdotal evidence: Veteran teachers consistently tell me that the increase in reading problems, learning disabilities, and attention-span difficulties has coincided with an increase in the number of hours children spend watching television. For another, there's cross-cultural evidence: In England and Europe, where children don't typically watch significant amounts of television, reading problems (that can't be attributed to low IQ), learning disabilities, and attention deficit disorder are almost unheard of. I recently heard an "expert" on attention deficit disorder attribute that discrepancy to different standards. She proposed that if foreign countries used the same diagnostic criteria, the numbers would be equivalent. Wrong. Two acquaintances of mine, both educational psychologists, conducted on-site studies of European schools for two years in the 1980s. Upon their return, they told me they could find, *by U.S. standards,* negligible evidence of reading problems, etc.

Finally, there's the scientific evidence: In 1991, psychologist Jane Healy compiled years of research she had done concerning the intellectual development of American children into a book entitled *Endangered Minds: Why Our Children Don't Think.* She proposed that television's electronic environment is actually altering the brains of children, both functionally (how the brain works) and structurally (its physical characteristics). Healy sees a connection between the increase in reading problems, learning disabilities, and attentional problems and the outrageous amount of time American kids spend splotched in front of television sets, especially during their preschool years. Like myself, Healy also emphasizes process over program. Television watching is inhibiting the development of language and listening skills, imagination, and various problem-solving processes essential to learning to read, she says.

The solution: Pull the plug. Ideally, preschool children should not watch any television at all. That's right. None. If that seems too radical for your blood, then I'll concede that thirty minutes a day probably will do no real harm, but the only program I can possibly recommend for preschoolers (and the recommendation is marginal) is *Mr. Rogers' Neighborhood.* By using only one camera that follows him around, Rogers maintains a low-key, easygoing pace that may actually strengthen attention span. It certainly won't hurt it.

"But what about *Sesame Street,* John," people ask. "I mean, my child watched it and learned to read!"

So? I learned to read without ever watching *Sesame Street.* So did you, if you were born before 1962. Watching *Sesame Street* is not necessary to learning to read. In fact, at least one independent study found that children who watched *Sesame Street* did less well in school than children who didn't. *Sesame Street* is not educational; it's antieducational. Children who watch it regularly are likely to come to school thinking education is (1) entertaining, and (2) something someone gives you. Indeed, teachers tell me that today's kids come to school expecting to be entertained; then they complain of "boredom" when teachers fail at making three-ring circuses of their classrooms.

For the elementary-age child, the only way to keep television at a minimum is to preselect a few programs and let the child watch them, and only them. At all cost, parents should disallow the "let's see what's on television" method. Random watching inevitably leads to overwatching. Older children who are reading, and reading well, can benefit from watching the occasional program that stimulates the desire to head for the library and learn more. Such programs include documentaries and specials on culture and science. Regardless of age or the programs being watched, no child should spend more than five hours a week in front of television.

"But, John," a parent somewhere cries, "television keeps my kids busy and allows me to get my work done!"

In the first place, television doesn't keep children "busy." It keeps them electronically drugged. (Since there is evidence that television watching begins, at some point, to resemble a bona fide addiction, I use the term *drugged* literally, not figuratively.) Parents who use television as a baby-sitter are their own worst enemies. The more a child watches television, the more the child becomes dependent on television as a source of occupation. He's not learning how to keep himself creatively occupied. When the television's not holding his "attention," he's likely to be whining at or clamoring for attention from his parents. Their solution to his oppressive demands: Turn on the television. The only way to break this vicious cycle is to shut the television off and keep it off. Eventually, free of distraction, the child's imagination, creativity, and resourcefulness will come out of hiding. I know this because I saw it happen with my own children. When Eric and Amy were nine and six, respectively, Willie and I moved the television to our bedroom. Several months later, realizing that the children were "stealing" television time every time our backs were turned (addictive behavior, by the way), we got rid of it altogether. The kids went through withdrawal for maybe four weeks: They acted tense and stressed much of the time, obsessed about watching television, and exhibited other behaviors indicative of detoxification. Finally, they got over "the hump" and began acting like normal children again. Here, I use the term *normal* to refer to what America's children once acted like, before television was introduced into their lives: playful, creative, spontaneous, independent little people who took responsibility for keeping themselves occupied. They began reading on their own, even asking to go to the library. Their grades improved, especially Eric's. They developed hobbies. Their manners improved. No longer constantly vying over which television program they were going to watch next, their relationship improved. Four weeks of upheaval was a price well worth paying, believe me.

And the story of Eric's and Amy's post-television rehabilitation is not, by any means, an isolated one. Because of my outspoken views on the subject, I am a lightning rod for stories concerning children and television. Time and time again, parents across the country have written, called, and approached me with tales of how marriages, families, and children have been "healed" by the simple act of banishing television from the house.

"But, John," I'm often asked, "won't a child who never watches television be at a social disadvantage among his or her peers?"

This is a myth, pure and simple. If there are social disadvantages, I've never heard parents of television-free children mention them, and Eric and Amy didn't experience any. Not being able to enter actively into conversations about what took place on the most recent episode of *Beverly Hills 90210* isn't going to put a kid on the "outs" with his peers. Children don't choose friends based on what television programs they watch, believe me.

"But, John," parents challenge, "won't a child who can't watch television at home just go watch it at a friend's house?"

No doubt about it. So what? You've still got a child who was watching twenty to thirty hours a week who's now watching maybe five. After we got rid of our television set, for example, Eric and Amy continued to watch occasional programs at other children's houses. We didn't allow them to go over to other kid's houses for the express purpose of watching television, but if some television was consumed in the course of a visit, so be it. The addiction was still destroyed.

In short, parents have absolutely no excuse when it comes to letting children consume more than five hours of television a week. None! It is naive to think that television watching is okay as long as the programs being watched pass some sort of moral muster. It is foolish to think that the rise in all manner of academic problems following the introduction of television into the lives of American children is nothing but coincidence.

So, dear reader, now that the choice is clear, what are *you* going to do?

. . . And Take a Sledgehammer to the Video-Game Console

I began speaking out against video games shortly after they were put on the market. After watching a number of kids play them, and seeing a common set of behaviors that didn't look healthy to me, I became as outspoken against letting children play them as I was/am concerning letting children watch much television.

Again, I'm in the minority. A significant number of psychologists around the nation have been quoted as saying video games are wonderful for children. That doesn't bother me in the least. After all, when it comes to child rearing, I don't agree with the majority of my colleagues about much of anything. Consistently, they seem beguiled by anything new, whether ideas or technologies. The March 3, 1990, issue of *TV Guide,* for example, featured an article on video games that quoted Patricia Marks Greenfield, professor of psychology at UCLA and author of *Mind and Media: The Effects of Television, Video Games, and Computers* as saying: "Video games develop a whole bunch of intellectual abilities, like problem solving and visual-spatial skills."

Greenfield also pooh-poohed the notion that children can become addicted to video games (a contention of mine). Commenting on the observation that some children seem to become obsessed with them, Greenfield said, "Of course kids are going to want to play until they've mastered a game, but I would call that mastery motivation rather than addiction."

Professor Greenfield needs to come down from her ivory tower and talk to people like the Kellys of Charlotte, North Carolina. After determining that they would never purchase a video game unit for their five-year-old son, Kenny, they finally relented and bought him a popular video-game system. Here's what they had to say about their decision a scant six months later: "We had two rules. Kenny was to share with his sister and they could play for forty minutes a day. After just a few days, we began seeing changes in Kenny's behavior. He became irritable and bossy. He would get very upset—crying, stomping his feet—when he couldn't get to the next level in [his favorite game]. He constantly tried to sneak additional time, and there were several nights when we awakened at three o'clock in the morning to find him playing.

"Kenny also began to balk at going to school. When we dropped him off, he would start crying and screaming. On several occasions, his teachers had to help pry him out of the car. He also started fighting with his classmates and sassing his teachers. He became sassy and belligerent with us and our baby-sitter.

"We couldn't figure out what was the matter, so we removed the video-game unit from the house and told Kenny it was broken. Within a few days, the real Kenny was back. No more tantrums, no more belligerent, sassy behavior, and he started happily going to school. Needless to say, the unit will never be 'fixed,' and we have happily gone back to being the only house in the neighborhood without one."

The Kellys' experience could be dismissed if it were an isolated one, but it isn't. Over the past eight years, more than five hundred (no exaggeration) parents have written me concerning similar video-game-related horror stories. These tales don't sound like descriptions of "mastery motivation" to me. They sound like tales of debilitating addiction. I've been around enough addicts and enough highly motivated people to know the difference.

Video games, I'm convinced, aren't games at all, not when it comes to children. They provoke high levels of stress and are indeed addictive in the sense that many children become obsessed with constantly increasing their scores (or "skill levels" as they are deceptively termed). Compared to the harm they are obviously capable of causing (unless these hundreds of parents are just making these stories up), the contention that video games improve certain problem-solving and visual/spatial skills rates a big "so what?" Playing with Lego blocks or building a model will do the same thing, and without risk.

. . . And Then, Stop Buying Toys

"I'm bored!" may be how the current generation of American kids is best remembered by parents who keep trying to find the one toy, the one interest, that will forever banish the "Nothin'-To-Do Blues." Meanwhile, most adults wonder how children with so many amusements can possibly think they have so little to do.

Over the past few years, I've conducted three informal polls that shed light on this contemporary enigma. In the first poll, I asked parents from foreign countries representing every populated continent (and subcontinent) on the planet, "Do children in your country frequently complain of being bored, of having nothing to do?" In every instance, the answer has been "no," accompanied by incredulity at the notion that such a complaint is even possible from a child. Frequent feelings of boredom, I've discovered, have nothing to do with being a child, but everything to do with being an *American* child.

In the second poll, I asked people who, like my parents, reared their children in the '40s and '50s, "Did we, as children, frequently complain of being bored, of having nothing to do?" The generic answer: "Oh, you children may have complained of that some, but certainly not often. Come to think of it, on those rare occasions when one of you had the audacity to complain of having nothing to do, we simply told you that if you couldn't find something to do, we'd find something for you." That nipped that particular complaint in the bud, now didn't it? Feeling bored, therefore, is only epidemic within the most recent generation of American children. Consider the implications of this as we make the transition to a global economy, one in which the rewards will accrue to those players who are the most resourceful.

In the third poll, I asked folks around my age (forty-seven) how many toys they remembered having when they were five years old. Their answers ranged from zero, as in "What toys Mom and Dad didn't make for us, we made ourselves from whatever odds and ends were lying around" to ten. Very few people reported having more than ten. The average number reported was five, which is my own remembrance. I had, at that age, a set of Lincoln Logs, a set of Tinker Toys, a set of lead cavalry and foot soldiers (this was before adults realized children were being poisoned by their toys), a "Hopalong Cassidy" six-shooter and black-and-white leather holster with fringe and a star on the side, and an electric train set that consisted simply of train, tracks, and transformer. Supplementing those meager possessions were things I rescued from the garbage, as well as things I collected from the yard. I used a shoe box for a tunnel, a Quaker Oats box for a water tower, and pinecones for pine trees. With a few basic toys and a reasonable amount of imagination, I was able to occupy myself for hours on end.

By contrast, today's typical American five-year-old has consumed close to 250 toys (that's a verified average!). To put this into perspective, consider that by his or her fifth birthday, a child has lived 260 weeks. For all intents and purposes, that's a toy a week!

Is today's "I've got nothin' to do!" kid trying to tell us something? You bet, and it's high time we all listened up. If this child could explain his boredom in adult terms, here's what parents would hear: "I know, Mom and Dad, that you bought me all this stuff to keep me happy, and in a sense you succeeded. Every time you bought me a toy, I was happy, for a while. But in the course of buying me all these toys, you convinced me, without ever intending to do so, that my ability to occupy and entertain myself is in direct proportion to the number of toys I can claim as my own.

"You should have been trying to convince me that my ability to occupy myself has nothing to do with the number of things I have out there [pointing around], but is simply a matter of how much I have up here [pointing to his head]. Mom and Dad, with the best of intentions, you caused me to believe in a trip to the toy store when you should have been teaching me to believe in *me*. Now, Mom and Dad, having explained all that, I have one question, and it may be the most important one I ever ask you: 'When are you going to cut it out?'"

Good question, don't you think? One that American parents (and grandparents!) had better lose no time in answering. It's one Willie and I confronted when our children were nine and six years old. Between them, Eric and Amy had at least three hundred toys. Despite this cornucopia of playthings, they constantly complained of being bored. We finally realized that no amount of toys was going to stop their whining; that, in fact, they were whining, in part, because this avalanche of good-intentioned giving had smothered their imaginations. They had both lost touch with what I call the "magical make-do of childhood"—the ability to improvise, create, do a lot with a little. We realized that Eric and Amy would never learn to do a lot with a little if we gave them a lot.

We sat them down and told them that since we rarely saw them play with their toys, and since there were children in the United States who had no toys, we had decided they were going to give most of their toys to charity. We told them they'd each be allowed to keep ten toys (five of Eric's "Matchbox" cars counted as one toy, as did—in the name of good family values—Barbie *and* Ken). Of the rest, those that were in good repair were going to an appropriately good cause. We were bowled over by their reaction: They actually became enthusiastic over the idea of making a contribution to the lives of children less fortunate than themselves. In no time at all, they had separated the wheat from the chaff and were busy making repairs to and boxing up their donations.

We encouraged them to keep toys that were high in "play value," meaning those that were not only durable, but could be utilized in a variety of creative ways, as opposed to being one thing and one thing only (e.g., a truck). Into this category fell toys similar to those Willie and I had played with as children. Eric kept his set of Lincoln Logs. Amy kept her Barbie and Ken, but donated her Barbie Dream House. (I have long felt, by the way, that nearly every toy invented since 1955 has simply been an attempt to reinvent an already-existing wheel.) Now get this: Willie and I *never* again bought either child what would be considered a toy. Never!

Eric and Amy quickly lost their interest in toys altogether. They developed hobbies, they became generally more focused, they read more, their grades improved, and so on. Some of this, I'm sure, wouldn't have happened without also banishing television from our household (which we did around this same time), but the one-two combination of no television and a handful of toys turned the tide in Eric's and Amy's lives. Sounds good, eh? Then do it! And help your children discover, as did Eric and Amy, that play doesn't come from Toys "R" Us. It comes from right up here. (I'm pointing to my head, folks.)

. . . And Then, Help Them Develop Hobbies

If you've noticed that today's kids don't spend as much time working on hobbies as you did when you were a child, you're right. In the last thirty years, the number of hours per week the average American child spends watching television has grown from five to twenty-five. Meanwhile, hobbies have become an endangered activity.

To make this point, I often ask my audiences, "How many of you, as children, spent significant time working on a hobby of one sort or another?" Almost everyone raises a hand. I then say, "Keep your hand in the air if at least one of your children has a hobby, meaning a self-directed, creative, and/or educational activity that occupies the child's time on a regular basis." (That definition serves to distinguish hobbies from adult-driven, after-school activities.) Most of the hands go down.

Thirty-five years ago, nearly every kid in my suburban-Chicago neighborhood had a hobby. Collecting and trading baseball cards was a popular pastime, as were coin and rock collections. One of my buddies was into building radios (he's now an electrical engineer), another built and raced go-carts (he's now a mechanic for an auto racing team). At various times, I collected rocks, newspapers from around the country, and pop records. I also played mad scientist with my chemistry and biology sets. All of us took immense pride in our hobbies and loved to show them off. Collecting newspapers from around the country distinguished me from the kid next door who collected postcards from around the world. As such, hobbies contributed not only to our self-respect, but also to our respect for one another.

Looking back on those glory days, I realize that hobbies benefit children in a number of important ways. As expressions of personal accomplishment, they help build feelings of personal competence. Hobbies are an educational medium, as well. A child who becomes interested in rocketry learns about propulsion and aerodynamics. Stamp collections contain mini-lessons in history and geography. Working on hobbies, children learn to set goals, make complex decisions, and solve all sorts of practical problems. Hobbies exercise imagination and creativity in addition to helping children focus their interests and talents. The list of benefits is virtually endless. In short, hobbies are catalysts for growth along almost every conceivable dimension.

The reasons why so few of today's kids have hobbies are obvious, and I've already talked about most of them:

❑ They watch entirely too much television.

❑ They have entirely too many toys.

❑ They are involved in entirely too many adult-driven after-school activities.

Continuing the story of Eric and Amy, when they were nine and six years old, a revolution occurred in their lives: We removed the television from the home, assigned each of them a daily routine of chores, stopped buying toys and had them give most of the toys they'd acquired to charity, and restricted after-school activities to no more than one at a time. All this happened, by the way, within a two-month period! After the kids recovered from the shock and adjusted to our new old-fashioned lifestyle, each developed a hobby, and their hobbies continue to enrich their lives today.

To help your child develop and sustain a hobby, I suggest you:

❑ *Set a good example.* Scott Harris, a buyer for John's Toy and Hobby Shop in Gastonia, North Carolina, finds that the parents of children who have hobbies almost always have hobbies themselves. Those parents provide not only the encouragement and support necessary to get their children interested in hobbies, but the role model as well.

❑ *Provide adequate space.* Your child will need a work area for hobby projects. It can be a special room, a corner of the basement, or part of the garage. When Eric became interested in model-building, we allowed him to convert one end of his walk-in closet into project space. A child should be able to walk away from his or her hobby, leaving unfinished work intact, and come back to it later. The area should definitely allow for paint spills, scratches, and other accidents.

❑ *Provide necessary guidance.* Nothing will kill a child's enthusiasm for a hobby more effectively than lots of frustration during the learning stage. Help your child off to a smooth start by demonstrating how to follow a set of directions and use hobby materials.

Last, but not least, understand that turning on a hobby all but requires turning *off* the television. As Scott Harris told me, "Children with hobbies tend to be those whose parents restrict, if not altogether disallow, television watching." You can't be engaged in constructive activity and watch television at the same time. It's as simple as that.

PART THREE

General Questions

On Values and Manners

Q: I don't have children, but I spend a lot of time with my nieces and nephews and the children of friends. Am I just getting old, or are today's children, by and large, a lot more sophisticated and worldly-wise than children of, say, forty years ago?

A: Yes, today's child is clearly more "sophisticated" than was the typical child of forty years past. In historical terms, however, the child of the 1950s is the exception to the rule. Childhood was not generally recognized as having distinct status until well into the nineteenth century. Prior to that time, children were often re-garded—especially within the "working" classes—as small adults who, because of original sin, were prone to misbehavior. The be-lated recognition that children were fundamentally different from adults brought about public education, child labor laws, child abuse reform, and the like. According to Professor Neil Postman, author of *The Disappearance of Childhood* (1982), the spread of literacy kindled this gradual change in the general perception of children. Quite simply, up to a certain age, children could not read. Further-more, until they themselves became adults, they could not under-stand most of what adults read. Differences in literacy and compre-hension levels not only created the state of childhood, but provided for its innocence as well.

Television, says Postman, has set that achievement into reverse. One need not *learn* to watch television, and because its content is presented visually, even a preschool child is able to comprehend—albeit at a naive level—adult situations. For example, whereas a young child reading a passage in an adult novel might not under-stand that two people are making love, what's going on becomes obvious to a child when that same scene is played out on a television screen. In this manner (and the issue does not begin and end with sexual matters), the innocence of children is no longer being sheltered. Exposed to the very things our grandparents believed should be hidden from them, children are, indeed, becoming more "sophisticated."

I compare this situation to that of a plant that's been hothoused and, as a result, has well-developed foliage but an inadequate root system. Likewise, the "hot-housed" child appears, on the surface, to be mature, knowledgeable, even charmingly wise beyond his years. Outward appearances, however, conceal a value system that is still underdeveloped. Values are prerequisite to being able to process knowledge effectively. Put another way, knowledge without values is a dangerous thing. To site but one concrete example: It is one thing to know how to participate in sexual intercourse; it is quite another to understand that to do so is wrong unless certain conditions are met. By watching television, today's child is able to learn how to engage in sex prior to developing a value system that will properly govern sexual behavior. And let us not forget that children are not only curious, but also tend to act out their understandings of adult life and adult relationships. It takes most of childhood for a solid set of values to develop. It takes watching one television program for a child to become "educated" concerning all manner of adult behaviors, receive the impression that the ends often justify the means, or learn that marriage is arbitrary to the social contract. Ironically, and tragically, the golden "Age of Innocence" in childhood lasted slightly more than half a century before it was undone by "progress." The good news is that the degree to which this "progress" touches a given child is still up to the child's parents.

Q: This may seem like a dumb question, but what is a moral value?

$\mathcal{A}$: Actually, I think it's an excellent question. A moral value is a learned internal standard against which we measure the rightness or wrongness of behavior, our own or someone else's. The relationship between a person's moral values and his social behavior is a two-way street. Not only does the framework of our value system influence our behavior, but our behavior and its consequences also have a modifying effect on our moral values. Moral values are learned, and are not the same from culture to culture, but it is my belief, rooted in my Christianity, that morals are not relative matters. Rather, they are absolute, timeless standards of right and wrong. I'm being so bold as to say, in other words, that the traditional Judeo-Christian ethic is the one and only one valid set of moral values.

Q: How do children learn their moral values?

A: Initially, at least, children learn moral values by watching and listening to their parents. Later, as the child becomes more involved with peers, the values he has learned from his parents become increasingly strained by the temptations he's exposed to, particularly during early adolescence. Whether those values stand the test of peer group pressure depends on how effectively the parents communicate them, model them, and reinforce them.

Q: How can parents make sure the moral values their children are learning are the ones they intend for them to learn?

A: By providing adequate supervision. If parents are going to provide effective guidance to their children they must take time to know what their children are doing, both at school and in the community, and who they are associating with. Parents who successfully guide their children into associations and activities that are desirable rather than undesirable maintain open lines of communication with their children. In turn, their children continue to listen to them and respect their opinions.

Q: What can parents do, in the case of older children in particular, if the values a child is learning through contact with peers are not the values the parents want him to learn?

A: Unfortunately, there is no cut-and-dried formula for handling problems of this sort. Facing facts, there isn't always going to be a perfect match between what parents have taught a child and what his peers expect of him. For instance, most parents teach their children honesty is important. Yet a child may find himself in a situation where, in order to remain in good standing with his peers, he is expected to lie to his parents. There isn't a teenager who hasn't been faced with conflicts like that, and there are times when they can be expected to go with the peer group. The occasional deviation isn't necessarily cause for alarm, but when a child is flagrantly and repeatedly rebelling against parental values, that is. By and large, that sort of pattern is usually an indication of communication problems at home, in which case family counseling would be advisable.

Q: What is the biggest obstacle parents face in communicating moral values to their children?

A: Themselves. The first problem is the parent who doesn't practice what he preaches. The parent who says for instance, "Always tell the truth," but then turns around and doesn't keep his promises to the child; the parent who says, "Don't use drugs," but keeps a cabinet full of tranquilizers and sleeping pills; the parent who says, "It's wrong to cheat," and then brags to his friends, in front of his children, about how he falsified his income tax form. The second problem is parents who may preach too much. In most cases, when a child makes a moral error, it is sufficient for parents to say a few words of explanation and encouragement and be done with it. A few words have a better chance of sinking in than a lot.

Q: How important is it for children to learn good manners?

A: A psychiatrist I know says that most of the counseling he does is a direct result of parents not teaching their children manners. Motivational speaker and author Zig Ziglar says that manners involve far more than what one does at the dinner table. "It's deportment, civility, and overall conduct in life," he says. "And yes, it very definitely does speak about respect [because] you will never be rude to anyone whom you respect."

Manners and respect are inseparable. Children begin developing respect for others by first developing it for their parents. Therefore, children should be taught to behave in mannerly ways toward their parents. That means children should not be allowed to call their parents (or any adult for that matter) by their first names, interrupt adult conversations unless in crisis, or—beyond age three—throw tantrums when they don't get their way. I'll even go so far as to recommend that children be taught to respond to all adults, including their parents, with "Yes, Sir," "Yes, Ma'am," and the like. When adults speak, children should pay attention; and when adults give instructions, children should carry them out. It's as simple as that.

If today's parents taught children the same things *they* were taught as children, the world would be a better place. Unfortunately, that doesn't seem to be happening. Veteran teachers tell me today's child is, in general, much less respectful and much less mannerly than the typical child of a generation ago. The tragedy of this is that unless children learn respect for others—beginning with parents and expanding outward from there—they can never develop true respect for themselves. Respect for others is the horse that pulls the cart of self-respect. Without respect for others, one never advances beyond the stage of self-absorption. So, in the final analysis, this isn't a matter of exalting adults, but a matter of helping children feel good about themselves.

Q: What are some tips for teaching good manners?

A: First, work on one thing at a time. If you try to teach too many social skills at once, you will end up teaching none of them well. Instead, teach table manners first. When those have been learned, advance to phone manners, and so on.

Second, praise young children for their successes. When your kids display proper manners at home or in public, give them immediate positive feedback. It's more critical that you do this during the early "learning phase" of manners instruction, but even older children need to occasionally hear how proud you are of their social deportment.

Third, be tolerant of your children's lapses, but do not overlook them. Children being children, they will make mistakes. The more patient you are, the more progress they will ultimately make. Under no circumstances should you reprimand a child's social errors in public, although firm reminders may at times be in order.

Remember that children want to please adults and that it's easier to catch the proverbial fly with honey than with vinegar.

Fourth, when it's obvious that your child has forgotten a certain social ritual, give a prompt. If, for example, your child forgets to extend his or her hand upon meeting an adult, quietly ask, "What are we supposed to do when we meet someone older than ourselves?" That gives the child the opportunity to do the right thing without feeling criticized.

Last, but not least, set a good example. A "do as I say, not as I do" approach to manners simply won't work. Your children must see you setting a good example when it comes to manners. And by the way, manners is not a one-way street. If you want your children to behave in a mannerly way toward you, then you must behave in a mannerly way toward them as well (not to be confused with treating them like equals, however).

Q: Our two children, ages twelve and nine, have been allowed to call us by our first names almost all of their lives, but we're no longer comfortable with it. Is it too late to turn this around? If not, how should we go about it? The added complication is that most of our adult friends seem to prefer it. What should we do in those cases? And what should we do about children whom we've let use our first names?

A: The disrespect adults often see in today's children is due, in large part, to the fact that over the last thirty years we've blurred the distinction between adults and children, creating the impression in the minds of children that the only distinction between the big guys and the little guys is one of size. Letting children call adults by their first names is both a cause and effect of this "leveling." I have to admit I'm guilty of letting children do likewise, but I've come to the conclusion it's not a desirable practice. Lately, when a child calls me by my first name, I'll say, with mock-seriousness, "It's Mr. Rosemond to you. When you're older and wiser, you can call me John." A semihumorous tone allows the child (and the parents) to get the point without feeling put down. If the child persists in using my first name, however, I don't make it an issue. In the final analysis, this is something only the child's parents can straighten out.

And it's never too late to straighten it out. To do so with your children, the keys are proactivity and practice. Hold a family conference at which you set forth the new policy. There's no need for any long explanations. Just tell the kids that using proper titles is more respectful, and that's the way you want it. If they want to know why it was okay to do otherwise until now, simply tell them it was a mistake on your part, but one you've decided to correct. From that point on, until the new habit is established, make a point of reminding them of the new rule just before going into social situations involving other adults. Should one of your children slip and call a familiar adult by his or her first name, wait until you can take the child aside for a private reminder. Handle their slip-ups discreetly, so they aren't embarrassed by them.

Unfortunately, it's inevitable that some adults will all but insist that your children address them using first names. In some cases, you might state your preference to the adult. In others, you might decide not to make it an issue. If the adult in question is a close family friend, you might suggest that the children use "Aunt" or "Uncle" in front of the adult's first name.

What should you do about children with whom you're on a first-name basis? Again, you're going to have to play that one by ear. If the child is young or a relatively recent acquaintance, you might want to quietly tell him the form of address you'd prefer. Otherwise, you might want to just let it go, as in "win a few, lose a few." Above all else, remember, it's hard to respect a neurotic.

Hey, what am I anyway? A psychologist or Mr. Manners?

On Television

Q: You come out strongly against letting preschool children watch television and recommend not letting school-age children watch more than five hours a week. What about family sitcoms?

A: Before I answer your question, I need to make a small, albeit significant, correction. To be exact, I'm opposed to letting *preliterate* children watch any television at all. The truly literate child not only has little difficulty recognizing words and comprehending passages, but also enjoys reading and reads independently. Using these criteria, the average child is not fully literate until age eight or nine. Ideally and according to Rosemond, most children should not be allowed exposure to television until that age. The problem has less to do with the content of programs generally considered appropriate for children than with the process—the nonact of watching. All television programs, irrespective of content, are watched in the same manner. It's my contention that the process, especially when imposed during the formative (preliterate) years, is inherently deprivational and interferes with the development of competency skills.

Yes, my five-hour rule is conservative, and yes, I even have problems with most family sitcoms. The overt themes of these programs (and I'm not talking about programs like *Roseanne* or *Married, With Children,* which aren't appropriate for viewing as a family, if at all) are certainly not going to warp a child's morals. There's no sex, no violence, no sexism or racism. Underneath the innocence, however, I see a not-so-harmless consistency: First, children are given disproportionate significance in these sitcoms. Second, the manner in which adult-child relationships are portrayed is inappropriate. Children are accorded at least as much, if not more, "presence" in these programs as are adults. In and of itself, this is nothing new. After all, Timmy enjoyed second billing on *Lassie,* and Ricky Nelson was the only reason I watched *Ozzie and Harriet.* What's different is that Timmy and Ricky never talked back to their parents. They may have been stars, but they respected their elders. By contrast, sarcasm between parents and child is standard in today's "family" sitcoms. Maybe I'm losing my sense of humor along with my hair, but this bothers me. It further bothers me that every time child "scores" against parent or vice versa, everyone's encouraged to guffaw right along with the laugh track. I wonder. Does this reinforce in the minds of children the idea that the parent-child relationship is one of equals, and that to verbally outwit one's parents is the pinnacle of achievement, not to mention humor? Do these programs lend to the already-insidious impression that the world revolves around children? Or is this just art imitating life? Come to think of it, the latter is what disturbs me most of all.

On Time-Out

Q: After reading an article on discipline in a parenting magazine, I began using time-out with my six-year-old son, who was either ignoring me when I told him to do something, or arguing, or both. The author of the article said time-out was the most effective disciplinary technique with all ages of children, including teens. At first, my son did a lot of testing, but when he found out I was determined to be consistent, his behavior began to improve. Within a couple of weeks, I was only putting him in time-out once or twice a day, if that. After six weeks of steady improvement, however, his behavior took a turn for the worse. I remained consistent, but his behavior slid quickly back to square one. As I write this letter, his behavior is worse than ever, but he no longer seems to care whether he goes to time-out or not. What happened?

A: You and I must have read the same article, except I just shook my head in dismay at the fact that professionals continue to beat this drum when the weight of anecdotal evidence clearly indicates time-out (a brief, specified period of confinement in a fairly boring area) has little, if any long-term effect on the highly oppositional child.

With a child who misbehaves only occasionally, sitting in the bathroom or an out-of-the-way chair for a few minutes serves as a generally effective reminder of the rules and the parent's authority. As was the case with your son, however, the difficult, disobedient child is likely to "immunize" to time-out rather quickly. Time-out may, at first, upend such a child, resulting in temporary improvement. In short order, however, it usually becomes no big deal. The child becomes willing to pay the relatively insignificant price of a few minutes in a chair in order to continue dominating the center of attention in the family.

In and of itself, time-out is a fairly weak response to misbehavior. The more pronounced the misbehavior, the weaker it is, by comparison. Highly oppositional children require powerful (not painful, *powerful*) consequences. Nothing less will keep their attention. Professionals are often reluctant to recommend powerful consequences because they cause children distress, thus (supposedly) lowering self-esteem. Ah, but unless the child's misbehavior results in more distress for the child than for the parent, the child has no reason to change his behavior.

It's time you stopped fooling around and made a powerful statement to your child concerning his disobedience. Hang three rectangles of construction paper on a hook in the kitchen. Call them "tickets." Every time your son responds disobediently to an instruction, put him in time-out for five minutes and remove a ticket from the hook. If he disobeys outside the home, remove a ticket when you get home. When the third ticket is taken, confine him to his room for the remainder of the day (yes, even if it's nine o'clock in the morning!) and put him to bed one hour early. If he loses his last ticket within an hour of his normal bedtime, put him immediately to bed. Under those circumstances, he may come out of his room to go to the bathroom, eat meals with the family, and run errands with you. The first two tickets, by the way, are his "margin of error" without which you create a "no-win" situation, thus making things worse instead of better.

Now you're making a powerful statement! Now he'll pay attention, and not just for a few weeks, I'll venture.

Q: My five-year-old simply refuses to go into time-out after she's misbehaved. We've actually gotten into physical struggles in which I've dragged her, kicking and screaming, through the house. I succeed at getting her into her time-out place—the downstairs bathroom—at great emotional cost to us both. Then comes the battle of getting her to stay there for five minutes, which I "win" only by holding the door. This simply isn't worth it, and I'd like your advice.

A: The scenario you describe is one I hear frequently from parents of difficult children. And you are certainly correct, the "price" you pay getting your daughter to time-out and keeping her there for five minutes is not worth the benefit. In fact, since your willingness to struggle with your daughter affirms that she holds the upper hand, the benefit to date has been less than zero.

Pairing time-out—which constitutes nothing but a relatively insignificant period of confinement—with loss of privilege, will probably solve your problems. First, on a sheet of paper, identify five "target" misbehaviors. The language should be specific, as in: "refusing to do what we tell you to do" and "calling us 'stupid' or other disrespectful names." When completed, the list is posted on the refrigerator. Then, using four index cards, write "free" on one and a privilege on each of the other three, as in: "going outside," "watching television," and "regular bedtime." Punch a hole in the top of each card and hang them on a hook somewhere in the kitchen with the "free" card on top. Every time your daughter displays a "target" behavior, she goes to time-out and loses a card. The first card is "free," but every card lost thereafter results in the loss of a privilege for the remainder of the day. So, the second misbehavior of the day means time-out and loss of outside play; the third misbehavior means time-out and loss of television; the fourth "earns" her both time-out and an early bedtime.

"But John," you say, "I told you she won't go to time-out!"

Right! So, every time she misbehaves, you say, "That's one of your targets, which means you must go to time-out and lose a card. But if you'd rather not go to time-out cooperatively and stay there your full five minutes, I'll just take two cards instead of one. The choice is yours." And just like that, your struggles are over!

"But what if she says she'll go to time-out, but then won't stay there until the bell rings?"

If she comes out before the bell rings, just shrug your shoulders and take another ticket. This system allows you to penalize your daughter even when time-out isn't an option. For example, if she misbehaves in a store or some other public place, simply inform her that a card will be removed from the hook as soon as soon as you return home. Keep this up for at least six months. If my experience serves me well, your problems will be at that point a thing of the past.

Q: Concerning sending children to their rooms for extended periods of time—as in, the remainder of the day—in addition to putting them to bed early, I have two questions: First, isn't sending a child to his room for several hours a bit extreme, especially if the infraction is relatively minor? Second, what about the fact that other people in your field maintain that punishing children in these ways causes them to develop negative feelings about their rooms and beds, both of which they should feel positive about?

A: It's perfectly appropriate to send a child to his or her room for an extended period of time when the misbehavior in question is either outrageous in nature (e.g., cursing an adult) or a frequent occurrence, albeit relatively minor. Take, for example, a six-year-old who has a habit of interrupting his parents' conversations. They might impose a ten-minute time-out for the first interruption on any given day, then banish him to his room for the rest of the day (with an early bedtime) upon the third. The banished child may come out of his room to use the bathroom, eat meals with the family, attend educational programs (school, piano lessons, and the like, but not after-school sports), perform chores, and accompany the family away from the home.

The fact is, nothing short of a powerful response will adequately address certain disciplinary issues. Confining a child to his room for the remainder of the day sends just such a forceful message. A child so disciplined—assuming the discipline is consistent—is not apt to continue the misbehavior in question for very long. Moving the child's bedtime back an hour serves to increase the strength of the message just that much more.

And yes, I've heard the rumor that children who are banished to their rooms and/or put to bed early develop room phobias and sleep disorders and are therefore entitled to later sue their parents for grievous psychological damages. All I can tell you is that in twenty-four years of working with children and families, and twenty-six years of parenthood, I have yet to see or hear any evidence to that effect. We're talking about doing nothing more than restricting a child's freedom. Nothing awful happens to the child while in the room. The child's parents don't lock the door, bombard the room with Mel Torme songs, or release a horde of roaches under the door. Assuming the room isn't a high-tech entertainment center, nothing is removed. It's the same room the child spends time in every day. What's the problem? Answer: There is none! Restricting the child's liberty in this fashion assists the child in making an important connection: To wit, freedom and responsible behavior go hand in hand.

My children, Eric and Amy, are both responsible, hard-working, well-adjusted young adults. As children, they both spent occasional days in their rooms. In fact, my wife and I once confined Eric to his room for four weeks (the above exceptions applying of course). Despite these "traumas," both children continued to enjoy their rooms and never had any trouble sleeping through the night. In fact, during the early teen years, my wife and I had a devil of a time getting them to come *out* of their rooms.

Q**:** What if you send a child to his room for the remainder of the day, and he comes out for an "illegal" reason? Do you move bedtime back another hour? Does he have to stay in his room the next day as well?

$\mathcal{A}$**:** You've described a typical problem, one parents tend to think is a big deal, but isn't. Keep three things in mind:

First, the child is only coming out of his room because he doesn't like being confined. Coming out, therefore, is proof positive the consequence is having the desired effect on the child. He doesn't want to be there. In other words, it's working! I'd be more concerned, in fact, if the child never came out of his room illegally.

Second, if in response to a nonproblem of this sort you begin escalating a consequence, or tacking on additional consequences, you run the risk of quickly painting yourself into the proverbial corner. Let's say you add a day onto the child's confinement every time he makes an illegal exit from his room. By the end of the day, he's likely to have earned several weeks' worth of confinement, which you simply cannot enforce. The point is that by escalating consequences, parents demonstrate not their power, but their powerlessness.

Third, and most important, children do not have to completely cooperate in a consequence in order for the consequence to work. More often than not, almost is good enough. Say the child comes out of his room: What would be accomplished by grounding a child for an even longer period? Answer: Nothing, except to gradually create a situation that is unenforceable.

So a child comes illegally out of his room? Just take him back. And rejoice! It's working!

On Who Sleeps Where

Q: What do you think about letting children sleep with their parents?

A: Generally speaking, I don't think it's a good idea. Sleeping in his or her own bed affirms that a child is an independent, autonomous individual. This facilitates identity-formation, which begins during early toddlerhood and is critical to the eventual success of the emancipation process.

In addition, the fact that parents sleep together and separate from the child helps the child understand that the marriage is the cornerstone and focal point of the family. This enhances the child's respect for his parents and lays the foundations of respect for other adults as well. When parents and child sleep together, the child may well draw the intuitive conclusion that the marriage is a threesome. My professional experience leads me to conclude that the "blendedness" inherent to this arrangement promotes an extended dependency, encumbers the child's ability to separate comfortably from parents, creates problems with peer relationships, and delays overall maturity.

For all these reasons, I say, "Children to their own beds at a reasonably early hour!" I would, however, under certain circumstances, not be opposed to breaking the rule. I have no problem, for example, letting children come into their parents' beds during illness or periods of stress and/or transition, such as might follow the death of a pet or a move from one house to another.

Q: What's the least disruptive way of moving my two-year-old son, who's been sleeping with me since he was a baby, to his own bed?

A: No doubt about it, a two-year-old who's been sleeping with a parent since infancy is not going to take kindly to being moved to his own bed, and this age child cannot be persuaded, rewarded, or punished into cooperating with this transition. Nonetheless, the move needs to be made, and the sooner, the better, because the longer you wait, the more upsetting it's going to be. Since there is no way of getting over this hump without at least a moderate (if you're lucky) amount of disruption, the best approach is to just make up your mind and do it. No build-up, no lengthy explanations, no attempts at sugarcoating—just do it! The more your determination shines through, the more security you will impact, and the sooner it will all be over.

In times like these, I recommend calling upon the mystical powers of the "doctor." Tell your son, with a shrug of the shoulders, that the "doctor" says he has to sleep in his own bed from now on. Simple as that. By invoking a third party—whose authority the child recognizes—you neatly defuse the otherwise inevitable power struggle.

Put your son in his own bed, read him a story, kiss him goodnight, walk out of the room, and be prepared to take him back, firmly but gently, over and over again. If he just lies there and screams, go back every five minutes or so, reassure him, kiss him, and exit, stage left. The first night, it might take him five hours to get to sleep. In two weeks, it should be down to thirty minutes. In two months, the whole process should be over, and both of you will be the better for it.

On Discipline

Q: Every time—and I do mean every time—I take my four-year-old son into a store, he quickly finds some reason to create a disturbance or throw a tantrum. I've tried everything from rewards to spankings to get him to behave himself, but nothing has worked. Besides leaving the store and taking him home—which isn't practical because I'd never get any shopping done—do you have any suggestions?

A: I suggest you leave the store and take him home. Bear with me, however, because what I have in mind won't require that you sacrifice your shopping—not much, that is.

This problem actually presents you with an ideal disciplinary opportunity. With relatively little time and effort, you can not only take positive control of your son's public behavior, but also establish an entirely new disciplinary "tone" in the relationship, one that will take you effectively out of the reward/punishment "rut" in which you're currently stuck.

As it stands, your son begins to misbehave in a store and you react. Your response to the problem is, in other words, after the fact and no doubt flooded with anger, frustration, and other negative emotions. The elements of reaction and emotion characterize a disciplinary style that's bound to fall flat on its face time after time after time. To turn your son around, you're going to have to first turn yourself around. You need to respond to his misbehavior proactively—before the fact. I refer to this as "striking while the iron is cold." A proactive response will enable you to remain in control of your emotions. As a result, your self-confidence—the essence of effective discipline—will shine through.

In your case, the proactive response of choice involves what I refer to as "making dry runs." Plan a trip to a store when you have no shopping to do. On the pretense of having to make a purchase, undertake the excursion as you normally would, taking your son along. Before you enter the store, however, stop outside and calmly inform him that should he create a disturbance, no matter how small, you will immediately take him home where he will not only spend the remainder of the day in his room, but also go to bed one hour early.

Now, instead of dreading an in-store disturbance, you're hoping for one. When it happens—and it will, believe me—you simply say, "You've just told me that you want to go home, so let's go." Take his hand, lead him immediately out of the store, take him directly home, and do exactly what you said you were going to do. Do not, under any circumstances, give him a second chance or renegotiate the consequences, regardless of what he might promise.

Now you have your son's attention. Instead of getting flustered when he misbehaved, you responded with calm, purposeful resolve. Having taken him by surprise, you can expect a dramatic reaction on his part. He will, in all likelihood, wail and wail and wail some more. Just say, "I'd be upset, too, if I had to spend the rest of the day in my room."

Over the next few weeks, plan as many unnecessary excursions to the store as you can, taking the same approach each time. Within a month, your son should be a model shopper. In the meantime, you may have to sacrifice one or two *necessary* shopping trips as well. If so, just remember there's a price to be paid for everything. In this case, however, the payment plan is virtually painless.

Q: Our ten-year-old son is supposedly responsible for the nourishment and exercise of Betsy, our family dog. I say "supposedly" because we must constantly nag him to remember to do either. He'd been asking for a dog for several years, and he agreed from the outset to accept these responsibilities, which amount to nothing more than feeding Betsy in the morning, keeping her water bowl filled, and exercising her in the afternoon. Everything we've thus far tried has been to no avail, so we're counting on you for a solution. Please don't recommend that we give Betsy away, however, because we've all grown very attached to her.

A: I assume that by "everything we've thus far tried" you mean cajoling, berating, complaining, bribing, reasoning, and threatening. Predictably, none of these has moved your son to begin living up to his promise to take care of Betsy, nor will they ever. That leaves you with no alternative but to stop beating around the bush and do something about his irresponsibility.

Your son isn't going to begin accepting his responsibilities toward Betsy until you dump the lock, stock, and barrel of this problem in his lap. At present, *you* have a problem, and Betsy has a problem, but other than a couple of nagging parents, your son has no problem at all. Who's upset concerning his irresponsibility? You! And who, pray tell, suffers the inconvenience of the problem? You! The proverbial monkey, in other words, is on your back. Ah, but the only person who can solve this problem is your son. He's the only person who can tame the monkey, which he cannot begin to do until it's on his back. In short, when, and only when, this problem upsets and inconveniences your son more than it does you, he will have reason to solve it. This is an example of what I call the Agony Principle: *Parents shouldn't agonize over anything a child does or fails to do if the child is perfectly capable of agonizing over it himself.*

If you haven't done so already, give your son a daily deadline for feeding Betsy and another for exercising her (unless they are one and the same). Vow to give no more reminders, hints, suggestions, or threats. If either deadline passes without his having carried out the assigned task, carry it out yourself and ground him to his room for the remainder of the day. If, through the week, he neglects his responsibilities toward Betsy more than once, ground him on the weekend as well. With these rules in place, if your son fails in his responsibilities toward Betsy, who will be upset and inconvenienced? Your son, that's who! Wonderful, because with the monkey on *his* back, *he* can get about the business of taming it.

People have occasionally asked whether this approach might not result in the child becoming resentful, even cruel, toward the family pet. If the child loves the pet in the first place, this is extremely unlikely. I've ventured this same recommendation many times and have yet to hear of it backfiring. At first, there may be some sulking, but pets—and especially dogs—give very positive feedback to their primary caretakers. It takes a hard-hearted child to reject a pet's expressions of gratitude and love. In the final analysis, responsibility begets not just self-esteem, but feelings of pride in the task itself. In short, this will no doubt improve your son's relationship with Betsy, and immeasurably so. But first, there's the matter of that monkey.

On Sibling Rivalry

Q: How should parents handle sibling rivalry?

A: First, parents should understand that sibling *conflict* and sibling rivalry are horses of entirely different colors. Sibling conflict is as inevitable as marital conflict. Like marital conflict, sibling conflict involves two people. Sibling rivalry, however, involves a third: a parent who believes it is his or her responsibility to "referee" the children's squabbles, thus helping them learn to be fair and get along with one another. But despite the parent's best intentions, all this "helping" has the ultimate effect of causing the children to compete for what I call the "Victim Award." The child who "wins" is always the child the parent designates as the victim—the child who was treated unjustly by the other sibling. As a consequence, the children learn that the way to get the parent's sympathies is to act like a victim. For every victim, there must be a villain. In this case, the child who is designated as such is angered at what he or she perceives as an injustice. The only way to discharge this anger is to retaliate—against the supposed victim. A vicious circle thus develops which drives a wedge into the sibling relationship and creates untold stress within the family. In most instances, therefore, I recommend a policy of nonintervention when it comes to sibling conflict. When intervention is necessary to restore peace to the family, parents should do so in ways that hold *both children equally responsible* for the disturbance. Reprimand them both, take away the object of contention, send them to their respective rooms (or some other neutral corners) for a time; regardless, take care not to confer the Victim Award. No victim, no villain, no escalating struggle to see who can come out on the bottom.

Q: There's research showing that children who are picked on constantly by older siblings are at high risk for later psychological problems. You advise parents to stay out of such conflicts and rivalries. Are you willing to admit that your advice is only applicable when children are fairly evenly matched?

A: No, but you've raised several interesting issues, not the least of which concerns the limitations of research in the social sciences. Because it's impossible to identify—much less control—all the variables that might effect the outcome of any scientific inquiry into human behavior, such research is inherently flawed. As a result, it proves nothing and almost always raises more questions than it answers.

Concerning the study you cite, the researchers indeed concluded that children who are consistently picked on by older siblings are at high risk for later emotional problems. I agree, but the question of "why?" is left begging. My general observation has been that when one child is picking relentlessly on another, the parents are unintentionally making matters worse. They respond punitively to the child they identify as the villain and sympathetically to the perceived victim. From an adult perspective, this may appear justified, but to the supposed villain, it is nothing but injustice. From his point of view, the younger sibling is at fault. The more, therefore, he is punished for what he believes are "right" responses to that sibling's irritating behavior, the more frustrated he becomes. The more frustrated he becomes, the more, and more violently, he retaliates. The younger sibling, meanwhile, sinks even deeper into the role of victim, central to which is a feeling of helplessness (a defining feature of depression). By constantly siding with him, the parents unwittingly enable his victimhood. Their interventions prevent him from developing, by trial and error, strategies for dealing competently with the older sibling. He develops, instead, strategies for provoking further villain behavior. The payoff? Watching his older sibling "get it."

Any way you look at it, this is a vicious circle. Any way you look at it, this is a mess. It is, in my estimation, simplistic (but such is the nature of psychological research) to conclude that the younger sibling's later emotional problems are caused by the older sibling's relentless attacks. It is, furthermore, shortsighted to imply that parents have a responsibility to always intervene protectively when that intervention may exacerbate the problem.

I do recommend that parents generally stay out of sibling conflicts. If, for whatever reasons, they feel they must get involved, I recommend they do so such that responsibility for the problem is assigned equally to both children. Because neither child profits at the expense of the other, they are equally motivated to solve the problem.

Granted, there are rare situations in which one child seems to take perverse pleasure in making younger siblings suffer physical pain and emotional humiliation. When that's the case, I'd be willing to bet the bully is himself the victim of physical and emotional abuse. And that's another story entirely.

$Q:$ Our children, ages eight and six, think that if one gets something—a privilege or a material thing—the other should receive it as well. We have tried to explain that this is not only unrealistic (as in, "the world isn't fair") but often inconvenient and unaffordable. We've also pointed out that in the long run both of them will have much the same privileges and so on. Our explanations have fallen on deaf ears. Is there some way of getting this across to them in a way they'll understand and accept?

A: No, because your explanations reflect your adult point of view. Children cannot even begin to understand an adult point of view, and no amount of words, however concrete, concise, or clever, will instill that understanding. By trying to explain yourself, you open the door to argument. The more you explain, the more stubbornly the child clings to his self-centered fantasies of how the world should work and demands that you see and do things his way.

Your goal should not be that of seeing to it that your children understand and accept your position while they are children. It should be that of building whatever foundation they will need to eventually understand and accept it when they themselves become parents.

Remember, there's a world of difference between a chronically unhappy child and a child who is *temporarily* unhappy because parents will not cooperate with his demands. Remember, too, children will react very badly to parental decisions that are clearly good for them. The issue is not, therefore, the child's reaction, but whether the parents' position is in the child's long-term best interests. I assure you, your position on this issue is a sound one. Stop trying to explain it.

By the way, your children are behaving normally. When our children, Eric and Amy, were much younger, each of them expected to receive exactly as had the other. When we realized how obsessed they were with this notion, we made a practice of not being "fair." If, for example, we bought Eric a pair of shoes, we would take Amy along, but tell her in advance the trip wasn't for her, that we didn't intend to purchase her anything. She'd say she understood, then raise Cain when we actually followed through on the promise. Things were no different when it was Eric's turn to be on the nonreceiving end of things. Finally, they stopped competing with one another for the "who got more" award. Their jealousy cooled, and slowly but surely they began to appreciate the benefits of having been raised "unfairly." They began to appreciate one another as well. Today, they get along just fine. What more could a parent ask for?

Q: What do you mean, what more could a parent ask for? For one thing, a parent could ask for children who love one another!

A: Personally, I think parents who expect siblings to really and truly love one another—while they are both still children, that is—are expecting too much. Think about it: Husbands and wives choose one another; friends choose one another; but siblings don't choose one another.

Someone might say, "But, John, children and parents don't choose one another, either, yet it isn't unreasonable to expect children and parents to love one another."

True, but we're talking apples and kumquats, believe me. Indeed, parents and children don't choose one another, but (1) children naturally develop a sense of obligation to their parents, and (2) parents naturally feel very protective of and responsible toward their children. Neither is the case with siblings. Some siblings get along, some even wind up loving one another, but some don't get along and don't love one another. More often than not, this has nothing to do with parents. It's chemistry. Parents who expect siblings to fall madly in love with one another set themselves up for disappointment and nearly always blame themselves if their expectations don't pan out. So, expect the worst, I say. That way, you can only be pleasantly surprised.

Q: Is it even possible for a parent to not have a "favorite child"?

A: Whether or not you have a "favorite" child is strictly in the eyes of the little beholders in question. In other words, if one or more of your children think you play favorites, then you may as well accept it: You play favorites. Believe me, you are not going to be able to persuade your kids that you lack bias when it comes to how you treat them.

To a child, you see, a parent who treats different children *differently* is playing favorites. If, for example, you allow your fifteen-year-old to stay out until ten-thirty on weekend nights, but insist that your thirteen-year-old be in by nine o'clock, you will undoubtedly be accused of being "unfair." (Take heart, however, because any time you do something that causes one of your children to cry "Not fair!" you must be doing the right thing. Keep on doing it.) Likewise, if your fifteen-year-old notices that his younger sibling is not required—as was he at that age—to mow the lawn every Saturday morning, then you are again playing favorites. No matter that the thirteen-year-old is accident-prone or can't tell the difference between flower beds and grass. Number One Son will no doubt take this as a personal affront, and no explanation will convince him otherwise.

Given that children will think whatever they want to think about such things, the best thing to do when you stand accused of prejudice is simply agree. In the first case, tell your thirteen-year-old that he's right, his curfew is not only unfair, it's a clear violation of the Equity in Child Rearing Act (ECRA). As such, he should consider hiring an attorney who specializes in such matters and suing you for everything you've got. (Then he could support you!) On the matter of mowing the lawn, simply tell your fifteen-year-old that scientists have discovered a connection between mowing the lawn and high intelligence. They speculate, tell him, that a substance released into the air by grass cuttings stimulates brain cell growth. You are simply making sure, therefore, that he has a lifetime advantage over his younger sibling. In other words, he must mow the lawn because he's your favorite!

In short, the less seriously you take these complaints, the less mileage the children will get for them. Likewise, the moment you begin trying to treat children "fairly," the more tangled up you will become. I know this because my wife and I tried it once. We tried to make sure we spent roughly the same amount of money on and time with each of our two children. The more fair we tried to be, however, the more the children carped, and the more fair we tried to be. We finally caught on. "Fair" is like a highly addictive drug. The more a child gets, the more the child wants, until finally, the child can't get enough. Actually, the problem with "fair" isn't children; it's parents who want their children to *like* them. So, withdrawing a child from "fair" first requires that the parent or parents in question accept their inevitable, irrevocable unpopularity. In doing so, keep one thing in mind: Children aren't supposed to like their parents all that much anyway. Children should *want* to leave home.

In all seriousness, now that my children are grown and living on their own, I realize that nearly every time one of them accused me of "liking" the other one better, the accusation was right on target—sort of. For example, I liked my son, Eric, for his sensitivity, his willingness to take risks, and his easy ability to make friends. On the other hand, I liked Amy for her madcap sense of humor, her insight into human nature, her flights of creativity. Unfortunately, my children, being children, failed to see that although assigned differently, my affections were balanced. So, when I laughed at one of Amy's impressions, Eric accused me of thinking she was "funnier." Translate: I "liked" her better. And Amy was equally sensitive to any attention I gave her brother. After years of talking myself blue in the face, I finally realized these were imagined "wounds" that only time would heal.

The bottom line: You, like all parents, play favorites. Stop denying it! Accept, admit, relax. Stop trying to explain yourself. Above all else, stop taking your children so seriously. When they're much older, and have children of their own who cannot get enough "fairness," they'll forgive you. To paraphrase Orson Welles, "No whine will stop before its time."

Q: The older of my two children, ages nine and three, was born out of wedlock. His skin is considerably darker than that of his sister, and he's recently started saying things like, "You love her more because she's whiter than me" and "You probably wish you didn't have me." He only says these sorts of things when I discipline him or become angry with him for some reason. I always take the time to point our that I also get angry at his sister and explain that his skin color has nothing to do with my love for him, but he keeps bringing it up. I'm beginning to feel like a broken record, but I don't know what else to do or say. Any advice?

A: Stop explaining yourself to him. In the first place, you've no doubt said all you can to reassure him. If talking were going to solve this problem, it would have solved it by now. In the second place, it sounds to me as if his complaints are distracting you away from important disciplinary issues. He misbehaves. You begin to discipline him. He complains. You become distracted. His behavior falls through the cracks as you deal, instead, with his complaint. Third, the more attention you give his complaints and expressions of insecurity, the more he will complain. The problem is that despite your denials, your continued attention fuels complaints that are both self-indulgent and self-destructive. You may also be feeling some guilt concerning the circumstances of your son's birth and your relationship with the father. If so, given that children are extremely intuitive about such things, your son probably senses your discomfort.

Your relationship with your son is snagged on this issue. You, therefore, must act to move the relationship forward. Instead of waiting for him to raise the issue again, take the bull by the horns. When things are relatively relaxed between you, sit down with him and tell him, in a calm but firm voice, that whether you want him or love him as much as his sister is no longer open for discussion. You want him, you love him, and that's that.

You might say, "People with light skin aren't better or more lovable than people with dark skin, any more than people with light hair are more lovable that people with dark hair. I'm not going to say these things to you ever again. They are a waste of my time. In the future, whenever you have these thoughts, you should find something to do that will take your mind off them. Go outside and play. Go to your room and read. Regardless, I don't give you permission to bring them up, and if you do, I'm just going to tell you to find something to do."

Make it short and sweet. When you've said your piece, give him a kiss and send him on his way. Over the next few weeks, he will surely test your resolve. When he does, demonstrate it! If you prove to him that you mean business, he will slowly but surely stop thinking of himself as a victim.

Q: We have three children, ages eight, six, and five. When it comes time to pick up toys, they argue with one another over who should pick up what, who put what where, and so on. More often than not, one of us ends up getting in there with them and helping. If we didn't, it would take all night. Bickering of this sort occurs every time we assign the three of them to a job, any job. Do you have a tried-and-true method for solving a problem such as this?

A: Yes, I do, and it's so obvious a solution that you're probably going to slap your forehead and exclaim, "Now why didn't I think of that myself?" But, you see, making the obvious seem brilliantly insightful is what being a psychologist is all about.

Solution: Don't ever again assign the three of them to the same job. I know, you want them to learn to work together cooperatively, and no one could argue with the logic of having all three children pick up toys that all three have been playing with, but there are times in the rearing of children when one must sacrifice ideals and logic in order to expedite the practical and preserve one's sanity. This is definitely one of those times.

Three unrelated children would probably cooperate willingly on just about any task you assigned to them (the operative word being *unrelated*). But siblings are another matter entirely. Siblings are always looking for ways of one-upping one another, of gaining the advantage, of passing the proverbial buck. If you assign siblings to the same chore—even one they cooperated in creating, like picking up toys—they are genetically programmed to point their fingers at one another and cry, "He/she did it!" If you manage, by threat or bribe, to override this program, then be prepared for them to complain that "he/she isn't doing his/her share."

You can live a longer, happier life by accepting the inevitable. Stop fighting the same battle every evening and be proactive. Instead of expecting all three children to work together on the same job, assign each child a separate task. One child can pick up toys. One can sweep the kitchen floor. And one can turn down everyone's beds and put mints on the pillows. If there aren't enough jobs to go around at bedtime, then rotate the one job of picking up toys. Put up a seven-day calendar on which picking up toys is the eight-year-old's responsibility on Monday, the six-year-old's on Tuesday, and so on. Over the first six days, therefore, each child will do the job twice. On the seventh day, draw straws, but put a straw in *the pot* for yourself and manage to always lose, much to your pretend chagrin. This will not only delight the children to no end, but will also, believe it or not, result in a more cooperative attitude on their part. Humor is the best of all family tonics.

Using the "one chore, one child" approach will circumvent lots of problems, but not eliminate them entirely. Your children will bicker until they are not longer children. But there will, I assure you, be later opportunities for revenge. For example, when it comes time to fund college educations, you and your husband could point at one another and cry "Make him/her do it!" That'll teach 'em.

On Disobedience

Q: My nine-year-old stepdaughter, who lives primarily with us, does not obey me as well as she does her mother. How would you suggest I deal with this?

A: If my experience in these matters serves me well, you're not going to resolve this problem with your stepdaughter until you resolve certain related issues with your wife, the woman you referred to—and not coincidentally—as "her mother."

One of the biggest problems typical of the so-called "stepfamily" involves the precedents set by the future husband and wife before their marriage. On the one hand, the single mother, following her divorce, often focuses on her child or children to the virtual exclusion of developing a life for herself. On the other, her future husband quickly sees that in order to win her hand, he must successfully court her child as well. Instead of commanding the child's respect, he becomes a "good-time Charlie." As a result, the child fails to see him as an authority figure.

Once these two adults are married, the patterns they've unwittingly set come back to haunt them. The child, often still at the focus of her mother's attention, views her stepfather as almost a "guest"—someone she and her mother have allowed to live with them. The stepfather's attempts to assert authority are either halfhearted or driven by frustration. In the latter case, the mother responds protectively to the child, further undermining the child's ability to see the stepfather as an authority figure. And around and around these people go, and where they stop, nobody has a clue.

Quite obviously, the real problem in a situation of this sort is not the child's refusal to recognize the stepfather's authority; it's the fact that the marriage exists in name only. In effect, the primary relationship in the family is that of the mother-child, not husband-wife. The female adult is more of a mother than a wife, and the male adult is trying to be the best *stepfather* he can be, instead of the best husband. Meanwhile, the child sits center stage in a family that has no substantial center.

Nothing will be solved by the mother telling the child that she must obey the stepfather. Nothing in fact, will be solved as long as the two adults in the family focus on parenting issues. It's as simple as this: When the mother becomes, first and foremost, a wife, and the stepfather becomes, first and foremost, a husband, and they position their marriage at the focal point of attention in the family, the child will have respect for them both and will obey them both. Another way of putting this is that you and your wife need to let your stepdaughter know that the marriage is not a threesome. Make it a point to go places without her. Assign her a bedtime that allows the two of you to spend quality time together every evening. Do not allow her to interrupt or invite herself into your conversations. Make yours a marriage in the true sense of the term.

When it comes to your responsibilities as a parent, remember that the prefix "step" is useful for legal purposes only. You are certainly not a biological father to this child, nor will you, in all likelihood, ever be considered her "daddy." Nevertheless, you are her *father* when she is in your care. If you quietly, yet confidently regard yourself as such, she will eventually come to also regard you as such. And she will love you for it.

Q: Our eleven-year-old will not obey his mother. In addition, he refuses to accept time-out (in a dining room chair) from her and becomes physical if she tries to make him go. There's not a weekday that goes by without an incident of this sort. He'll cooperate with me, perhaps because he knows if he doesn't, I'll spank him. I don't like being the "heavy," but I certainly don't want Freddie thinking he can run over his mother without penalty. What should we do?

A: First, I agree you have an obligation to support your wife and if that means playing the heavy, then play the heavy you must. There are, in fact, ways of doing so that will, in the long run, lead to a strengthening of your wife's authority and effectiveness.

A "wait until your father gets home" policy can, on the one hand, be an admission of weakness by a mother. On the other, it can be an affirmation of solidarity between husband and wife concerning disciplinary matters. The difference depends on the manner in which it's communicated as well as the follow-through. Under no circumstances should your wife enter into physical struggle with your son. As you've no doubt already discovered, altercations of this sort between parent and child escalate rather rapidly. They also set the stage for increasingly out-of-control behavior during the teen years. It's imperative, therefore, that you and your wife act quickly to nip this situation in the bud.

Using a standard-size sheet of paper, make a sign that reads, "Freddie is to do what we tell him to do without delay, argument, disrespect, or loud complaint" and affix it to the refrigerator. (Visual aids of this sort help keep everyone on track concerning disciplinary matters, enhancing cooperation on the part of the child as well as consistency on the part of the parents.) Every time Freddie breaks the rule, he has a choice: he may either sit in the time-out chair for fifteen minutes or he may go to bed fifteen minutes early.

Say your wife tells Freddie to take out the garbage and he ignores her or refuses. She must not repeat herself or threaten, but simply say, "You've broken the rule. What's it going to be, time-out or early bedtime?" The "default arrow" always points in the direction of early bedtime. If, in other words, Freddie doesn't state his choice within a few seconds, your wife is to say, "Then it's early to bed," and walk away. It's absolutely imperative that she remain calm, in control, and consistent. Every time he refuses time-out, it's another fifteen minutes off bedtime, to a cap of one hour.

If Freddie chooses time-out in the dining room chair, his fifteen minutes should be defined with a kitchen timer. Should he so much as stand up before the bell rings, however, time-out is over and the full fifteen minutes comes off his bedtime. If Freddie initially refuses time-out, but later decides he doesn't want to go to bed quite so early, you can give him the option of serving thirty minutes in the dining room chair in exchange for eliminating one fifteen-minute "early to bed" period.

This procedure accomplishes several things: First, your wife has a means of exercising authority without entering into power struggles of any sort with Freddie. Second, the penalty for misbehavior is shifted to the evening, when you're home to enforce it. Third, there's no longer a payoff to Freddie for not cooperating with your wife. Fourth, should Freddie have to go to bed early, you and your wife have more time to spend together in the evening. Use it creatively!

On Discipline

Q: You frequently stress the need for disciplinary consistency. Is it inconsistent for parents to change their minds if they realize they've make a bad decision? Also, if parents realize they've mishandled a certain situation, is it all right for them to apologize to their children, or are apologies a display of weakness that children will ultimately take advantage of?

A: Properly conceived and delivered, parental discipline enables the gradual development of self-control or self-discipline. The crux of self-control is the ability to anticipate consequences and adjust one's behavior accordingly. It follows that children cannot develop self-control unless they're able to successfully predict the consequences of their actions. That becomes impossible when parents are inconsistent. Inconsistency, therefore, prevents the development of self-control. This all boils down to one point of fact: In order to successfully discipline children, parents must themselves be self-disciplined.

Self-discipline and self-confidence go hand in hand. They are, in effect, synonymous. As I've already said (but cannot overemphasize), the successful discipline of a child is not a matter of proper selection of consequences. It's a matter of communicating one's self-confidence to the child—of communicating that you know where you stand and where you want the child to stand as well. This means that consistency is not necessarily a matter of delivering the same consequence each and every time the child misbehaves in a certain way; it is more a matter of always communicating your resolute, yet loving disapproval of that misbehavior. In other words, when it comes to the discipline of a child, form is secondary to substance.

Both of your questions can be stated thusly: Is there anything wrong with a parent admitting to a child that he or she has made a mistake? Answer: The only parent who cannot admit to having made a mistake is a parent lacking in self-confidence. Changing one's mind is not necessarily an example of inconsistency, nor is making an apology to a child a sign of weakness. There's a critical difference, however, between changing one's mind and flip-flopping. Likewise, there's a difference between apologizing from a position of self-confidence and apologizing from a position of guilt.

Insecure parents, because they are not certain of where to stand, flip-flop. In general, all this flipping and flopping takes place because they are only comfortable when their children are happy. Secure parents, upon realizing they've made a mistake, change their minds. In changing their minds, their primary concern is not making their children happy, but doing the right thing. So there are times when they change their minds and their children are happy with the change, and times when they change their minds and their children are unhappy with the change. In other words, secure parents have no more problem changing a "yes" to a "no" than they do a "no" to a "yes," whereas insecure parents have great difficulty with the former.

Secure parents have no problem saying "I'm sorry," but tend to make no big deal of it when they do. They accept their own imperfections as no big deal. Their children come to see them not as ideal, but real; faulted, but blameless. As a consequence, their children come to better grips with the realities of life. And that, my friends, is what raising children is all about.

Q: Our nine-year-old son has a way of drawing us into conflict with him, and it's driving us nuts. The "game" generally begins with him refusing to do something—go to his piano lesson, do a chore, etc. We become upset, and he stands his ground until we levy a threat meaningful enough and believable enough to convince him we mean business. At this point, he will comply, but not without a great show of displeasure. Even though we always win these battles, the frequency of them is wearing us out. Do you have any idea why he's doing this and any suggestions for what we can do, if anything, to stop it?

A: I would guess your son is playing this "game" with you because you so willingly play it with him. He throws down the gauntlet and you pick it right up. In the exchange that follows, he has absolutely nothing to lose. So, he pushes it to the limit. Meanwhile, you bluster and threaten, but in the final analysis, you do absolutely nothing! Your son has learned, therefore, that refusing to do what he's told is inconsequential—to him, that is. You, on the other hand, suffer all manner of angst as a result of the power struggles that ensue.

I've said many times that parents need to consistently demonstrate their power to their children. Why? Because children feel more secure with parents who demonstrate that they are perfectly clear on what they want their children to do and not do. Children may not always be happy with the decisions their parents make, but they will always feel more secure with parents who are firm and resolute when it comes to making decisions. And secure children are happier children, yes?

The moment a parent steps into a power struggle with a child, however, the parent loses all power. The child wins. Period. Even if the parent is ultimately successful at getting the child to do what he wants, the child has won by virtue of the fact that he succeeded at pulling you down to his level, however temporarily. Breaking this pattern is going to require that you give your son the "last word." As it stands, *you're* trying to have the last word. You ultimately prevail (in a sense), but at great cost to yourself emotionally and in terms of the steady erosion of your authority. One of these days, if you don't pull yourself out of this quicksand, and fast, you're going to find yourself faced with a son who's no longer fazed by your threats. Then what?

So, the next time he refuses to do what you tell him to do, simply say, with a shrug of your shoulders, "Oh well, I guess that's up to you." And walk away. If he persists in trying to draw you into a struggle, simply repeat that the decision to obey is his. There's a chance he may, after some posturing, do what you've told him to do.

He probably won't, however. In that event, later that day (or even the next or the next), when he asks if he can watch television or go outside with his friends, tell him no, he can't. When he demands to know why not, say, "Well, you see, whether or not you [whatever it was you told him to do] is up to you, but whether or not you can go outside with your friends is up to me. So, you can't go outside."

From that point on, every time he refuses to do something, just say, "It's up to you." In no time at all, your son will figure out those four words mean that if he doesn't do what you tell him to do, something evil and unfair is in store for him. He'll become much more cooperative, I assure you. But the best thing is, he'll be much more secure and, therefore, much happier. Everyone wins!

Q: We're having a problem coming up with appropriate punishments for our twelve-year-old son. He's not a big problem, but like all children his age, he occasionally misbehaves. You generally recommend a restriction of one sort or another for punishment. My husband and I run a busy retail business, which means neither of us is home after school to supervise a restriction. I divide my Saturdays between home and the shop, and I never know when business is going to demand my presence. How can we restrict when we're not there to supervise? In lieu of that, are there other, equally effective means of punishing a child of this age?

A: Your question raises several equally interesting issues, the first of which concerns the commonly held belief that when a child misbehaves, punishment (a corporal, material, or recreational penalty) is in order. Not so. When a child misbehaves, some consequence is due; punishment, however, is but one of the available options. Other options include a stern (albeit calm) reprimand, an open discussion of why the behavior took place and how it can be prevented in the future, or even a simple acknowledgment of the misdeed along with an equally simple statement of disapproval, as in "I know you got in trouble at school today, and all I have to say is I'm not pleased."

Your choice is determined by a number of variables, including the child's age, the nature of the misbehavior in question and whether or not it's chronic, the child's emotional status, and whether it tends to take place in public or only in the home. It is not necessarily true that consequences must escalate as the "severity" of the "crime" increases. It is sometimes, in fact, more strategic to take a low-key approach with a serious infraction. Likewise, it might be best to impose a heavy penalty for a problem that's relatively minor, but occurs fairly often. As is the case with adults, children are highly motivated to maintain their standards of living. For adults, the standard is a matter of money; for children, privilege. A child who knows certain misbehavior will result in curtailment of freedom is a child more likely to walk the straight and narrow.

Then there's the matter of your dilemma. While it's certainly not prudent to assign a restriction you can't enforce, a restriction can still be effective even when enforcement can't be completely guaranteed. Let's say you tell your son he cannot leave the house on Saturday. At noon on Saturday, you leave the house for the shop, returning at three o'clock. During your absence, your son goes outside for two hours to visit with a group of friends. He will probably go no farther than the yard. After all, he's got to stay close enough to the house to get back inside quickly, as soon as your car comes into view. Even considering his "escape," which was hardly satisfactory, he still served the better part of his sentence. Furthermore, he knows there's no guarantee that the next time you put him on restriction, you'll give him the opportunity to escape. Therefore, the restriction has still served its purpose, which is to penalize the misbehavior in question and deter a repeat performance.

Any punishment has its drawbacks. The fact is, however, *a child does not have to completely cooperate in a punishment for it to be effective.* Just as there is no perfect child, there is no perfect means of discipline.

Q: When we sit down to eat, our ten-year-old complains about the food on her plate. Trying to persuade her to take even one bite of something she doesn't like is worse than pulling teeth. On several occasions, after we insisted that she eat something, she ran to the bathroom and threw up. We have made her sit at the table until she finishes everything on her plate. She sits and sits, but still refuses to eat. I know it's wrong, but guilt-ridden Mom here has sometimes given up and fixed her something she would eat, in the name of peace. Do you have a better way?

A: Sure. But first, let's untangle the situation. The overriding issue has nothing to do with nutrition. It is a matter of manners and your daughter's proper place in the family. It is rude to complain about food that someone else has prepared. It is equally rude to refuse to eat it because of some neurotic prejudice. You don't want your daughter going to someone else's home and complaining about food her hosts prepare for her, now do you? Then don't allow her to complain about the food *you* prepare.

With regard to her place in the family, it seems necessary to remind you that she is a *child*. By allowing her to disrupt family meals with her complaints, by pleading with her to eat, by fixing her special food, you are aiding and abetting her need to occupy center stage in the family. As long as she can control the family by whining and complaining at the dinner table, she will.

Stop catering to her! From now on, serve her plate with ridiculously small portions of the same foods everyone else in the family is eating—two or three forkfuls of each item. (As time goes on, and the problem is nearing solution, you should gradually increase her portions until they are reasonable for her age and appetite.) Tell her she doesn't have to eat anything not to her liking, but that she may not, under any circumstances, complain. If she violates this rule, either verbally or facially, take away whatever privileges she usually enjoys after dinner and move her bedtime back one hour. Refuse to let her have seconds of anything (or dessert) until she cleans her plate. Do not make any remarks about what she eats or doesn't eat and don't make any effort to persuade her to eat. In fact, pay no more attention to her than you do to anyone else at the table. If she eats everything, allow her seconds of anything. If she acts like she's going to throw up after eating something, simply tell her to go to the bathroom. When she returns, inform her that throwing up or acting like she has to is tantamount to a nonverbal complaint and earns the same punishment. When the meal is over, clear her place along with everyone else's. If any food remains, cover it and set it aside. Later, if she complains of hunger and asks for food, show her plate and tell her that when she finishes what remains, she may have whatever snacks you normally allow.

She will test the new rules. She will complain, throw up, refuse to eat, and then later complain of hunger pains. In other words, you ain't seen nothin' yet. Take heart! Two or three weeks of hurling herself upon the barricades is all it will take for her to begin cooperating. Take your choice: Three weeks or eight more years?

Q: How should parents deal with lying?

$\mathcal{A}$: The child who lies and steals is perhaps the most provocative and frustrating of all children, capable of driving both parents and therapists up the proverbial wall. These are problems that slip through the grasp and manage to dance through the best of traps.

"The pearl earrings I've been looking for were under your mattress, Susie," asks Susie's mother. "How did they get there?"

"I don't know."

"What do you mean, you don't know? You must have put them there."

"I didn't. Really."

"What, did they just walk into your room and climb under your mattress all by themselves?"

"I don't know. Maybe."

And up the wall Susie's mother goes. She tells Susie her punishment will be worse if she continues to lie. Susie continues to lie. Her mother then tells Susie she won't be punished at all if she tells the truth. Susie continues to lie. Susie's mother banishes her to her room until she's ready to tell the truth. Susie, however, is capable of outlasting her mother. Eventually, at wit's end, Susie's mother (a) begins to scream, (b) starts to cry, (c) spanks Susie, (d) promises her a new bicycle if she'll just please, please tell the truth. Susie continues to lie.

Some experts say children lie and steal because of low self-esteem. Others say it's a means of controlling the family, or winning a power struggle. Some say it's all of the above. Some will tell you they don't know. Trying to explain why a child lies and steals is, at best, an exercise in speculation. Explanations, furthermore, often get in the way of solutions. For those reasons, I generally vote for "I don't know." Onward, then, to a possible solution.

First, trust your instincts. Then, ask the child no questions. If you're past denying the problem exists, and you have a good "feel" for your child, you're going to know, at least 90 percent of the time, who "done it" when you're being told a lie. When you discover your earrings are missing, instead of asking "Susie" if she took them, say "When you're finished with my pearl earrings, Susie, please put them back where you found them."

When you feel you're being told a lie, simply say "This sounds like a lie to me. When you're ready to tell the truth, let me know and we can continue this discussion." Put the ball in the child's court and walk away. Experience should tell you nothing will be accomplished by trying to catch this elusive butterfly. In fact, pursuit only adds fuel to the fire. Next, don't let lies distract you and bump you off track. The earrings are the immediate issue, not Susie's lying.

"The next time you want to wear my earrings, Susie, just tell me. If I'm not planning on wearing them, they're yours."

Punish the deed (but only if the deed truly deserves punishment), not the lie. Don't promise that things will go better if the child tells the truth. Don't threaten to make the punishment worse if the lie continues. Stay on track.

Lastly, provide the child the opportunity to become a more responsible member of the family. Stop spending so much energy trying to catch the lies and concentrate, instead, on helping the child adjust to performing a daily routine of chores around the home. I find, fairly consistently, that the more responsible these errant kids become within their families, the less they lie and steal.

Why? I don't know. Who cares?

Q: Our sixteen-year-old daughter is seeing a seventeen-year-old boy whose reputation leaves much to be desired. When we confronted her with what reliable adult sources had told us about him, Angela admitted knowing about his past, but said he'd changed. We told her she was naive to think she could make a leopard change his spots, but she is adamant about wanting to continue the relationship. She says they've done nothing wrong, and that we have no right to interfere on the basis of rumor alone. We feel as if we're in a bind. What would you advise us to do?

A: If you can't beat 'em—and you certainly can't—then join 'em. You're making the most common of all mistakes made by parents of teens: You're letting your emotions drive your decisions. As a result, you're in danger of not only making decisions that will almost certainly come back to haunt you, but also of being pulled into a power struggle you can only lose. In short, you risk creating lots of problems and solving none.

Fear and danger are arousing your protective instincts. No one could fault you for wanting to keep your daughter out of harm's way, but the only way you can protect Angela is to restrict her from seeing this young man, and she's made it clear she won't stand for that. If you restrict, she's bound to rebel, and that's when your heartaches begin. Didn't you guys ever read *Romeo and Juliet,* by Will Shakespeare? If you haven't, you should. Shakespeare was the most brilliant psychologist of all time.

As the father of a young adult woman, I am in complete empathy (that's a psychology word) with your feelings. Nonetheless, you need to rein in your emotions and adopt a more strategic approach to the problem. In so doing, things may get slightly worse from your point of view before they get better, but a good tactician is always willing to lose the battle if doing so means winning the war.

In the first place, Angela is as right as rain. She and her boyfriend have done nothing wrong (that you know about). Therefore, you lack just cause to do anything but trust her. Begin your strategic campaign by putting your concern on the table while at the same time admitting to overreaction. Apologize for underestimating her ability to conduct herself properly and make responsible decisions, whatever the pressure this young man puts on her. Don't lapse into lecture or try to extract promises from her. Just move the ball of responsibility gently into her court.

Your next move should be to begin including the young man in family activities. Invite him to be a regular guest at dinner. Request his presence on family outings. If he's hiding ulterior motives, an open-arms policy on your part will make him more than a bit uncomfortable, in which case he's likely to back quickly out of Angela's life. If he's legit concerning his feelings for Angela, then your family's values can do nothing but have a positive effect on him. Beside, where Angela is concerned, trust breeds trustworthiness. In the final analysis, Angela can only take responsible control over her life through trial and error. Your job is not to prevent her from making mistakes, it's to control the consequences of those mistakes and see to it she learns from them.

Parents who overcontrol by trying to catch their children every time they fall inadvertently set them up for even bigger, more catastrophic tumbles.

(A personal note: My in-laws felt Willie had fallen in with a "bum," as they put it, when she began seeing me during her first year of college. At the time, I deeply resented their characterization of me, but am now able to clearly understand their concerns. After all, my hair was shoulder-length, I played in a hard-rock band, and I wore sunglasses at night. I was, by their standards, a punk, and I was indeed in need of reforming, which Willie patiently accomplished. So, a punk at seventeen is not necessarily a punk for life.)

On Aggression

Q: Our four-year-old gets very mad when we don't give him his way. On occasion, he's hit, or tried to hit, us. How should we respond to his aggression?

A: It's not unusual for children this age to hit, or attempt to hit, their parents when they don't get their way. When a child loses control to this degree, parents should act quickly and authoritatively. In most cases, I'll just bet you can "read" your youngster's behavior well enough to know when an attack is coming. Demonstrate your control and power by intercepting the blow. Hold his wrists, look him straight in the eye, and say something like, "I will not allow you to hit me. You are *not* getting your way. Furthermore, you're going to your room until you've calmed down."

Later, when things have cooled off, you can say, "It's okay to be upset when we won't let you do what you want, but it's not okay to try to hit us. If you want to tell us you're upset, that's fine. We might even be able to talk about it. If you don't feel like talking, or you're too upset to talk, you can go be mad in your room."

Keep conversations of this sort short. A long-winded discourse on the "why nots" of hitting won't accomplish anything. In fact, the more you overstate the issue, the more likely it is your child will continue to try to hit you when he gets upset.

Q: Our eight-year-old daughter has a low tolerance for frustration with her peers. Ever since she was a toddler, she's been bossy with other children, but it's getting worse as she gets older. If her playmates don't allow her to be the leader and make all the rules, she becomes verbally aggressive, even abusive, toward them. We don't know whether to get involved or just let them work things out on their own. We're inclined toward the latter, but don't want our daughter to think that outbursts of temper are the way to handle conflict. What would you recommend?

A: My general rule of thumb is to let children work out their own conflicts, but the general rule works when playmates are fairly evenly matched in terms of strength of personality. In this case, it appears that not only is your daughter's typical reaction to interpersonal frustration completely out of proportion to the circumstances, but also that she is frequently able to successfully intimidate her playmates into cooperating with her. Indeed, she's not learning how to give and take with her friends. Rather, her friends —by acquiescing in the face of her outbursts—are inadvertently helping to exaggerate what is probably nothing more than a personality disposition toward dominance.

Research suggests that the tendency toward being either dominant or submissive in social situations is inborn. The average person, however, while tending to lean in one direction, is able to lean in the other—albeit temporarily—if circumstances demand it. A minority of people seem "stuck" at the extremes, either inadvertently shy or insistently controlling. Long-term studies of shy children show that their genetic program can be overridden by parents who are gently encouraging and model outgoing behavior. Left to his or her own devices, however, a shy child is likely to become a shy adult.

Your daughter may be in danger of becoming stuck at the controlling end of this particular personality spectrum. As would be the case if she were painfully shy, your job is to "unstick" her. Doing so will require equal amounts of patience and firmness.

To begin with, outbursts of temper toward her friends should not, under any circumstances, be allowed. Not getting one's way is not an excuse for abusing other people, and you need to communicate that to your daughter in no uncertain terms. When she blows her top at her friends, you need to remove her from the group until she calms down. When she's able to talk about the events that precipitated the outburst, you can talk with her about what she could have done instead of exploding. Do not, however, allow her to justify her behavior. Make it clear that there is absolutely no excuse for being verbally abusive toward other people, especially one's friends. Before allowing her to rejoin her friends, you must require that she (1) acknowledge that she overreacted, and (2) apologize to all concerned.

Sometimes, exaggerated displays of frustration on the part of a child indicate the youngster is dealing with an overload of stress in some area of his or her life. In this sort of situation, however, the resulting behavior would be *uncharacteristic*. Since your daughter has been demandingly bossy since toddlerhood, a search for sources of undue stress in her life is likely to be fruitless. In effect, she is her own worst source of stress, her own worst enemy. She's going to need your help in order to make peace with herself.

Q: We're concerned that our ten-year-old may be becoming a bully. What should we do?

A: A bully generally feels inadequate, perhaps even rejected, and takes his or her feelings out on children who can't defend themselves. I tend to be extremely conservative when it comes to recommending professional help, but this is one situation where I think it can be helpful. Don't, however, get involved with a therapist who's going to talk solely with your son. My experience in matters of this sort has convinced me that counseling won't be very successful, if at all, unless the child's parents, and perhaps the entire family, participate in every session.

Meanwhile, ask other parents in the neighborhood to inform you of any acts of aggression by your son. When an incident comes to your attention, keep him inside (preferably confined to his room) for several days without television and with an early bedtime.

Until the problem is completely resolved, your son should not be allowed to participate in any highly competitive or aggressive sport. I'd recommend instead that he take part in one or more structured, supervised, noncompetitive peer-group activities such as scouting or a church youth group. Preferably, these activities should not require your attendance. The adults who direct these activities should be aware of your son's problem so they can help him develop more appropriate social skills.

On Money Matters

Q: At what age should parents start a child on an allowance?

A: It makes sense (har, har) to start a child on a small allowance when he's learned the names of the various pieces of currency and how to count them. Start with a small amount; say, two dollars a week. Take him to several stores and help him learn what two dollars will buy. Once he's learned to read price tags fairly well, teach him to look for bargains and do comparison shopping. Above all else, teach him to save by pointing out that if he holds onto his allowance for several weeks, he'll be able to purchase something bigger and better.

Q: How much allowance should a child receive each week?

A: Somewhere between too little and too much. If the amount is insufficient, money management will become an exercise in frustration. If it's excessive, the child won't learn to set limits on his spending. Determine the actual amount by taking into consideration such things as your family's income level, the socioeconomic level of the child's peers, his age, the extent of his involvement in activities at school and in the community, and the cost of living in your community. In the final analysis, a child should have enough money to fund a reasonable amount of recreation and nonessentials like soda, snacks, and toys.

Q: Should a child be required to earn his allowance by doing chores around the house?

A: No, but children should have plenty of household chores to do. Chores help children develop responsibility, self-discipline, and other essential values. An allowance helps a child develop money management skills. Parents need to make sure the two lessons don't get confused. An allowance should not be used to persuade a child to carry out his assigned duties, nor should it be suddenly withdrawn to punish him for inappropriate behavior. When all is said and done, children should do chores for one reason only: because they are told to do them by parents who are wise enough to realize their value.

Q: Is it all right for parents to give a child the chance to earn additional money by doing extra chores?

A: Certainly. Whereas parents should not pay a child for doing jobs which are part of the household routine—taking out the garbage, feeding the pet tarantula, and so on—it's perfectly okay for parents to contract with a child for work over and above the daily call of duty. Deals of this sort should be the exception, however, rather than the rule.

Q: Should parents set rules on how a child can use an allowance?

A: Oh, absolutely, especially with a young child. Parents should keep tabs on how a child uses or intends to use an allowance and exercise the right of refusing to let money be spent irresponsibly or in ways which are incompatible with the values of the family. Parents should take every available opportunity to teach children how to be intelligent consumers—how to recognize quality in an item, how to comparison shop, and so on.

When our son, Eric, was about seven years old, he took two dollars we'd given him and bought two cheap plastic cars (the kind that hold together for no longer than thirty minutes once they're out of the package) that were on a rack in a grocery store. When we found out what he'd done with his money, we made him take one of them back for a refund. Several days later, we casually inquired about the car he had kept. "It broke," he said, with a chagrined look. Lesson learned.

Q: How should parents deal with grandparents who hand out money to grandchildren as though it grows on trees?

A: As long as grandparents don't see the children often, this really isn't a problem. Grandparents can relax the rules a bit without undermining parents' authority or the values they're trying to teach their children. By trial and error, my wife and I discovered that the best policy concerning grandparents is "when in Rome, do as the Romans do, and when the Romans come to you, do as the Romans do." In other words, don't interfere in how grandparents choose to dote on grandchildren. There's just no point in letting conflicts over trivia like this spoil family get-togethers, especially when the family doesn't get together that often.

Q: What kinds of things should a child be expected to pay for himself, using his allowance?

A: A child should *not* be required to use his allowance for essentials like food, clothing, books, or school supplies. An allowance is not meant to establish a child's standard of living, but to supplement it. A child should use an allowance to pay for certain recreational activities as well as nonessentials like toys. If the child runs out of money before the end of a given week and then finds something he wants to buy, parents should *not* give him an advance on the next week's allowance. Rather, he should have to wait until "payday." Parents who give advances might as well do away with an allowance altogether and simply give the child money on demand.

Q: What are the most important lessons parents can teach their children about money?

A: Perhaps the most important lessons of all are those parents communicate not with words, but primarily through example. Ask yourself these questions: Do my children see me using money wisely, or do they often see me wasting it frivolously or using it as a means of impressing others? Do they see me sharing it with others through contributions to my church and/or other charitable organizations, or do they see me being tightfisted? Do they often see me tense and agitated about money, or do they see me relaxed, and yet sensible, in my attitude toward it? In the final analysis, it's just as important that parents instill in their children a set of healthy, humanitarian values concerning money as it is that they teach the everyday pragmatics of money management.

Q: Are there additional exercises in money management appropriate to the high school years?

A: Once a child begins earning regular income from part-time and summer jobs, a checking account becomes an excellent tool for teaching how to budget. When a child's savings account is sufficiently large, parents should acquaint him with the full range of bank services—different savings and checking options, certificates of deposit, saving bonds, and even money-market accounts. Parents might consider letting an older teen—one who will be leaving home within a year or so—have a credit card. Some credit card companies offer "student cards" which carry lower credit limits and require that parents cosign for the child's debt.

Q: If a teenage child works, should he be completely free to spend his money any way he wants, or should parents still set some rules on how he must manage his money?

A: As a child gets older, the amount of control his parents exercise over his spending should decrease and be gradually replaced by guidance, but no child who's living at home should have permission to spend money irresponsibly or in ways that are incompatible with the values of the family. For the teen who works, a helpful rule is: "For the most part, you can spend your money as you choose; however, if the item you want to purchase costs more than fifty dollars, you must first discuss it with us."

Q: Our two children have been required to help with housework for the last five years. They're now in their early teens and are capable of doing just about anything around the house, including washing and ironing their own clothes and cooking simple meals. We have never paid them for chores, nor have we ever given them allowances. If they wanted money for something, they asked, we evaluated the request, and funded only what we felt was reasonable. They recently asked if we'd start giving them an allowance, however, and we wanted your advice on this. Do you have guidelines on determining how much is enough and how to dole it out?

A: It sounds as if you've done a good job of instilling a sense of responsibility in your children. Unfortunately, too many of today's hyperbusy parents fail to realize that in the course of striving to keep their children happy and racing them from one after-school activity to another, they're neglecting the fundamentals of good citizenship, which begin in the home. In the final analysis, being a "star" in one's own family is infinitely more character-building than becoming a star on the soccer team.

Like your children, ours were expected to perform a daily routine of chores around the home. By the time they were in their early teens, Eric and Amy were doing most of the housework. For all this, we paid them absolutely nothing. As a result, their acts of contribution took on the kind of value one can never measure in dollars and cents. The kids took pride in what they did for the family, began to understand the basics of good citizenship, and became ever more independent in the process.

If they wanted money for something, they asked and heard

"no" fairly often. Because it wasn't easy to get money out of Mom and Dad, the children were forced to put more thought into their requests. By the time they were teens, they had become fairly smart shoppers. At this point, we decided to start them on allowances. We set up two checking accounts, one for each of them, into which we deposited one hundred dollars per month. They used their allowances to pay for all nonessential clothing and any recreational activities (movies, amusements parks, concerts, etc.) that did not include other family members. Willie and I continued to purchase such things as winter coats, socks, underwear, and any clothing that needed replacement. Even concerning necessary clothing, however, it became the responsibility of the child in question to pay the difference between a "stock" item and the latest "in" brand.

At age sixteen, each of the kids was required to get a part-time job in order to pay his or her own car insurance. In order to keep their jobs, however, their grades had to stay at previous levels. The sum total of these family policies forced the children to learn to manage both time and money—two giant steps toward a successful adulthood.

If all of this sounds old-fashioned, that's because it is. Today's parents need to wake up to the fact that thirty years of nouveau parenting hasn't worked and begin bringing lots and lots of "old-fashioned" back into their children's lives.

On Setting Family Priorities

Q: You've said children don't need a lot of attention, that too much is addicting, and that families should be adult-centered. How much attention is too much?

A: There is no formula. Suffice to say it is high during infancy and toddlerhood and diminishes significantly and steadily thereafter.

During the first eighteen months of life, a period of all but complete helplessness, it is essential that the child be the center of parental attention. From eighteen to thirty months or so, one notices the child wanting lots of attention one minute and complete autonomy the next. If parents are appropriately responsive, patient, and authoritative, the conflict between wanting to prolong dependency and strive for independence is resolved by age three.

At this time, it is essential that the center of attention in the family shift from child to parents.

The tendency among middle- and upper-middle-class parents in our culture is to give children too much attention. Their good intentions cause their children to become "stuck" at the center of their families. As a consequence, they become demanding, disrespectful, and unappreciative.

To paraphrase Ecclesiastes, we need to keep in mind that there's a time for giving attention, and a time for expecting it. If you give too much, you'll get too little in return.

Q: I subscribe to your philosophy that in a two-parent family, the marriage should come first. Trying to get my husband to feel and do likewise has proven to be an uphill battle, however.

He comes home from work feeling that since he's been gone all day, he needs to spend most of the evening with the kids, ages seven and four.

My position is he's been apart from me all day, too, and the marriage should be his first priority. He agrees in principle but can't seem to put his principle into practice.

Meanwhile, the children are becoming increasingly demanding and disrespectful of any attempt on our part to separate ourselves from them. Any advice?

A: A short forty years ago, a good father was a male who was first a good husband, and second a good provider. The amount of time he actually spent with his children was largely irrelevant to the consideration. Contrary to the myth, he wasn't remote, just busy.

He was involved with his work and involved with his wife, and together, they were involved with their friends and activities.

When his children needed him, he was there; not immediately, perhaps, but nonetheless in reasonable time. In short, a father's effectiveness as a role model was accorded more importance than the amount of attention given his children. Thus, the maxim: "The greatest thing a father can do for his children is love their mother with all his heart."

Gradually, all that changed. Today, the "good" in the "good father" is a matter of how much "quality" time he spends with his children, how involved he becomes in their after-school activities, and the like.

As the masculinity pendulum swings from machoism toward sensitivity and caring, being a buddy to one's children has become the mark of a sensitive, caring dad.

The result of this renewed focus on fatherhood is that marriages become that much further displaced in America's families.

It's bad enough that parenting professionals have for thirty years encouraged women to believe that their primary role was that of mother; now, we have the media and professionals telling men that fathering is where it's at. The fatherer, the better, or something like that.

In the first place, children should not have adults of either gender overly involved in their lives. Adults should interact primarily with other adults, children primarily with other children.

There is a time and a place for the twain to meet, but God did not intend the twain to be every evening and through the weekends. That's why marriage vows read "till death do us part" and not "till children do us part."

If words haven't succeeded at transforming your ex-husband back into a husband, then you're going to have to take the bull by the horns. The key is getting him out of the house.

As often as you can, arrange for a sitter after he gets home so the two of you can go shopping, to restaurants, concerts, or whatever. Find a mature woman or couple who'll take the kids on occasional weekends, so the two of you can get away on mini-honeymoons. If he resists, and he probably will, put your foot down.

Make two hours of time with one another for every hour you spend with the kids. After all, there's nothing that makes children feel more secure than knowing their parents are taking good care of one another.

Q: You emphasize the importance of children having respect for adults. I'm a teenager, and it seems to me that some adults have little respect for children. Isn't respect a two-way street?

A: You're absolutely right. Respect is a two-way street. It is important that adults demonstrate proper respect for children, just as they expect it in return.

Unfortunately, a lot of adults—perhaps most—want the respect of children, but don't understand why that's so important to a child's development or how to achieve it.

These adults seem to think this is a matter of children acknowledging the superiority of adults and demonstrating gratitude for being fed, clothed, and protected from the elements. Because they think in superficial terms, these adults (and I hope I'm stepping on a lot of toes) get all bent out of shape when children act the least rebellious or ungrateful.

The objective is not to uplift adults by having children feed their egos, but to assist children toward their own uplifting. Jesus, Buddha, Muhammad, and Confucius all said that one must develop respect for others in order to develop self-respect. What goes around, comes around. The young child takes the first step toward self-respect by learning respect for his or her parents. Respect then expands to other adult authority figures, to the immediate social group, and eventually, to all mankind. In bestowing respect upon others, respect for self matures.

Yes, it is necessary for adults to demonstrate respect for children, but the adult-child relationship cannot be democratic. Therefore, showing respect for children is not a matter of treating them like equals. Rather, it's a matter of accepting children for what they are; patiently nurturing them toward what they are capable of becoming; expecting a lot of them.

Accepting children for what they are means accepting their misbehavior—not approving of it, mind you, but accepting it. It takes most of eighteen years to civilize a child, and the process is one of trial and error, with an emphasis on error. As the errors occur, adults must be ready to correct them. To effectively correct, one must communicate well, and to communicate well, one must be reasonably composed (albeit disapproving). One cannot remain composed in the face of a child's errors unless one accepts (respects) that the child is a child.

To patiently nurture means not only to give adequate love and affection, but also to deliver proper discipline. These are the two sides of the coin of good parenting. Love without discipline in equal measure is indulgent, and discipline without an equal measure of love is punitive. Walking this balance beam, with grace, is the task set before parents.

Expecting a lot of children means setting high standards. It is, of course, possible to set unreasonably high standards. But the more common mistake is to set standards too low. In the real world, mediocrity is not rewarded. To accept mediocrity of any sort from a child is disrespectful. Parents should expect children to do well in school, display excellent manners, treat other children fairly, and perform chores (for no pay) around the home.

Within reason, the higher parents set standards, the more they elevate their children. And that, in the final analysis, is what respecting children is all about.

Q: I read a recent column of yours in which you said three-year-olds who demand lots of attention have probably received too much to begin with. You were talking about my thirty-four-month-old son. As a result of my excessive "mommying," he follows me around the house all day, wanting me to play with him, read to him, get him this, do that. As soon as I begin to do something for myself, he interrupts. I feel like I have no time to myself, no life outside that of being Ryan's mother. Is it too late to undo all this?

A: First of all, you are not guilty as charged. As I said in that column, women have been encouraged to buy into the falsehood that the more attention a mother pays her child, the better a mother she is. Female parents in our culture do not have full, unfettered permission to have lives of their own, to pursue personal or professional goals, much less say "no" to their kids and mean it.

You're not guilty. You've just fallen into what I call the "Parent

Trap." In the process of paying so much attention to Ryan, you've neglected yourself. If you want to help Ryan become more independent, you must begin controlling his access to you. You must let him know, in no uncertain terms, that you are not at his beck and call. If you can stand some temporary unhappiness (temporary, I assure you) on his part, here are some tried and proven suggestions:

❑ Make it easier for Ryan to do certain things on his own. If, for example, he frequently asks you to get him a cup of juice, put a small easy-pour container of juice on a low table every morning and teach him to pour his own. Refill it when empty.

❑ Pick three things Ryan frequently wants you to do for him, but which he can do for himself. Cut pictures out of magazines to represent each demand and glue them on a piece of construction paper onto which you've already glued a photo of Ryan. When finished, you have a poster that says, in effect, "Ryan can do these things on his own." Put the poster on the refrigerator, telling him what it means. Tell him you can't—not won't, but can't—do them for him anymore because he's a "big boy." From then on, when Ryan asks you for one of the things on the poster, take him over to it and say, "This means you can do that for yourself. I can't do it anymore, remember?"

❑ Try your best to set aside thirty minutes every morning and afternoon for Ryan. When you have the time to play with him or read to him, announce that it's "Mommy Time" and set your stove or microwave timer to ring in thirty minutes. Tell him that when the bell rings, it means you have to stop and go back to your own work (or reading, or whatever).

He will, no doubt, be initially unhappy with these limits. But if you're firm and consistent, he'll make a relatively quick adjustment.

Q: My husband and I don't always agree on how to handle situations that come up with our two children, ages six and three. I'm concerned that this may be confusing for the children and might contribute to later insecurities. My husband says I worry too much. Who's right?

A: The real issue is not that you and your husband don't always agree, but how you negotiate your disagreements.

In any healthy relationship, one in which the two people involved retain autonomy while maintaining commitment, a certain amount of disagreement is inevitable. Because of differences in background and biology, each of you sees and responds to things differently. It's inevitable, therefore, that your parenting styles will at times be on slightly different wavelengths.

There are several advantages to disagreement. First, different people bring more than one point of view to a situation. Your differences create options. This has the potential of imparting more flexibility and adaptability to the manner in which you raise your children. Second, your differences create a more exciting dynamic within your relationship and increase your potential for growth both as individuals and as a couple. Third, assuming you find creative ways of resolving your differences, your children not only learn a lot about conflict resolution but also see there is more than one way to do it.

Disagreement can quickly become a barrier to, rather than a vehicle for, growth and change if you focus too much energy on it. The more attention you pay to disagreement, the further apart you'll seem and the worse your disagreements will be. Under these circumstances, you can quickly lose sight of the fact that you actually agree about more than you disagree.

For example, although you might differ on how to get the children to bed at night, you may agree on such things as the time you want them in bed, that it's important for the two of you to have time together in the evening without children, that you're not going to get in bed with them, and so on. Finding your common ground makes it easier to find mutually acceptable solutions.

Discussing your differences within earshot of, or even in front of, the children is okay as long as the discussion is low-key and creative. Children need to see that conflict and hostility are not the same.

Children have a tendency to want to rescue their parents from conflict, regardless of how low-key it is. When our children were younger and tried to rescue Willie and me from conflict by interrupting or trying to distract, we'd say something like, "We know it makes you uncomfortable to hear us argue, but we'll be just fine. Meanwhile, you aren't allowed to interrupt." If they persisted, we sent them to their rooms until we finished our discussion. Eventually, they learned the old-fashioned virtue of minding their own business.

Q: My ex-husband and I have been divorced now for nearly two years, but he doesn't seem to be able to let go of his bitterness. Almost every time our two children, ages nine and seven, visit with him, they come home with tales of negative, critical things he's said about me. Making matters worse, most of them are completely untrue. I don't want to put the kids in the middle, but it's becoming increasingly difficult to bite my tongue. What would you suggest I say to them?

A: As little as possible. Or, put another way, a lot less than you'd like to say. This is definitely more a matter of don't than do, as in: Don't try to explain to them why their father is saying these things about you; don't even deny what he's telling them; and don't, under any circumstances, try to "one up" him in the scandalous-tales department.

In the first place, responding to your ex-husband's vitriol lends it credence. The more you talk, explain, deny, whatever, the more you invoke the Me Thinks Thou Dost Protest Too Much Principle. Put another way, the more you defend yourself against his "assaults by proxy," the guiltier you begin to appear.

Your husband is undoubtedly well aware that the children are relating his gossip. This is a fairly common way for one ex to get the other's goat, and you are evidence of the fact that it usually works. Do yourself a big favor by not making the mistake of thinking that the children are your allies and will keep your rebuttals in confidence. They are no one's allies; rather, they are in the middle, where their father has put them. Therefore, just as they blab to you, they will blab to him. In a situation of this sort, the children are always double agents, albeit unwittingly. The more you say in defense of yourself, the more he will hear, and more his criticisms of you will escalate. In short, don't be your own worst enemy.

Your number one objective is to come to the aid of the children. Their father is manipulating them, pure and simple. He probably feels justified in what he's telling them, but it's manipulation nonetheless. You can't stop him from doing what he's doing, but you can limit the damage by acting completely unfazed by anything he says (or, more accurately, the children say he says). In keeping with the fact that the more adults talk, the less children understand, and the more anxious they become, you need to act completely unfazed by your ex-husband's childishness. The next time the kids come to you with a "guess what Dad said," listen politely and say (pick one that feels comfortable):

(a) "Oh, I understand why your father would say such a thing. Look, kids, your father and I are divorced. Therefore, he can talk about me all he likes."

(b) "I'm sorry that your father tells you such things. It must confuse you a great deal. I'm not going to confuse you any more than you already are; therefore, we're not going to talk about it."

(c) "You know, kids, if you don't want to hear this kind of thing from your father, you should tell him so. I can't do anything about it, but you can."

(d) All of the above.

In any or all of these ways, you project self-confidence, which is what the children need from you. Their father is undermining their sense of security. You need to shore it up. If you do so successfully, then regardless of what he says about you, you are the champion.

Q: How can parents know when they've reached the point of diminishing returns and are about to "cross the line" in some area of their child's life?

A: Parents are always wanting to have these matters quantified. How much is too much? they ask, wanting to know precisely how many toys a child of, say, six should have, how many minutes of one-on-one attention a child of three needs from his or her parents on a daily basis, when to give help with homework and when not to, and how many times in a week, and for what length, etc. What these parents don't understand is that knowing where to draw the line isn't a matter of quantities; rather, it's a matter of common sense. Willie and I eventually decided that by simply asking ourselves, "Where, in this situation, would *our parents* have drawn the line?" we would, more often than not, end up drawing the line in a proper place for the child in question. Our parents raised us according to common sense, not books. And as all parents will, they made mistakes, but their successes outweighed their mistakes; in the final analysis, their successes, not their mistakes, defined their child rearing.

On Homework and Other School Matters

Q: Can you give a concrete example of where to draw the line? Take helping with homework, for instance.

A: Early on, like most parents of our generation, Willie and I thought good parents help their children with their homework whenever they ask for help. It took us awhile to realize that the more we answered the children's questions, the more questions they asked, and the more trivial their questions were. So, we asked ourselves, "How did our parents handle *our* requests for help with homework?" We remembered that when we went to our parents for such assistance, they sometimes helped, but briefly. If we didn't "get it" within a few minutes, the parent in question would say, "Well, it's obvious I'm not the person to explain this to you, in which case you'd better just put this problem on hold until you can ask your teacher about it tomorrow." More often than not, however, our parents would refuse to give us help. They'd say:

❑ "You are perfectly capable of doing that on your own, and to prove that to you, I'm not going to give you any help." And so we went back to the drawing boards, and we sweated, and we became frustrated, and we agonized, and we usually figured whatever it was out for ourselves.

❑ Or "I don't have time right now; besides, your homework is your responsibility, not mine. If I have time later, and you still are having a problem, I'll see what I can do." Today's parents don't think they have the right to say such blunt things to their kids. Watching them, one gets the impression today's parents think they are obligated to be at their children's beck and call; that they must drop whatever they're doing if their kids yell "Help!" concerning something, especially if the something is as earth-shaking (I'm being facetious) as homework. But when our parents told us they didn't have time right then and there to help us with our homework, Willie and I went back to trying to figure it out on our own, and we usually did. So, the fact that our parents had other, more important things to do at whatever moment resulted in Willie and me both realizing a higher level of belief in ourselves. We'd like to take this moment, therefore, to thank our parents for having lives of their own.

❑ Or "I can't help but feel that if you had been paying better attention to your teacher, you wouldn't be asking this question." And they were right, probably nine out of ten times. What about the tenth time? you ask. Well, neither Willie nor I can actually remember any tenth times, although we're sure there were some. Perhaps the way to answer that question is to point out that Willie and I both finished high school, went to college, and have made successes of our lives. Therefore, the tenth time didn't matter.

Taking a lesson from our parents, we began giving those same four responses to Eric and Amy when they asked for help with homework. And the most amazing thing happened. They began asking for help less and less often. And their grades remained the same. No, I'm not telling the truth. The truth is, their grades *improved.* In 1991, my third book, *Ending the Homework Hassle,* was published by Andrews and McMeel. It was nothing more than a comprehensive summation of the conclusions I'd drawn from having worked with academic underachievers for more than a decade. It contained these same recommendations concerning when and when not to give help with homework. Since its publication, parents and professionals across the country have implemented the "plan" detailed in the book and shared their results with me. The overwhelming consensus: It works! The less help parents give their children with homework, the better they do in school. And that feedback is consistent regardless of any problems—learning disabilities, attention deficit disorder, whatever—a child may have been diagnosed as "having."

Q: Are you saying that parents should only give help one out of four times a child asks for it? If so, that sounds more than just a bit lazy.

A: It sounds lazy by today's standards of "good parenting," but then today's parents have been led to believe that the harder they work and the more exhausted, in the process, they become, the better parents they are. That's not the way things work in any other area of life, so why parenting? In business, for example, the best employee is not the one who is constantly running himself ragged, constantly exhausted, constantly working his/her fingers to the proverbial bone. The best employee is the most *efficient,* the one who finds ways to save on effort and time. The most valued employee is the one who accomplishes his or her objectives with a minimum of sweat, not the one who sweats the most. And so it is with rearing a child.

What parents need to understand is that more often than not, when a child says "I need help," the request is not legitimate. Oh, the *child* thinks it's legitimate, all right, but in truth the child's complaint of "I can't!" is nothing more than a knee-jerk response to frustration of one sort or another. This is the case in any area, but schoolwork is a prime example of what I'm saying, so we're going to stay with it.

I conduct approximately fifty teacher-training ("in-service") sessions a year. At one point in these workshops, I ask, "Raise your hand if you think that when a child asks for help from you, you have a responsibility to give it." It never fails that nearly everyone in the audience will raise a hand. (And interestingly enough, the ones who don't are almost always the *older* teachers.)

Then, I pose this problem: "Let's think, for the moment, in terms of an average-ability child in a typical classroom. Over a certain period of time, this average child asks the teacher for help ten times. He asks her to clarify directions, demonstrate solutions to problems, check his work, or whatever. You're all teachers, so I want you to tell me how many times, as a general rule, out of the ten times this average kid requests your help, he actually, truly needs it. In other words, how many of those requests, if you weren't there to respond to them, would he be *unable* to eventually work through on his own?"

Inevitably, someone will say, "Two." Then, someone else will say, "No, just one." And someone will even say, "None."

And I, at that point, begin "auctioning" the answer: "I have two, someone says two, this teacher says the child in question only needs help two out the ten times he asks for it. Do I have three? Three? No one says three? Two going once; two going twice, two it is, then, and this audience has answered that question exactly the same way every audience of teachers has ever answered it."

Two. The average child needs help approximately two out of ten times he or she asks for it. The other eight requests represent the child's knee-jerk reaction to frustration.

Having made one point, I go on to another. "And what," I ask, "is it called when someone accepts responsibility for someone who is capable of accepting it on his own?"

At first, there is an embarrassed silence. Finally, someone will say it: "Enabling."

Right. Enabling. One of the most slanderous terms in our culture. People enable alcoholics, right? And drug addicts and gamblers and other people who are beset with addictions that unravel their moral fiber, right? Yes, that's right, but these days, children are being enabled more than any other single "class" of people in our culture. And all that enabling, all that good-intentioned "helping," is unraveling, if not their moral fiber, then certainly their ability to stand on their own two feet; their ability to stand up to the challenges of life and say, "I can! I know I can!"

Q: But, John, whereas it may be true that I'm giving my ten-year-old too much help with his homework, it's also true that he's making good grades. What's wrong with that?

A: What's wrong with that is that in the final analysis, success in life is not primarily a matter of what grades you made in school. Interestingly enough, the same question is always asked at those training sessions I conduct for teachers. When it is, I ask the group a series of questions:

"How many of you on a regular basis find yourselves needing to use what you learned in high school algebra?" In an audience of, say, one hundred, maybe three hands will rise.

"Chemistry?" A few hands.

"American literature?" Maybe ten hands.

"World history?" Five hands, maybe.

At this point, I change my tack. "How many of you have found that in order to be successful, you need to manage your time effectively almost every day of your lives?" Every member of the audience raises a hand.

"Keep your hand up if you have found you find that in order to be successful, you need to accept responsibility for things you'd really rather avoid doing." All the hands stay up.

"Keep your hand up if you have found that exercising initiative is critical to success." Every right arm in the place is getting numb at this point, so I tell 'em to put their hands down.

My point is that whether we realize it or not, most of the subject matter a child learns in school is not going to matter one way or another in his life. What's going to matter is what the child learned in the *process* of struggling to master the subject matter. And the operative word in the last sentence is struggling. In other words, the more effort parents expend, the less children struggle, and the less they learn what they need to learn to make successes of their lives.

Q: Our son, Turner, is now in the third grade. Late last school year, after many problems involving homework, we started following your advice. Turner is responsible for his homework and we are not. Turner is doing his homework and we are not. Turner's grades and attitude toward school have improved. As you recommend, we are making him stop working on homework at eight P.M. every evening, done or not. He's getting slowly better at managing his time, but he's recently discovered a way to beat the system. The clever little guy has started doing whatever homework he didn't finish the night before during our ride to school the next morning. I say we should not allow him to do this; my wife says, "Who cares?" I say the quality of his work suffers; my wife says, "Let him take the consequences." Whose side are you on?

A: Your wife's, but before I tell you why, allow me to let readers in on my plan, which consists of three understandings:

❑ First, the child does homework only in his room or some other equally personal, private "homework place." This physical boundary communicates to the child that homework is his responsibility, and no one else's. It is fact, not theory, that when a child is allowed to do homework in the family area, homework will become, to one degree or another, a family affair. The more of a family affair it becomes, the less benefit there is to the child.

❑ Second, the child receives help only when help is needed, not necessarily every time he asks for it.

❑ Third, to help the child develop time-management skills, parents set a time at which the child must put homework away, done or not. When our two children were in elementary school, their "homework deadline" was eight P.M. After several weeks of trial and error, they learned to plan their after-school time accordingly.

Generally speaking, the plan takes four to six weeks to take full effect. As with any other long-term solution, things usually get worse before they get better. If parents hang in there, however, the result is a child who assumes full responsibility for homework, thus taking control of an important facet of his or her life, thus adding another brick in the wall of self-esteem.

So you think Turner's learned how to beat the system, eh? Put that way, one is led to conclude that doing homework on the way to school in the morning is devious and manipulative and must be stopped. If, on the other hand, we say Turner's found a way to take full advantage of the system, then he rightfully deserves our admiration. He's ingenious, not devious; resourceful rather than manipulative.

The missing link in all this is the teacher. In order for the plan to work, she must hold Turner to strict, yet reasonable, quality control standards. In other words, she must not accept work that is sloppy, unfinished, or clearly below his caliber. (She will undoubtedly be delighted to meet parents who actually want her to educate.)

Under these circumstances, as sharp as he is, Turner will quickly see the folly of doing homework during the ride to school.

Q: For the last year we've been using the homework-management system from your book on school performance problems to help our second-grade daughter, with much success. She does her homework on her own, and asks for help only occasionally. After finishing her work, however, she does ask us to check it. If we understand correctly, that's okay, but we want to know what to do when we find mistakes. Should we point them out to her, or be less specific and let her figure them out for herself?

A: Yes, checking a child's work is perfectly okay, as long as the child initiates the request, as your daughter is doing. How you deal with mistakes is a judgment call; there is no one answer to your question. Sometimes, it's more appropriate to refer specifically to the mistake, saying, "You might want to give this problem some more thought." Take note: This is different than saying, "You need to redo this." Just put the ball in the child's court and let her decide what she wants to do with it.

At other times, it's more appropriate to say, "You've made several errors on this page. They look like careless mistakes to me. I'm sure you'll catch them yourself if you go over the assignment one more time."

In general, I'd lean toward the second option unless: a) the child was obviously tired or "burned out" that evening; b) the assignment was long, and going over it problem by problem would take a good deal of time; or c) the mistake was an isolated one and nothing would be gained by having the child find it on her own.

I'd also prefer the first option when, instead of pointing out an error, you're simply making a suggestion, as in, "This sentence is a bit long. What you're trying to say might be clearer if you made two sentences out of it, but that's up to you."

In the final analysis, the answer to your question is, "Use your common sense."

Q: I attended one of your talks and was surprised to hear you say that reward-based methods of motivating improvements in behavior or school performance are generally ineffectual. Why?

A: The primary problem with reward-based motivational strategies is that they bear little, if any, relationship to the way the world actually works.

To illustrate: Let's suppose your job performance is consistently below par. You come in late, fail to fill your quota or turn in reports on time, and often leave early. Your supervisor counsels you concerning these problems, but his words and warnings fall on deaf ears.

One day, he posts a chart above your desk and announces, "Every day you come to work on time, turn in your reports, fill your quotas and stay until closing, I'll glue a star in one of the fifty blocks on the chart. When you've filled all the blocks of the stars, we're going to reward you with a new car, any car you want!"

Fat chance, eh? But for purposes of discussion, let's pretend your supervisor does exactly that. Would you get your act in gear and begin earning stars for cars? Sure you would! And once you were behind the wheel of your new Messerschmidt Turbo 2001 Sport Convertible, you'd slowly but surely begin reverting to your old, irresponsible ways at work. You'd even take certain pleasure in your supervisor's mounting exasperation, knowing that the more exasperated he becomes, the more likely he is to make you an even better offer than the first one. Earning the new car didn't, therefore, make you a better employee. Quite the contrary, it taught you how to be manipulative.

Reward-based motivational plans carry a built-in time bomb I call the Saturation Principal. Sooner or later, any child will saturate any reward. Whereas the reward might have been initially enticing enough to leverage improved performance, when saturation occurs—when, in other words, the child has "had his fill" of the reward—the child's interest in the reward will decline along with his performance.

At this point, in order to pump the child's performance up again, the adult must make the child another offer, more interesting than the first. Under the circumstances, therefore, the adult is taking responsibility for maintaining the child's performance at adequate levels. As such, this cannot be helping the child appreciate the intrinsic value of improved behavior/performance.

You run the risk with reward-based systems of teaching children that misbehavior/underachievement is the ticket to getting special things and privileges. It doesn't take them long to realize—at an intuitive level—that adults aren't making well-behaved, highly motivated children these offers. Conclusion: Misbehavior pays.

Q: You've written you are not in favor of giving rewards for good report-card grades. Do you feel the same way about criticizing or punishing children for making bad grades?

A: I do not, under most circumstances, recommend that parents either reward children for good grades or punish/criticize them for bad ones.

Before elaborating, I need to distinguish between a reward and reinforcement. A reward is any out-of-the-ordinary tangible item intended for either the child's mouth (e.g., a treat) or hands (e.g., a toy), given contingent upon the child meeting a certain standard of performance, in school or otherwise.

On the other hand, anything that strengthens a particular behavior is reinforcement. Reinforcements, however, are not necessarily tangible. A smile is reinforcing, as is a pat on the back or a word of encouragement.

Furthermore, reinforcement is usually noncontingent. In other words, reinforcements can be dispensed even if the child doesn't meet certain standards. For example, if a child makes a C on a science project, it would still be appropriate to hug him and say, "That's all right. The important thing is that you did your best and did it without any help."

Our son Eric had great difficulty mastering academics during his first three years of school. When grades weren't the best, we continued to be encouraging and focus on the positive. If, for instance, he received a bad grade, we might ask him for an explanation. As long as his answer wasn't along the lines of "The teacher doesn't like me," we would say something like, "If you know what the problem is—and you obviously do—you can correct it. We trust that's what you'll do."

That was that. Short and sweet. No anger, no threats, no lectures of the "if you want to get into the college of your choice" variety. Just a few words to let him know that in our eyes he was just as swell after a report card as he was before, regardless of grades. It was, quite obviously, the right approach.

$Q:$ As a parent contemplating home schooling, I'm interested in your thoughts on the subject. What, in your estimation, are its advantages and disadvantages?

$A:$ The conversations I've had with parents who home-school their children lead me to conclude that this is more often than not a decision driven by values rather that purely practical considerations. These parents often voice objections to what, in their view, are "politically correct" or "secular humanist" themes running through public school curricula, especially in the language arts and social sciences.

They often echo former secretary of education William Bennett's warnings concerning outcome-based education—which has found a home in many a public school system—feeling that its hidden agenda is that of liberalizing the attitudes of children toward a number of controversial social issues. In addition, they tend to feel that the approach taken toward drug, sex, and AIDS education in public schools tends to promote a relativist attitude toward moral issues.

Every home-schooling parent I've talked to is of the opinion that public school standards, behaviorally and academically, are outrageously lax, exacerbating the potential of untoward peer influences.

Understandably, the educational establishment does not have a positive view of home schooling and has consistently attempted to discredit it, even disallow it. Home-schooling parents have been unjustifiably characterized as fanatics with an almost paranoid distrust of the government.

My impression, on the other hand, is that by and large these are knowledgeable, rational folks whose concerns are well founded. Whether you agree with them or not, it's hard not to admire the strength behind their convictions.

Are public-school standards lax? Does the social climate of many a public school warrant concerns about peer influence? Are politically correct, liberal attitudes insidious in many public school texts, programs, and teaching methods? Is it possible that outcome-based education might result in even lower standards, along with an escalating emphasis on raising the "social consciousness" of America's youth?

The answer to every one of the above questions is "yes." And that's precisely why an isolated phenomenon has grown, in little more than a decade, into a national movement that does, indeed, threaten America's educational establishment.

The downside of home schooling includes the child-centeredness of the arrangement, the fact that unresolved problems in the parent/child relationship are likely to contaminate and interfere with the teaching/learning process, the disproportionate amount of parenting required of the instructional parent and the limited social experience inherent to the arrangement.

When parents have solicited my advice on home schooling, I've recommended that they get together with other like-minded parents and form a home-schooling cooperative involving shared responsibilities. This arrangement would not only give each parent some precious time off, but would provide the children with a peer group and take some pressure off each of the parent/child relationships involved.

For further information on home schooling, contact the National Home School Association, (513) 772-9580 (answering machine). Many states have their own home-schooling associations, the addresses of which can also be obtained through the national office.

On Toys and "The Grandparent Problem"

Q**:** We want to sharply reduce the number of toys our kids have, but how do we handle grandparents who want to give, give, give?

A: I'll let other parents answer your question, beginning with a mother from Jackson, Mississippi:

"In 1991, when my husband and I started our family, we decided then not to overindulge our children with toys. Grandparents, however, didn't always comply, and the sheer number of children we had (five) left our closets overflowing. We solved that problem a few years ago by dividing all the toys into four piles labeled winter, spring, summer, and fall. We bagged them up, and into the attic they went. We pull the appropriate bag down the first day of each December, March, June, and September. The children love it! It's as if Christmas comes to our house four times a year! When it's time to repack them, each child donates a toy to charity. As a result, what was once a clutter is now quite manageable."

A mother from Nashville suggests that parents ask grandparents to keep all toys purchased for the grandchildren at their house. She correctly points out that asking grandparents not to make toy purchases, or only one on the child's birthday and one at Christmas or Hanukkah, is likely to generate hard feelings, interfering as it might with the grandparents' need to dote.

That's a good idea, but one that's likely to work only if the grandparents live nearby. If they don't, then regular care packages are a means of reminding the grandchildren of their love, and that's certainly unimpeachable. But instead of toys, I suggest books. Or the grandparents could introduce the grandchild in question to a hobby and advance the child's interests with regular gifts of hobby supplies and equipment.

Some friends of ours, after drastically reducing their children's toy stocks, sent their very generous relations a letter explaining what they'd done. The children, the relatives were told, had readily agreed that from that day forward for every toy they received as a gift, they would give a toy of equal value away to charity. Books, hobby-related items, and creative materials were exempted. Not surprisingly, while their generosity did not wane, the relatives never gave the children another toy.

For every problem, there's a solution.

Bibliography and Recommended Reading

The Open Bible: New American Standard. Nashville: Thomas Nelson, Publishers, 1960.

Bennett, William J. *The Index of Leading Cultural Indicators.* New York: Touchstone, 1994.

Briggs, Dorothy Corkille. *Your Child's Self-Esteem.* Garden City, N.Y.: Doubleday & Company, 1970.

Council on Families in America/Institute for American Values. *Marriage In America: A Report To The Nation.* New York: Institute for American Values, 1995.

Dobson, James. (All of his books.)

Gordon, Thomas. *P.E.T.: Parent Effectiveness Training.* New York: Peter H. Wyden, 1970.

Gordon, Thomas. *Teaching Children Self-Discipline.* New York: Times Books, 1989.

Henry, William A. *In Defense of Elitism.* New York: Doubleday, 1994.

Kilpatrick, William. *Why Johnny Can't Tell Right From Wrong.* New York: Touchstone, 1993.

Marlin, George, Richard Rabatin, and Heather Higgins eds. *The Quotable Paul Johnson: A Topical Compilation of His Wit, Wisdom and Satire.* New York: Farrar, Straus and Giroux, 1994.

Spock, Benjamin. *The Common Sense Book of Baby and Child Care.* New York: Duel, Sloan and Pearce, 1946.

About the Heretic

*J*ohn Rosemond is a family psychologist whose syndicated newspaper column appears in more than one hundred newspapers around the country. He writes a regular column for *Better Homes and Gardens* magazine and a monthly column for *Hemispheres*, United Air Lines' award-winning in-flight magazine. He's written six books—including this one—for Andrews and McMeel. To date, John's best books are the other five, but this one, he says, is his "masterpiece." He hopes to make enough moolah off this one to retire from being a "parenting expert" and pursue his lifelong dream of being a rock 'n' roll star.

John is director of The Center for Affirmative Parenting, which provides print, audio, and video resources for parents, schools, and professionals who work with families. By the way, John hates the word "parenting," and will only use it if the correct term, child rearing, sounds awkward, as in The Center for Affirmative Child Rearing. He's also one of America's busiest and most popular public speakers, known for making his audiences laugh a lot. On August 21, 1995, John debuted his daily syndicated radio talk-show, "Because I Said So," which airs live from three o'clock to five o'clock in the afternoon (Eastern time) on more than sixty stations coast-to-coast. If you can't hear him in your area, call your local AM talk station and tell the station manager that if he doesn't begin carrying John's show, you'll start having pizzas delivered to his house in the middle of the night.

John and his wife, Willie, have been married twenty-seven years. She's a very tolerant woman. They have two children, Eric— twenty-six, a commercial pilot, married to Nancy (the daughter-in-law of John's dreams)—and Amy—twenty-three, a recent graduate of the University of North Carolina (journalism and public relations), and currently working in the marketing department of a major hospital in Charlotte. On January 1, 1995, at seven o'clock in the morning, John and Willie became grandparents to John McHenry Rosemond. About Jack Henry, as he is affectionately called, John says, "He's gifted. No, really, he is. I know, because I'm a psychologist."

For more information, write: The Center for Affirmative Parenting, P.O. Box 4124, Gastonia, NC, 28054, or call (704) 864-1012.